Paul's Missionary Methods

Paul's Missionary Methods

In His Time and Ours

EDITED BY

ROBERT L. PLUMMER & JOHN MARK TERRY

INTER-VARSITY PRESS
Norton Street, Nottingham NG7 3HR, England
Email: ivp@ivpbooks.com
Website: www.ivpbooks.com

First published 2013

British Library Cataloguing in Publication Data
A catalogue record for this book is available from the British Library.

ISBN: 978–1–84474–615–6

Typeset in the United States of America
Printed and bound in Great Britain by Ashford Colour Press Ltd, Gosport, Hampshire

Inter-Varsity Press publishes Christian books that are true to the Bible and that communicate the gospel, develop discipleship and strengthen the church for its mission in the world.

Inter-Varsity Press is closely linked with the Universities and Colleges Christian Fellowship, a student movement connecting Christian Unions in universities and colleges throughout Great Britain, and a member movement of the International Fellowship of Evangelical Students. Website: www.uccf.org.uk

To our former students
serving in mission fields
around the world.

CONTENTS

POSTSCRIPT

Preface

♦ ♦ ♦

In 1912 Roland Allen, a missions researcher and former missionary to
China, published his book *Missionary Methods: St. Paul's or Ours?* In the
next one hundred years, Allen's book came to be regarded as a missiological
classic. Because this year marks the centennial of the publication of *Missionary Methods,* it is fitting to revisit the book. What contributions has it
made to missiology? How has Allen affected New Testament studies? Are
the teachings found in his book still valid today? In what ways do our
current missiological questions and concerns differ from Allen's day? These
questions prompted us to undertake this volume.

We decided to divide the book into two sections: "Paul's Message" and
"Paul's Missiology." Robert Plummer agreed to edit the section on Paul's
message. He is a rising star in New Testament studies, and the Pauline literature is his specialty. I (Mark) am proud to claim him as my student. He
studied with me at both the master's and doctoral levels at The Southern
Baptist Theological Seminary, where he now teaches. When he took my
PhD seminar on missions strategy, he wrote the paper on the apostle Paul's
strategy. Later, that seminar paper became the seed from which his dissertation grew.

In the section which I (Rob) edited, the contributors focused on Paul's
message in the first-century context. What was Paul's gospel? How did he
envision the organization of the churches that he started? How were these

churches to relate to the ongoing advance of the gospel? For Paul, what is the role of suffering in missions? These and other questions are answered in this book by an impressive lineup of New Testament scholars. As the contributors wrote, they gave hermeneutical priority to the biblical text, followed by reference to broader data, including Roland Allen's writings.

For my (Mark's) part, I was introduced to Roland Allen by my beloved professor, Dr. Calvin Guy, who taught missions for many years at Southwestern Baptist Theological Seminary. That introduction has led me to a career-long fascination with Roland Allen's work. I have been delighted to direct my students, both in Asia and in North America, to Allen's writings. One of those students, J. D. Payne, wrote his dissertation on Roland Allen, and his chapter at the end of this book will help you understand Allen's life and ministry.

The missiological section of this book addresses several important questions, much discussed by missiologists: Did the apostle Paul have a strategy? If he did, what was it? Is Paul's strategy still applicable today? These questions, and more, are answered with reference to both the New Testament and Allen's book. The astute reader will notice that there are differences of opinion regarding how Allen would have engaged in contemporary debates, for example, his view on insider movements.

We believe that Roland Allen's book is still helpful a century after its publication. Allen's emphases on planting indigenous churches, trusting in the power of the Holy Spirit and encouraging national workers to lead the new congregations are essential today. Few books remain in print after one hundred years, but *Missionary Methods* is still in print. This is because Allen's work presents the principles that characterized the apostle Paul's missionary work. Roland Allen believed that imitating Paul's approach would enhance the results of missions work in his day. We believe that contemporary missionaries would do well to imitate Paul also. Roland Allen did the cause of Christ a great service in writing *Missionary Methods*. He wanted to reconnect the missionaries of his day with the example of the greatest missionary—Paul of Tarsus. We hope to reconnect the missionaries of our day to both Paul and Roland Allen.

We are grateful to Volney James, formerly of Biblica Books, for his encouragement, and to Ben McCoy of InterVarsity Press for his cheerful assistance in editing this volume. We are thankful for the contributors who prepared their essays without promise or hope of financial reward. They saw this as a project for the kingdom, and they have laid up treasure in heaven. Thanks to others who offered feedback or corrections to earlier drafts, including Donnie Hale, Rod Elledge, Mike Cosper, Tim Beougher, Caleb Davis, Justin Abercrombie, Cammie Abercrombie, Luke Bray, Samuel Wilwerding and Philip Van Steenburgh. Finally, we are grateful to God for the joy of collaborating together on this project. It has been a labor of love.

John Mark Terry and Robert L. Plummer
December 2012

Abbreviations

AB	Anchor Bible
AGJU	Arbeiten zur Geschichte des antiken Judentums und des Urchristentums
Josephus *Ant.*	*Antiquities of the Jews*
Dionysius of Halicarnassus *Ant. Rom.*	*Antiquitates Romanae*
Aristides *Apol.*	*Apology*
Justin *Apol.*	*Apology*
Tertullian *Apol.*	*Apology*
Asc. Isa.	*Ascension of Isaiah*
Suetonius *Aug.*	*Augustus (The Twelve Caesars)*
AV	Authorized Version (= KJV)
BECNT	Baker Exegetical Commentary on the New Testament
BBR	Bulletin for Biblical Research
Apollodorus *Bib.*	*Bibliotheca*
CEJ	*Christian Education Journal*
Origen *Cont. Cels.*	*Contra Celsum*
Lucan *C.W.*	*Civil War*
Hippolytus *Dem. Chr.*	*Demonstratio de Christo et Antichristo*
DNTB	*Dictionary of New Testament Background*
DPL	*Dictionary of Paul and his Letters*
EDNT	*Exegetical Dictionary of the New Testament*
EBC	The Expositor's Bible Commentary
EJ	*Enrichment Journal*
1 En.	*1 Enoch*
Diogenes *Ep.*	*Epistula*
ESV	English Standard Version
Irenaeus *Haer*	*Adversus Haereses*
Herm	Hermeneia
Polybius *Hist.*	*Histories*
Tacitus *Hist.*	*Historiae*
Eusebius *Hist. Eccl*	*Historia Ecclesiastica*
HCSB	Holman Christian Standard Bible

HolNTC	Holman New Testament Commentary
ICC	International Critical Commentary
Int	*Interpretation*
JPastCare	*Journal of Pastoral Care & Counseling*
Jub.	*Jubilees*
LABC	Life Application Bible Commentary
LCC	Library of Christian Classics
Seneca (the Younger)	
Lucil.	*Epistles to Lucilius*
NASB	New American Standard Bible
NAC	New American Commentary
NIGTC	New International Greek Testament Commentary
NIV	New International Version
NRSV	New Revised Standard Version
NovT	*Novum Testamentum*
NTC	New Testament Commentary (Kistemaker and Hendrikson)
NTM	New Testament Monographs (Sheffield Academic)
Num. Rab.	*Numbers Rabbah*
Dio Chrysostom *Or.*	*Orationes*
Maximus of Tyre *Or.*	*Oratio*
PBM	Paternoster Biblical Monographs
Silius Italicus *Pun.*	*Punica*
1QS	*Serek hayyad / Rule of the Community, Manual of Discipline*
SBJT	*Southern Baptist Journal of Theology*
SGC	Study Guide Commentary
SNTSMS	Society for New Testament Studies Monograph Series
Test. Benj.	*Testament of Benjamin*
TJ	*Trinity Journal*
TNTC	Tyndale New Testament Commentary
WBC	Word Biblical Commentary
Wis.	*Wisdom of Solomon*
WUNT	Wissenschaftliche Untersuchungen zum Neuen Testament

Part One

Paul in the
New Testament

♦♦♦

1

Paul's Religious and Historical Milieu

♦ ♦ ♦

Michael F. Bird

It was Martin Kähler who first said that mission was "the mother of all theology."[1] Roland Allen's *Missionary Methods: St. Paul's or Ours?* was a resolute confirmation of Kähler's dictum. The doctrines that Paul taught emerged principally out of his missionary situation. Consequently, any contemporary practice of mission has to appropriate Paul's missionary methods and the theological rationale undergirding them.[2] In fact, the more we learn about Paul's missionary methods, the more we might learn something about his theology too!

Allen also stressed that Paul's missionary endeavors did not occur in a cultural vacuum. He pointed out that: (1) Paul focused his missionary work on certain provinces that contained a Roman administration, Greek culture, and Jewish influence and that bustled with commercial activity, because these centers were the most conducive to promoting the gospel in its wider environs. (2) Paul did not focus his efforts on any particular class or group of people, but engaged all hearers and inquirers. Paul entered cities as a Jew,

---

[1] Martin Kähler, *Schriften zur Christologie und Mission* (Munich: Verlag, 1971 [1908]), p. 190.
[2] Roland Allen, *Missionary Methods: St. Paul's or Ours?* 2nd ed. (Grand Rapids: Eerdmans, 1962), esp. pp. 6-7.

a teacher of a form of Judaism, and claimed to be preaching a new revelation about the Messiah, but he did so in terms that addressed the sophistication of the Greek mind. (3) Paul's missionary preaching tackled the
worldview of his audience and features of their beliefs in things such as evil
spirits, morality and religion, slavery, and the amphitheater.[3] Thus, Paul's
missionary success is partly attributable to his ability to understand and
utilize his own peculiar contexts.

Allen's discussion of Paul's missionary context was rather terse and
lacked the sophistication of someone like Adolf von Harnack, who meticu-
lously described the forces and factors in the Greco-Roman world that
made the expansion and growth of the early Christian mission possible.[4]
Sociologist of religion Rodney Stark has also utilized sociological studies
and appealed to factors as wide ranging as immunology to account for the
rapid growth of the Christian movement.[5] In what follows, I want to describe briefly those features of Paul's Jewish, Greek and Roman contexts
that explain the success of the Pauline mission. Obviously, Paul's faith in
God and in the Lord Jesus—and the work of the Holy Spirit through him—
drove his mission. However, we still have to be mindful of the geographical,
political, cultural, linguistic and religious factors that God actually used to
promote the gospel in the Greco-Roman world through the apostle Paul
and his companions. That, I hope, will lead to a more thorough knowledge
of the context of Paul's missionary activities.

THE GEOGRAPHICAL CONTEXT OF PAUL'S MISSION

Ancient authors knew of different people groups, ethnicities, tribes and nations spread across the inhabitable world. Luke records how, on the Day of
Pentecost, the Galilean followers of Jesus began speaking in other tongues
and praising God in the languages of the "Parthians and Medes and Elamites
and residents of Mesopotamia, Judea and Cappadocia, Pontus and Asia,
Phrygia and Pamphylia, Egypt and the parts of Libya belonging to Cyrene,
and visitors from Rome, both Jews and proselytes, Cretans and Arabians—we

---

[3]Ibid., pp. 10-37.
[4]Adolf von Harnack, *The Expansion of Christianity in the First Three Centuries,* 2 vols., trans. J. Mof-
fatt (New York: Williams & Norgate, 1904-5) 1:1-39.
[5]Rodney Stark, *The Rise of Christianity: A Sociologist Reconsiders History* (Princeton: Princeton
University Press, 1996).

hear them telling in our own tongues the mighty works of God" (Acts 2:9-11). Luke also records the words of Jesus to the disciples, that they will be "witnesses in Jerusalem and in all Judea and Samaria, and to the end of the earth" (Acts 1:8) which is virtually a table of contents for the Acts of the Apostles. But what was the "end of the earth" for people living in the Greco-Roman world?[6]

The world as the Romans knew it was a world basically cordoned off with Ethiopia in the south of Africa, India and mysterious lands to the east, Spain and the British Isles to the west, and the Germanic tribes to the north of Italy. Many ancient geographers such as Demetrios of Kallatis, Strabo, Pliny the Elder and Dionysius of Alexandria had written accounts of the peoples, lands and nations that they encountered in their journeys or had heard about from others. For most of the geographers, the major continents were Europe, Africa and Asia. It is interesting that Jerusalem lies close to the intersection of all three! This was the world known to the ancient Romans, though Parthian (i.e., Persian) authors obviously had better knowledge of the East such as India and China, as they came into contact with travelers from those regions more frequently.

The explosion of Christianity in the first two centuries meant that missionaries had reached many of these lands. By A.D. 70, not long after Paul's death, there was a network of small Christian communities comprised of Jewish and Gentile adherents spread across Alexandria, Syria-Cilicia, Cyprus, Galatia, Asia, Mysia, Macedonia, Achaia, Cappadocia, Pontus-Bithynia, Dalmatia, Crete, Edessa and Damascus. The gospel had spread to all the lands that the early Christians knew. But the evangelistic work continued in the postapostolic era, and Eusebius records that a certain Pantaenus of Alexandria reportedly set off for India for evangelical work early in the second century.[7] In the developing church of the second and third centuries, the expansion of the church was regarded as part of the Christian message itself.[8] Some second century church fathers even thought that the Christian mission to the "end of the earth" had actually been achieved during the apostolic and subapostolic ages. Christians spread in such a pro-

---

[6]Cf. Eckhard J. Schnabel, *Early Christian Mission* (Downers Grove, Ill.: InterVarsity Press, 2004), 1:455-99.

[7]Eusebius *Hist. Eccl.* 5.10.

[8]Aristides *Apol.* 2 (Syriac); Justin *Apol.* 1.39; Tertullian *Apol.* 21; Hippolytus *Dem. Chr.* 61; Origen *Cont. Cels.* 3.28; *Asc. Isa.* 3.13-21; cf. Acts 26:22-23.

fusion all over the Mediterranean and even into the Parthian regions that Tertullian could say to Roman critics of Christianity: "We [Christians] are but of yesterday, and yet we already fill your cities, islands, camps, your palace, senate, and forum. We have left you only your temples."[9]

Paul wrote this to the Gentile churches in Rome:

> For I will not venture to speak of anything except what Christ has accomplished through me to bring the Gentiles to obedience—by word and deed, by the power of signs and wonders, by the power of the Spirit of God—so that from Jerusalem and all the way around to Illyricum I have fulfilled the ministry of the gospel of Christ; and thus I make it my ambition to preach the gospel, not where Christ has already been named, lest I build on someone else's foundation. . . . But now, since I no longer have any room for work in these regions, and since I have longed for many years to come to you, I hope to see you in passing as I go to Spain, any to be helped on my journey there by you, once I have enjoyed your company for a while. (Rom 15:18-24)

Evidently, Paul considered his work in the East complete—complete in the sense that he had established clusters of churches in many major urban areas, churches capable of reproducing his own evangelical efforts in that location and beyond it (it was the church in Ephesus that probably established the churches in Laodicea and Colossae!).[10] Paul now intended to continue his missionary work in the West after a brief visit first to Jerusalem to deliver the collection to the saints there.

In terms of a pattern, Paul consciously worked in areas that were under Roman control and usually had a Jewish community of some form. Paul appears to have spent most of his time in and around coastal cities in the eastern Mediterranean, perhaps because travel was easier to come by and they were major population centers bustling with people and commerce. There were exceptions to this. Early in his career Paul had spent some time ministering in Arabia and Damascus (2 Cor 11:32; Gal 1:17). But thereafter he focused on Roman provinces in the East. For instance, Luke tells us that when Paul and his companions "had come up to Mysia, they attempted to

---

[9]Tertullian *Apol.* 37.
[10]Cf. Robert L. Plummer, *Paul's Understanding of the Church's Mission: Did the Apostle Paul Expect the Early Christian Communities to Evangelize?* PBM (Milton Keynes: Paternoster, 2008).

go into Bithynia, but the Spirit of Jesus did not allow them" (Acts 16:7). From there Paul could have stayed in any number of the Hellenistic cities that existed between Damascus and Babylon, among the northern cites of the Decapolis, or as far south as Petra, and ministered among Jewish communities in the Far East all the way to Babylon. Yet Paul went west instead, into Greece and eventually onto Italy. There might be more going on here that just travelling convenience as Paul's ambition to go to Spain might imply that he was influenced by Is 66:19, "I will set a sign among them. And from them I will send survivors to the nations, to Tarshish, Pul, and Lud [Libyans and Lydians, famous as archers], who draw the bow, to Tubal and Javan [Greece], to the coastlands far away that have not heard my fame or seen my glory. And they shall declare my glory among the nations." Although Spain did not have a thriving Jewish population and it was more Latin-speaking than Greek-speaking, Paul's plan for visiting Spain (= Tarshish) was part of the itinerary in his role to declare God's glory in Christ Jesus to *Jews and Gentiles* among the nations as part of the Isaianic script for the end of Israel's exile and the beginning of the new creation.[11] Paul probably saw himself as a postcard for God's glory that was being delivered all over the Roman world.

THE GRECO-ROMAN CONTEXT OF PAUL'S MISSIONARY WORK

There are several important facets to the Greco-Roman world of Paul's day that enabled and facilitated his missionary work and communication with a network of Christian churches.[12]

Successive empires including the Assyrian, Babylonian, Persian, Greek and Roman kingdoms had dominated the Ancient Near East. Alexander the Great (356-323 B.C.) led Greek armies to conquer Egypt, Asia Minor, Palestine, Persia and even parts of India. Alexander established Hellenistic cities throughout his conquests with the express purpose of spreading Greek language, learning and culture. This attempt to disseminate Greek culture was successful to the point that the Greek language became the *lingua franca* of the eastern Mediterranean. That is not to say that everyone in the East spoke Greek (see Acts 21:37). Indigenous languages persisted for

---

[11] Cf. Rainer Riesner, *Paul's Early Period: Chronology, Mission Strategy, Theology,* trans. Doug Stott (Grand Rapids: Eerdmans, 1998), pp. 245-53, 305-6.
[12] Cf. further Schnabel, *Early Christian Mission*, 1:557-652.

some time. But Greek became the international language of commerce, politics and literature. The widespread usage of Greek enabled the spread of ideas and information through various oral and written media in the ancient world. Paul the Greek-speaking Jew from Tarsus (Acts 21:39; 22:3) was well acquainted with Greek language and customs, which enabled him to navigate effectively the socioreligious complexities of life in the eastern Mediterranean. Greek philosophy, concerned as it was with both ethics and religion, lent itself to thought about creation, god, religion, the immortality of the soul and the highest good. The schools of Platonic, Pythagorean, Epicurean and Stoic thinkers concerned themselves with asking questions about supernatural realities that Judaism and Christianity sought also to engage with the resources of their sacred texts and traditions.

The nature of the Roman Empire changed markedly after the accession of Augustus who, after successive civil wars, eventually became the unchallenged ruler of Rome and the Roman provinces in 27 B.C. Augustus reorganized the empire into imperial and senatorial provinces and embarked on a process of fiscal reforms. The Romans ruled provinces directly through proconsuls and legates, but often allowed client kings to rule as long as they kept the peace and taxes kept flowing back to Rome. Legions did not occupy all provinces, but were stationed in key points such as Italy, Gaul, the Danube and Syria. Paul found himself frequently caught between Roman officials and local authorities and was often imprisoned in Roman garrisons. Importantly, the Romans strove to propagate through the ancient media of coins, inscriptions, imperial decrees and even poetry the myth that Rome's ascent to power had been divinely determined and, therefore, the peoples of the world should acquiesce and submit to Roman authority for its own good (see especially Virgil's *Aeneid*). The Romans rewarded faithful subjects with citizenship and enabled others to come under the protection of its military might and legal system—something Paul too could use for his own advantage when he required it (Acts 16:35-40).

The Romans revolutionized travel in the ancient world. This is significant because travel was "the transmission belt for the gospel."[13] Lines of communication were improved during the Roman period in a number of ways. First,

---

[13]Reinhold Reck, cited in Schnabel, *Early Christian Mission*, 1:632.

Gnaeus Pompeius successfully led a campaign around 70–67 B.C. to rid the eastern Mediterranean of pirates who terrorized sea farers, threatened Rome's grain supply from Africa and interfered with communications with the provinces. Second, by building roads and bridges, the Romans provided reliable and well-used forms of travel over land. Third, governors and local authorities were charged with protecting travel routes from bandits and thus ensured a degree of security for merchants and officials in their journeys. Travel by both sea and land became safer and faster during the Roman period. Not only travel but also the transmission of written communication became far more effective and reliable during this period. Augustus even introduced a postal system for the whole empire.[14] The international mobility afforded by Roman engineering and military presence meant that Paul's various missionary journeys through Palestine, Syria, Asia, Greece and Rome were in a large measure possible because of the new routes that had been opened up and maintained by Roman infrastructure.

The urban centers in Greece and Asia Minor show a clear interface of Greek and Roman culture. Places like Corinth were reestablished as colonies for retired veterans. Corinth is full of Greek and Latin inscriptions. The cities were filled with temples, markets, various shops, baths, gymnasia and amphitheaters that provided means of entertainment and employment. Life in the cities was often crowded, and multistory tenements, called *insulae*, were densely inhabited. Early Christian meetings probably took place in many of these *insulae* but also in the apartments or houses of richer members who had significantly more spacious living quarters. Many of the Pauline churches were established in these dense and multicultural urban centers and probably met in a mixture of house churches, shops and lecture theatres.

Greco-Roman religion was inherently pluralistic. Veneration of local deities as well as Greek and Roman gods took place side by side. The Romans and Greeks often incorporated Eastern deities into their pantheon by identifying them with existing gods like Zeus or Jupiter. The Greco-Roman world contained a potpourri of public and private cults that developed out of archaic Roman and Greek religions and often absorbed Near Eastern religions such as the mystery cults. This was often combined with beliefs in

---

[14]Suetonius *Aug.* 49.3.

astrology and folk religion centered on demons and spirits. Temples and shrines were common in both private and public places. Importantly, religion was not a private individual affair but affected politics, various guilds and associations, festivals and public events. Leaders attempted to show themselves as exemplifying the trait of *pietas*, that is, as religiously devout to the ancient gods and rites. Added to that we can note the growth of the imperial cult, especially in Asia, where Ephesus and Pergamum competed for the honor of being the official seat of imperial worship in the East. Although many of Paul's converts were drawn from the ranks of Jewish proselytes and "God-fearers" with varied exposure and adherence to the Jewish way of life, many came from pagan religion and were among those "who turned to God from idols" (1 Thess 1:9).[15]

In sum, the political and social context of the Greco-Roman world provided an environment favorable to the spread of Christianity in general and to the conduct of the Pauline mission in particular.

THE JEWISH CONTEXT OF PAUL'S MISSIONARY WORK

Jesus was a Jew, his closest followers were all Jews, and the Gentile mission into the Greco-Roman world was launched by Jewish Christians like the apostle Paul. The Jewish Diaspora and the effusion of Judaism into the eastern Mediterranean was a key mechanism by which the good news of salvation through faith in Israel's Messiah was spread among Greeks, Barbarians and Romans.

Jewish communities could be found widely all over the Mediterranean basin and comprised up to 20 percent of the population in the Roman Empire. Jewish Diaspora locations were located in the major centers of the Mediterranean such as Alexandria, Syrian Antioch, Ephesus, Corinth and Rome. These Jewish communities, distant as they were from Judea, had constantly had to face the struggle of how to navigate life in a pagan society where they were a minority group with a string of socioreligious convictions clearly out of sync with the surrounding culture. In many cases this led to various forms of acculturation and assimilation, even to the point of apostasy, but in most cases it seems that Jews of the Diaspora were able to

---

[15]Most helpful here is the summary by D. E. Aune, "Religion, Greco-Roman," in *DNTB*, pp. 917-26.

retain something of their Jewish heritage, identity, and customs, despite living far from their ancestral homes. Synagogues served as important centers of Jewish social and religious life, and it is entirely unsurprising that Paul and other Christian missionaries began their evangelistic work in the synagogues of the Jewish Diaspora.

In the eyes of the Romans, the Jews were known for several things. First, they were known for their peculiar religious devotion to a single God (i.e., monotheism) and their aniconic worship that was void of physical representations of deity and with their refusal to offer sacrifices to other deities (which was the principal form of worship for pagans). Second, they stood out for their peculiar customs like abstaining from pork and observing the Sabbath. Third, Jews of the Diaspora often formed cohesive and identifiable communities that looked after their own members, often withdrawing contact from the wider pagan community, so much so that the Jews were thought to be haters of humanity.[16]

In scholarship it has often been alleged that there was during the first century an active and concerted Jewish mission to convert Gentiles to Judaism.[17] There is some credence to this theory, and it was a popular view in an older generation of scholarship; however, there does not seem to be much explicit evidence for widespread missionary activity by Jews directed towards Gentiles.[18] What "missionary" work took place was largely exceptional and spasmodic. Jewish attitudes on the whole seem more oriented towards a warm willingness to receive converts than a clear agenda to seek them out. That said, there were, quite clearly, several contextual factors that made conversion to Judaism an attractive option for non-Jews living in the ancient world. Of course, what pagans saw in Judaism would depend entirely on what they saw of it, and this would differ from city to city from Gaul to Galilee. The magnetic attraction of Judaism to some non-Jews was on account of several factors.

First, Eastern practices and rites held a certain fascination in some circles of the Roman west, especially those from Greece, Egypt and Persia. The

---

[16]For a good example of these kind of attitudes see Tacitus *Hist.* 5.5.

[17]For recent discussion on this see Michael F. Bird, *Crossing Over Sea and Land: Jewish Missionary Activity in the Second Temple Period* (Peabody, Mass.: Hendrickson, 2009).

[18]Cf. Mt 23:15 and Josephus *Ant.* 20.17-50.

influx of foreign cults and religions even led the Roman authorities to inter-
mittently expel foreign religious leaders if they grew too numerous or when
Roman rulers wanted to appear to be the guardians of the purity of Roman
religious culture (which perhaps explains Claudius' expulsion of the Jews
from Rome in A.D. 49 as narrated in Acts 18:2). The assumption was that too
many foreign rites seeping into Rome could lead to a neglect of the ancestral customs and the traditional deities. As Rome permeated further east
in its military exploits, eventually conquering parts of Parthia in the second
century A.D., so too did religions like Judaism begin to be drawn into the
Roman world and find ready devotees who were interested in all things
mysterious and Eastern.

Second, another reason why Judaism gained a following from some was
because it had a distinguished antiquity in its history. Though our modern
culture disdains old and traditional things, in the ancient world, the antiquity and longevity of a religious tradition was the very grounds for its
authenticity. That is why the first book of Josephus' *Against Apion* invests so
much time establishing the ancient roots of the Jewish people and their religious customs.

Third, practices in common Judaism such as prayer, giving alms, observance of holy days and festivals, instruction in Scripture, and a system of
purity laws held some esteem in the eyes of many ancient peoples. Though
in our day we tend to think of ritual as a stale act of almost meaningless
repetition of antiquated practices, for ancient people, ritual was a key mechanism for demonstrating one's piety and establishing a connection with the
supernatural world. Ritual was the gateway into a whole new reality of gods
and apprehending their benevolence.

Fourth, the Jewish religion was widely considered to be effective in peti-
tioning gods for healing and for defeating evil magic and evil spirits. One of
the purposes for magic and divination in the ancient world was to coerce
gods or divine powers to accomplish certain tasks like healing, cursing or
blessing. We find this in the book of Acts where Paul on Cyprus encounters
a Jewish magician named Bar-Jesus/Elymas (Acts 13:6). Paul also came
upon itinerant Jewish exorcists in the sons of Sceva that operated in Ephesus
(Acts 19:13-14). The effectiveness of Jewish prayers and ritual for exorcisms
and other magic explains one reason for pagan attraction to Judaism.

Fifth, monotheism was not unknown in the ancient world, but it was rare. More common was henotheism, or the belief that one god was superior to others. Yet monotheism was clearly a distinctive trait of the Jewish religion. The most basic confession of Israel's faith was that "The LORD our God, the LORD is one" (Deut 6:4). Jewish monotheism, even with its accommodation of intermediaries like angels and spirits, was intellectually compelling for many pagan thinkers because it described the simplicity and unity of God. Jewish prophetic and apologetic literature also did a wonderful job of mocking idol worship and its domestication of deity to material matter which may have inclined some minds towards a monotheistic faith (e.g., Is 44; *Wis.* 13).

Sixth, members of Jewish communities experienced the civic and economic benefits of being a Jew. In the eyes of pagan authors who wrote on Judaism, Jews were known for looking after each other, even at the expense of their obligations to wider society.[19] Jews also secured a number of political privileges that included exemption from participation in the imperial cult and from military service. Combined with that was a unique ethical stance that integrated religion, ethics and social life. In addition, the well-defined social identity and group boundaries made Jewish communities socially and politically visible. Judaism was, then, an alluring option if one sought an identity that was concrete and yet flexible enough to exist within the Greco-Roman polis. On the whole, Judaism, as both a religion and a nationality, represented an attractive way of life for many outsiders.

One must not overlook, then, the significance of Jewish synagogues in the Diaspora as places where Christian missionaries like Paul began his evangelistic activities. Synagogues were places of prayer and instruction in the Torah; they also served as schools, charities, libraries, hostels and even hospitals. They were the hub of Jewish life and functioned as virtual outposts of Judaism in the Greco-Roman world.

CONCLUSION

Roland Allen was correct that contemporary mission methods need to get more in line with the model laid down by Paul in his own apostolic and

---

[19]Once more, see Tacitus, *Hist.* 5.5.

evangelistic work to establish churches in the Mediterranean basin. There is no point and no reason to reinvent the missiological wheel every few years. Although every generation tries to do it, they kick against the goads, since the best resources we have for developing a theory and praxis of missiology should come from a close reading of Paul's letters and the Acts of the Apostles with our minds clicking over as to how we can replicate it in our own context. We have our own agoras and our own Areopaguses where we need to preach. Paul is the exemplary model not for us to follow blindly, but to appropriate and replicate intelligently. Importantly, just like Paul, we need to be able to navigate the geographical, social, political, religious and cultural contexts of our day to be able to achieve that. Mission does not occur in a cultureless and valueless vacuum. Even though the "end of the earth" encompasses more people than many of the ancients thought, the message and method for reaching these people remains the same. In our own day, lands in Africa, Central Asia, parts of Oceania, South America and even in secular Europe are filled with people who desperately need to hear the good news of Jesus Christ. It is true in our day as it was in both Paul's day and in Isaiah's day that: "How beautiful are the feet of those bringing good news!" (see Is 52:7; Rom 10:15).

2

Paul the Missionary

♦ ♦ ♦

Eckhard J. Schnabel

Paul preached the good news of God's undeserved grace after he had personally experienced God's undeserved, powerful grace transforming him from a persecutor of Israel's Messiah and his people to an ambassador of God and a witness of Jesus Christ to all the world. Paul's missionary work rests squarely on his encounter with the crucified, risen and glorified Jesus on the road to Damascus.[1] We will first look at Paul's call to proclaim Jesus Christ to Jews and Gentiles, and then we will investigate how his encounter with the risen Messiah motivated his missionary work and informed his understanding of the missionary task before we survey his missionary activities.

Paul's Call

When Paul recounts his past in his letter to the Christians in southern

---

[1]Roland Allen refers only once, briefly, to Paul's call: "It is argued that as a matter of fact St Paul was an exceptional man living in exceptional times, preaching under exceptional circumstances; that he enjoyed advantages in his birth, his education, his call, his mission, his relationship to his hearers, such as have been enjoyed by no other" (Roland Allen, *Missionary Methods: St. Paul's or Ours?* [Grand Rapids: Eerdmans, 2001(1912)], p. 4). Allen argues that it is problematic if church leaders and missionaries regard Paul as exceptional in this sense: it prevents them from learning from Paul what Scripture teaches about missionary work. He writes, "However highly we may estimate St Paul's personal advantages or the assistance which the conditions of his age afforded, they cannot be so great as to rob his example of all value for us" (ibid.).

Galatia, he asserts that God "called me by his grace" as he was pleased "to reveal his Son to me, in order that I might preach him among the Gentiles" (Gal 1:15-16). First, Paul emphasizes that his conversion and call were the result of the sovereign will of God. The term translated "grace" (*charis*) describes God's favor, God's generous gift which includes forgiveness of Paul's prior activities as a persecutor of the messianic people of God (Gal 1:13-14) and inclusion among those who had seen the risen Jesus and who have been commissioned to be God's envoys (1 Cor 15:5-10). Paul is a follower of Jesus and a missionary not because of a personal decision by which he volunteered to preach the gospel, but on account of the grace of God who forgave his sins, who effectively convinced him of the significance of the life, death and resurrection of Jesus, and who summoned him to proclaim the saving message of Jesus Christ.[2] Second, Paul emphasizes that God's commission is fundamentally connected with Jesus, the Son of God, a title that "connotes Jesus' special relationship with God, his royal-messianic status, his unique significance in God's plan, and God's close involvement in Jesus' appearance."[3] Third, Paul asserts that he has been commissioned by God to preach Jesus Christ "among the Gentiles." This phrase can be interpreted in ethnic terms (Gentiles, non-Jews) or in territorial terms (regions outside of Judea, including Jews living in the Greek and Roman Diaspora).

Luke's account of Paul's conversion relates a revelation that Ananias, a Damascene Christian, received from God: "Go, for he is a chosen instrument of mine to carry my name before the Gentiles and kings and the children of Israel. For I will show him how much he must suffer for the sake of my name" (Acts 9:15-16).[4] This revelation of the risen Jesus describes Paul's missionary commission in terms of four emphases. First, Paul is Jesus' "chosen instrument." This means that Paul has been chosen by God to be an

---

[2]Note that Paul understands his conversion and call in terms similar to the calling of Isaiah and Jeremiah as God's prophets (compare Gal 1:15 with Is 49:1 and Jer 1:5). See Roy E. Ciampa, *The Presence and Function of Scripture in Galatians 1 and 2*, WUNT 2/102 (Tübingen: Mohr-Siebeck, 1998), pp. 111-12.

[3]See Larry W. Hurtado, *Lord Jesus Christ: Devotion to Jesus in Earliest Christianity* (Grand Rapids: Eerdmans, 2003), p. 107.

[4]On Paul's conversion see Dean S. Gilliland, *Pauline Theology and Mission Practice* (Grand Rapids: Baker, 1983), pp. 71-117; Richard N. Longenecker, ed., *The Road from Damascus: The Impact of Paul's Conversion on His Life, Thought, and Ministry* (Grand Rapids: Eerdmans, 1997).

instrument in Jesus' hands, fulfilling Jesus' purposes. Second, the purpose of Paul's life after his conversion is the proclamation of the message of Jesus as Israel's Messiah and the Savior (Acts 9:15). Paul is called to proclaim Jesus in front of people who have not heard this message. Third, the focus of Paul's proclamation of Jesus is the Gentiles—that is, people who worship other gods—but he is also sent to the people of Israel, and he will proclaim Jesus even before kings (Acts 25:23–26:29). Paul's call as a missionary to Gentiles (Rom 11:13; 15:15-16) does not preclude the proclamation of Jesus among the Jewish people: he preaches the gospel to the uncircumcised and to the circumcised (1 Cor 9:19-23). Luke reports on Saul's preaching in synagogues in the subsequent narrative (Acts 13:5, 15-41; 14:1; 17:2-4, 10-12, 17; 18:4-5; 19:8). Fourth, Paul will suffer as he proclaims the gospel of Jesus Christ before Gentiles and Jews.[5] The proclamation of Jesus who suffered, died and rose from the dead involves suffering on the part of Jesus' witnesses.

Paul's accounts of his conversion as recounted by Luke in Acts 22:4-16 and 26:9-18 restate these emphases in terms adapted to the contexts in which Paul gives these two speeches of defense in Jerusalem and in Caesarea. First, Paul asserts that God chose him to see and hear Jesus and to be Jesus' witness (Acts 22:14-15). He asserts that Jesus has appointed him as his servant and witness (Acts 26:16). As a servant he assists Jesus in what Jesus continues to do in the world (see Acts 1:1). As a witness he communicates to others what he has seen of Jesus—the reality of Jesus as risen from the dead, as alive and active from heavenly glory. He is sent as a "witness with us to his resurrection" (Acts 1:22 NRSV) just as the Twelve had been sent by Jesus. Second, Paul asserts that he has been commissioned to be Jesus' witness "to all the world" (Acts 22:15 NRSV), that is to all people, wherever they live, irrespective of ethnic identity or social status. He asserts that he will proclaim Jesus among his own people, that is, among Jews, as well as among Gentiles (Acts 26:17). Third, Paul describes (for King Agrippa) the mission and message he proclaims among Jews and Gentiles (Acts 26:18). Paul proclaims the gospel before Jews and Gentiles so that they will see the reality of Jesus as crucified, risen and exalted Messiah, Savior and Lord who fulfills God's promises. Paul proclaims the gospel so that Jews and Gentiles will turn

---

[5]For Paul's suffering see Rom 8:35; 1 Cor 4:11-13; 2 Cor 4:7-12; 6:4-10; 11:23-33; 12:10; Phil 4:12-13.

from darkness to light, which is a turn from the enslaving power of Satan to God.[6] Paul proclaims the gospel to Jews and Gentiles so that they may receive forgiveness of sins—the sin of living in darkness instead of seeing and accepting the reality of God and his revelation, the sin of serving Satan instead of God, the sin of refusing faith in Jesus, the sin of trusting in other gods. People who come to faith in Jesus, whom Paul is sent to proclaim, will be given a place in the community of God's people who enjoy fellowship with God.

Paul's call to missionary service emphasizes God's initiative, the encounter with Jesus, Jesus' authority over the life of Paul, the people to whom he is sent, and the content of the message that he will proclaim. Paul is an instrument in the hands of the Lord, sent particularly to Gentiles but to Jews as well. The message that he is to proclaim is focused on faith in the one true God and on the crucified and risen Jesus who grants forgiveness of sins and who grants them a place in God's messianic people.

PAUL'S MOTIVATION

Paul's encounter with the crucified, risen and glorified Jesus Christ who commissioned him to preach the good news of forgiveness of sins for Jews and Gentiles remained a fundamental motivation in his ministry. He emphasizes in his first letter to the Corinthian Christians, written twenty or so years after his conversion and call, that "if I preach the gospel, that gives me no ground for boasting. For necessity is laid upon me. Woe to me if I do not preach the gospel! For if I do this of my own will, I have a reward, but if not of my own will, I am still entrusted with a stewardship" (1 Cor 9:16-17). Paul's missionary work is not a matter of personal preference but a necessity, a compulsion that God has laid upon him. Like the prophet Jeremiah (Jer 1:5; 20:9), Paul is constrained by God: he has to do what God commissioned him to do. Unlike the prophet Jeremiah, "Paul laments neither the overpowering nature of his calling nor the hardship that preaching the gospel of the cross free of charge creates for him."[7]

---

[6]This "mission statement" in Acts 26:18 echoes Isaiah 42:6 where the Servant of the Lord is sent "as . . . a light for the nations," and Isaiah 42:16 where God promises that he will "turn the darkness before them into light."

[7]David E. Garland, *1 Corinthians*, BECNT (Grand Rapids: Baker, 2003), p. 424; he continues to emphasize that Paul does not bemoan his suffering "but welcomes it as something that reveals to

Paul's description of the obligation under which he works as an apostle is connected with his description of his status as a "slave of the Messiah Jesus" (Rom 1:1; Phil 1:1, author's translation). Paul obeys Jesus as a slave (Greek *doulos*; Latin *servus*) obeys his master. This does not mean that Paul is a reluctant missionary, anticipating the day when he can shed the shackles of this bondage. On the contrary, since his status as a slave is determined by the status of his master, he regards it as a privilege to speak for Jesus Christ, the exalted Lord: he expects that "by my speaking with all boldness, Christ will be exalted now as always in my body" (Phil 1:20 NRSV). He asserts that for him "living is Christ and dying is gain" while for him living in the flesh means "fruitful labor" in his missionary work. If he had to chose between the two, he would be hard pressed: "my desire is to depart and be with Christ, for that is far better; but to remain in the flesh is more necessary for you" (Phil 1:21, 23-24 NRSV). As he continues to serve Jesus Christ by serving the churches, he will "continue with all of you for your progress and joy in faith" (Phil 1:25 NRSV).

Thus, while Paul is motivated by the divine call and commission to be a witness of Jesus Christ before Jews and Gentiles, he is motivated by other factors and realities as well: by his desire to win Jews and Gentiles for Christ (1 Cor 9:20-23); his yearning for the salvation of the Jewish people (Rom 9:2-3); his concern for the believers' progress in the faith (Rom 1:11; Phil 1:8-11; 4:1); the reality of God's power (1 Cor 1:18; 2:5); the reality of the Holy Spirit (1 Cor 2:4; 2 Cor 3:8; Gal 3:3, 5; 5:25; Eph 6:17; Phil 1:19; 1 Thess 1:5); the example of Jesus (Phil 2:5-11); the example of Abraham and other people described in the Scriptures (see Rom 4:12; 1 Cor 10:6, 11); past experiences (Acts 15:37-38; compare 1 Cor 3:10, 13-15 with 9:1; also 15:10); divine guidance through dreams and revelations (Acts 16:6-10; 18:9-11; 22:17-21); and consultation with coworkers (Acts 16:10).[8]

---

others the life of Christ (2 Cor. 4:7-12)."

[8] Allen emphasizes progress in the faith in the section titled "The Training of Converts" (Allen, *Missionary Methods,* pp. 81-107), and he repeatedly and strongly emphasizes the power of the Spirit as the cause of the "success" of Paul's missionary work; cf. Allen, *Missionary Methods,* pp. 16, 25, 28, 48, 76, 91, 93-95, 113, 124, 131, 142, 121, 146-47, 149-50, 152. He ends Chapter 12 ("Principles and Spirit") with the following sentences: "We have not to do with mere men; we have to do with the Holy Ghost. What systems, forms, safeguards of every kind cannot do, He can do. When we believe in the Holy Ghost, we shall teach our converts to believe in Him, and when they believe in Him they will be able to face all difficulties and dangers. They will justify our faith.

THE MISSIONARY TASK ACCORDING TO PAUL

In two texts in 1 Corinthians, Paul provides extended descriptions of his missionary work.[9] In 1 Corinthians 3:5-15 we find seven convictions that characterize Paul's understanding of the missionary task. First, Paul sees himself as a servant (Greek *diakonos*; Latin *famulus*, meaning *minister* or *administer*). Since other missionaries, preachers and teachers are also servants, there is no place for arrogance and striving for superior prestige: missionary work is not about personal honor and status, but about getting work done at the behest of God.[10] Second, God is the Lord (*kyrios*) of missionary work. He is the master who directs the work of his "assistants" who serve him; both the task that God has assigned and the gift with which the various tasks are carried out are God's gracious gifts. Third, the missionary who "plants" a church and the teacher who "waters" the new believers in the emerging and established church are involved in one and the same task: they are "one" as they are both dependent upon the Lord and as they have a common purpose. Fourth, Paul is a pioneer missionary who establishes new churches, a task that involves "laying the foundation" of proclamation and explanation of the saving message of the crucified, risen and exalted Messiah. This Messiah forgives the sins of Jews and Gentiles and brings about reconciliation with God and transformation of the lives of the repentant sinners. The foundation is Jesus Christ, specifically Jesus the crucified Messiah (1 Cor 1:23; 2:2). The focus on the crucified and risen Jesus is the content of the missionary proclamation, the foundation of the church and the standard for measuring the authenticity of the church's growth. Fifth, the positive outcome of missionary work is due only to the power of God: only God gives growth, only God renders the proclamation of the gospel effective. Sixth, the churches that emerge as the result of missionary work do not belong to the missionary: the church is "God's field, God's building" (1 Cor 3:9) and thus belongs to God. Seventh, missionaries are

---

The Holy Ghost will justify our faith in Him. 'This is the Victory which overcometh the world, even our faith'" (p. 150).

[9]For a more detailed exposition see Eckhard J. Schnabel, *Paul the Missionary: Realities, Strategies and Methods* (Downers Grove, Ill.: InterVarsity Press, 2008), pp. 130-37. Unfortunately, Allen does not discuss these important passages.

[10]See Andrew D. Clarke, *Secular and Christian Leadership in Corinth: A Socio-Historical and Exegetical Study of 1 Corinthians 1-6*, AGJU 18 (Leiden: Brill, 1993), pp. 119-20.

accountable to God: God alone decides what constitutes success. While Paul seems to indicate that there are different "wages" which God grants according to the "work" of the individual missionary, preacher or teacher, he does not elaborate on the specific differences concerning these wages. The preachers and teachers of the church are responsible for the way in which they build on the "foundation" which is Jesus Christ. Their theological perspectives, their strategic priorities, their motivations and their methods must be squarely based on the reality of Jesus' death and resurrection. Missionaries and teachers whose ministry is the result of the central reality of the crucified and risen Jesus Christ do not have to be afraid of the fire of the Last Judgment. Yet those who marginalize the message of the crucified and risen Savior and focus on other matters will "suffer loss" (1 Cor 3:15) in the Last Judgment.

In 1 Corinthians 9:19-23 Paul formulates seven fundamental elements of missionary work. First, the basic rule of missionary existence states that missionaries take the hearers of the message seriously. Paul's behavior is subordinated to preaching the gospel, which will not be heard if he does not take his audience seriously. Second, Paul makes himself dependent upon the audience in the sense that he listens to the people so that they will listen to him. His behavior is informed by the needs of his audience. This means that he lives with the people he seeks to reach with the gospel. Third, Paul does not exclude anybody from his preaching. He is obligated to preach the gospel to all people, irrespective of ethnic background, social status or gender. He preaches to Jews and Gentiles, to the free and to slaves. Fourth, missionary accommodation does not formulate limitations in advance: Paul becomes "all things" to all people (1 Cor 9:22). Among Jews he lives as a Jew, among Gentiles he lives as a Gentile (although without engaging in sinful behaviors in which Gentiles often engage). Fifth, Paul seeks to win more people: he never stops evangelizing. Sixth, the goal of his missionary work is to "win" people, to rescue sinners so that they will receive salvation and adoption into God's family. Seventh, the benchmark of Paul's behavior is the gospel, not pragmatic effectiveness: "I do it all for the sake of the gospel, that I may share with them in its blessings" (1 Cor 9:23). The gospel of the crucified and risen Jesus Christ determines the scope and the limits of missionary accommodation.

PAUL'S MISSIONARY ACTIVITIES

While church tradition has long assumed three "missionary journeys" of the apostle Paul, a close look at Paul's comments on his missionary work in his letters and Luke's report in the book of Acts allows us to distinguish sixteen phases of Paul's missionary activities.[11]

Damascus (A.D. 32).[12] Paul preached in the synagogues of Damascus soon after his conversion (Acts 9:19-22) and again before he returned to Jerusalem (Gal 1:17; Acts 9:23-26), demonstrating that Jesus was the Son of God, Israel's promised Messiah (Acts 9:20, 22). The fact that the Jewish community of Damascus cooperated with the local representative of Aretas IV, the Nabatean king, in the attempted arrest of Paul (2 Cor 11:32) suggests that the Jews of Damascus regarded Paul's activities as a threat. This implies that Paul's preaching in the synagogues of Damascus had met with considerable success. Why would Paul start his missionary work in Damascus? The answer is simple: he found himself in Damascus when he was converted to faith in Jesus, and as he had received a divine commission to be Jesus' witness among Jews and Gentiles, he started to carry out the task that God had given him immediately, right where he was.

Arabia (A.D. 32/33).[13] Paul describes in Galatians 1:17 how he preached the gospel after his conversion without first consulting with the apostles in Jerusalem, going to Arabia (also called Nabatea). He relates in 2 Corinthians 11:32-33 that the ethnarch of King Aretas in Damascus wanted to arrest him (see also Acts 9:23-25), which suggests that Paul was not in Arabia to meditate in the desert but to preach the gospel in the Nabatean cities (perhaps in Selaima, Shahba, Kanatha, Soada, Bostra, Gerasa, Philadelphia and other cities, including the capital Petra). He went to Arabia presumably because it was the area adjacent to Damascus, allowing him to reach not only Jews but Gentiles as well. Also, the Jews regarded the Nabateans as descendants of Ishmael the son of Abraham; the translators of

---

[11]Allen spends very little time discussing the details of Paul's missionary work in chapter 2 titled "Strategic Points" (Allen, *Missionary Methods,* pp. 10-17).

[12]This date assumes that Paul's conversion took place in A.D. 31/32, the second year after Jesus' crucifixion and resurrection. See Rainer Riesner, *Paul's Early Period: Chronology, Mission Strategy, Theology* (Grand Rapids: Eerdmans, 1998), pp. 64-74.

[13]See Martin Hengel, "Paul in Arabia," BBR 12 (2002): 47–66; Eckhard J. Schnabel, *Early Christian Mission* (Downers Grove, Ill.: InterVarsity Press, 2004), 2:1032-45; for the following phases of Paul's missionary work see ibid. 1045-1292; Schnabel, *Paul the Missionary,* pp. 60-122, 258-85.

the Hebrew Bible into Greek identified the Nabateans with Nabaioth, the firstborn of the twelve sons of Ishmael.[14] Since the Idumeans, the descendants of Esau, were converted (by force) to Judaism by John Hyrcanus (135/34-104 B.C.), the Arab Nabateans would have appeared to the Jews as their closest relatives who were still Gentiles.

Jerusalem (A.D. 33/34). After his forced departure from Arabia and Damascus, Paul returned to Jerusalem, where he had been based as a persecutor of the church three years earlier. Paul preached in the meetings of the Christian congregation as well as in the local synagogues; the strong opposition forced him to leave Jerusalem after two weeks, despite his desire to stay (Acts 9:26-30; 22:17-21; Gal 1:18-19).

Syria and Cilicia (A.D. 34-42).[15] Paul traveled via Caesarea to Tarsus (Acts 9:30), his home town (Acts 21:39; 22:3), the metropolis of Cilicia that was administered by the Roman governor of the Province of Syria throughout much of the first century. Paul preached the gospel in the regions of Syria and Cilicia, a fact that was known in the Judean churches (Gal 1:21-24). Paul certainly engaged in missionary work in Tarsus, but he established churches in other cities as well: the letter drafted at the conclusion of the Apostles' Council is sent to Gentile Christians in Antioch, in Syria and in Cilicia (Acts 15:23), a fact that presupposes churches in cities besides Antioch (see also Acts 15:41). This period of Paul's missionary work, about which we have no detailed information, lasted for ten years. Why did Paul preach the gospel and establish churches in Syria and Cilicia? Tarsus was his home town, in which, presumably, relatives and friends lived; Paul's Tarsian citizenship gave him protection from the kind of opposition that forced him to leave Arabia, Damascus and Jerusalem. Also, Tarsus was the most significant city in the region north of Antioch, Tarsus had a Jewish community, and Tarsus was a center of communication in the region.

Antioch (A.D. 42-44). Barnabas recruited Paul to help with missionary and pastoral work in Antioch (Acts 11:25-26; see Acts 13:1), the capital of the province of Syria, the third largest city in the Roman empire. The church in

---

[14]See Gen 25:13 LXX; 28:9 LXX; 36:3 LXX; 1 Chron 1:29 LXX.

[15]The fact that both Luke and Paul refer to provinces does not prove that "in St Paul's view the unit was the province rather than the city" (Allen, *Missionary Methods,* p. 12). It is impossible to evangelize provinces if the missionary does not reach people who live in the cities (and the villages that the cities control).

Antioch had been established by Greek-speaking Jewish believers from Jerusalem who had left the Jewish capital in connection with the persecution of A.D. 31/32, following the killing of Stephen (Acts 11:19-24). Paul accepted Barnabas' invitation, perhaps because his missionary work in Cilicia, "as later in Corinth and Ephesus or then in the eastern Mediterranean generally, had come to a certain conclusion. Presumably the communities that he had founded had to some degree become independent. On the other hand, Barnabas, who must have regarded Paul as a missionary authority 'with equal rights,' must have convinced him that he was *urgently needed* in Antioch, at least at that very moment," perhaps because the situation in the capital of the Province of Syria "became more critical, so that a theologian with Paul's competence in the scriptures, capacity to argue strongly, resolution and capacity for organization was urgently needed."[16]

Cyprus (A.D. 45). Paul, together with Barnabas and accompanied by John Mark, traveled from Antioch to the eastern coast of Cyprus and preached the gospel in the synagogues of Salamis, probably in other cities along the coastal road (perhaps in Kition and Amathus) and eventually in Paphos, the capital (Acts 13:4-12). Luke relates the power encounter with a Jewish magician and the conversion of Sergius Paulus, the governor of the province of Cyprus. Paul and Barnabas went to Cyprus perhaps because Barnabas was a native of Cyprus (Acts 4:36), and perhaps because Greek speaking Jewish believers from Jerusalem whom Barnabas knew had been active on Cyprus (Acts 11:19), presumably to consolidate and expand the work of these missionaries in the cities of the island.

Southern Galatia (A.D. 46-47). Paul preached the gospel and established churches in Pisidian Antioch, Iconium, Lystra and Derbe (Acts 13:14–14:23). He preached in the local synagogues, he spoke before Gentile audiences, and he established churches whose ministry he consolidated by appointing elders (Acts 14:22-23).[17] Why did Paul bypass Perge, the capital of the province of Pamphylia, and other large towns in Pamphylia and Pi-

---

[16]Martin Hengel and Anna Maria Schwemer, *Paul Between Damascus and Antioch: The Unknown Years,* trans. John Bowden (Louisville: Westminster John Knox, 1997), pp. 179-80, 218 (emphasis Hengel and Schwemer).

[17]Note Luke's summary of Paul's sermon in the synagogue of Pisidian Antioch in Acts 13:16-41. In Lystra he spoke before pagans who wanted to honor him and Barnabas with sacrifices after a man who was crippled from birth had been healed (Acts 14:15-17).

sidia, going straight from Paphos to Pisidian Antioch, which had only about ten thousand inhabitants?[18] Paul may have moved to Pisidian Antioch, located on the Anatolian plateau, as the result of having contracted malaria.[19] Another reason for Paul's move to Pisidian Antioch has been suggested: Sergius Paulus, the governor of Cyprus, who was converted in Paphos (Acts 13:12), belonged to the family of the Sergii Paulli who owned estates in the region of Vetissus (mod. Emirler) in the Province of Galatia in central Anatolia, with members of the family living in Pisidian Antioch.[20] Paul's missionary work in Pisidian Antioch may have been suggested by Sergius Paulus who proposed "that he make it his next port of call, no doubt proving him with letters of introduction to aid his passage and his stay."[21]

Pamphylia (A.D. 47). Paul preached in Perge, the capital of Pamphylia (Acts 14:24-25). While Luke reports neither conversions nor the establishment of a church, both are likely: since Luke's account is selective, even the very brief remark about Paul speaking "the word" in Perge suggests that people heard the gospel and responded by coming to faith in Jesus.

Macedonia (A.D. 49-50). After a visit to Antioch in Syria and the Apostles Council in Jerusalem, Paul planned missionary work in the province of Asia and in the province of Pontus-Bithynia (Acts 16:6-7). He then crossed from Asia Minor to Europe and preached the gospel in Macedonia (Acts 16:6–17:15). Accompanied by Silas, Luke and Timothy (who had been recruited as a coworker during a visit to Lystra; Acts 16:1-3), Paul established churches in Philippi, Thessalonica and Berea. Luke reports missionary ministry in the local synagogues, conversion of Gentiles (Lydia, who was a God-fearer), an encounter with a demon-possessed slave girl who earned money for her owners as a medium, encounters with city officials, imprisonment (in Philippi) and forced departures on account of

---

[18]See Barbara Levick, *Roman Colonies in Southern Asia Minor* (Oxford: Clarendon, 1967), pp. 93-94. The theater of Perge could seat 14,000 spectators, while the theater of Pisidian Antioch had room for 5,000 inhabitants.

[19]Paul states in Gal 4:13 that he came to Galatia and preached the gospel there "because of a bodily ailment." See F. F. Bruce, *Commentary on Galatians*, NIGTC (Grand Rapids: Eerdmans, 1982), pp. 208-9.

[20]For the latest discussion of the Sergii Paulii and their relationship to Pisidian Antioch see Michel Christol and Thomas Drew-Bear, "Les Sergii Paulli et Antioche," in *Actes du Ier congres international sur Antioche de Pisidie*, Collection archéologie et histoire de l'antiquité 5, ed. T. Drew-Bear, M. Tashalan and C. J. Thomas (Lyon/Paris: Université Lumière-Lyon / Boccard, 2002), pp. 177-91.

[21]Stephen Mitchell, *Anatolia: Land, Men, and Gods in Asia Minor* (Oxford: Oxford University Press, 1995) 2:7.

strong local opposition. The move across the Aegean Sea to Macedonia was not motivated by a strategic decision to reach cities in Europe but by a dream-vision (Acts 16:9-10). Thessalonica was the most populous city of Macedonia and was thus an obvious choice as a location for missionary work. The move to Berea, a town that was certainly not more attractive than the Macedonian cities of Pella or Edessa for missionaries who had just been forced to leave the provincial capital, was probably motivated by contacts that the Jews of Thessalonica had with the Jewish community in Berea: the Jewish converts in Thessalonica "sent Paul and Silas away by night to Berea" (Acts 17:10).

Achaia (A.D. 50-51). Leaving Macedonia, Paul traveled south to the province of Achaia and preached the gospel in Athens and Corinth (Acts 17:16–18:28). The stay in Athens was not a mere stopover on the journey to Corinth: the fact that Luke provides an extensive account of Paul's visit (Acts 17:16-34) and the summary statement in Acts 17:17 ("so he argued in the synagogue with the Jews and the God-fearers and in the agora day by day with those who happened to be there," author's translation) indicates that Paul engaged in missionary work in Athens along the lines of his missionary work in other cities. Luke's report focuses on Paul's conversations with Epicurean and Stoic philosophers, which prompted the notion that Paul wanted to introduce new deities into the pantheon of gods worshiped in Athens (perhaps the deities "Jesus" and "Anastasis" or "Resurrection" as the personification of a central reality that Paul emphasized in his messages). Despite the religious tolerance of the Greco-Roman period, there was no freedom of religion in the sense that one could introduce new cults into a city.[22] Paul is thus invited to explain his activities before the Areopagus Council of the city whose members would assess the novelty of a cult, the desirability of allowing the new cult and the requirements of the cult such as the need for a temple or an altar, sacrifices, festivals and processions. The Council assumed that Paul, who had evidently found a sub-

---

[22]See Robert Garland, *Introducing New Gods: The Politics of Athenian Religion* (Ithaca: Cornell University Press, 1992). Isocrates praises the Athenians for guarding "against the elimination of any of the ancestral sacrifices and against the addition of any sacrifices outside the traditional ones" (*Areopagiticus* 30). On the deities which were worshiped in Athens see John M. Camp, *Gods and Heroes in the Athenian Agora* (Princeton: American School of Classical Studies at Athens, 1980).

stantial following among the Athenians, would want to claim for his new religious cult a rightful place in the pantheon of Athenian gods. In his speech before the Areopagus Council (Acts 17:22-31), Paul asserts that he is not introducing new deities to Athens; rather, he proclaims the deity who is honored at the altar with the inscription "To the unknown god" (Acts 17:23)—the God who needs neither a temple nor festivals or sacrifices (Acts 17:24-26), the God who is present everywhere because he created the world and everything in it (Acts 17:24-28), but also the God who no longer overlooks the times of human ignorance, commanding all people everywhere to repent as the Day of Judgment is coming and the judge has been appointed, whose name is Jesus (Acts 17:30-31). Luke reports the conversion of Dionysius, a member of the Areopagus Council, a woman with the name Damaris and of other Athenians (Acts 17:34). The missionary work in Corinth begins in the local synagogue and then relocates to the house of a certain Titius Justus, a Gentile God-fearer who had evidently come to faith in Jesus (Acts 18:4-5, 6-7). The attempt of the leaders of the Jewish community to indict Paul before Gallio, the governor of the province, is unsuccessful, which allows Paul to preach and teach in Corinth for one and a half years (Acts 18:11).

Ephesus (A.D. 52-55). After visiting Antioch in Syria and Jerusalem as well as the churches that he has established in Galatia and Phrygia, Paul travels to Ephesus, the capital of the province of Asia, where he preaches and teaches the gospel for over two years (Acts 19:1-41). Luke reports the negative effect that the evidently numerous conversions of Gentiles in the city had on the trade of the producers of religious objects connected with the famous cult of Artemis Ephesia (Acts 19:21-41). And he reports the effect that Paul's missionary work had on the entire province: "all the residents of [the Province of] Asia, both Jews and Greeks, heard the word of the Lord" (Acts 19:10 NRSV). Paul's references to "the churches of Asia" in 1 Corinthians 16:19 confirms that other churches were established in the province of Asia during this period.

Illyricum (A.D. 56). As Paul traveled from Ephesus to Macedonia and Achaia before returning to Jerusalem, he evidently visited cities in the province of Illyricum. Paul asserts in Romans 15:19 that he preached the gospel "from Jerusalem and all the way around to Illyricum." Since he engaged in missionary outreach in Jerusalem, even though only for a short period of time, it is plausible to assume that he also preached in Illyricum. Since Paul was planning a mission to Spain, a region in which Latin was the common language, and as the people in the cities of Illyricum also used Latin, Paul may have tried to find out how he would be able to operate in a Latin speaking environment after leaving the Greek speaking regions in the eastern Mediterranean.

Judea (A.D. 57-59). When Paul was arrested in Jerusalem, he was accused of "teaching everyone everywhere against the people and the law and this place" (Acts 21:28). Paul explains and defends the gospel that he has been preaching in the Temple (Acts 22:3-21) and before the Sanhedrin (Acts 23:1-6). When he waits as a prisoner in Caesarea for Felix and then Festus, the Roman governors, to decide his case, he explains the gospel before the Roman authorities (Acts 24:10-21) and the Jewish King Agrippa (Acts 26:2-29), whom he seeks to lead to faith in Jesus as Israel's Messiah (Acts 26:27-29).

Rome (A.D. 60-62). During Paul's imprisonment in Rome, where he was able to rent his own accommodations and meet with the leaders of the Jewish community, he tries "to convince them about Jesus both from the law of Moses and from the Prophets," which leads to conversions (Acts 28:23-24).

Spain (63-64?). According to early church tradition, Paul was released from Roman imprisonment in A.D. 62, enabling him to engage in missionary work in Spain.[23] Clement of Rome, in his letter to the Corinthian Christians written in A.D. 95, says concerning Paul: "Seven times he bore chains; he was sent into exile and stoned; he served as a herald in both the East and the West; and he received the noble reputation for his faith. He taught righteousness to the whole world, and came to the limits of the West, bearing his witness before the rulers" (1 Clement 5:6-7). The phrase "the limits of the West" is sometimes used for Gaul (France) and Britain, but usually designates Spain, which was regarded to be located at the western "end of the world." If Paul indeed traveled to Spain and preached the gospel, perhaps in Tarraco, the capital of the province Hispania Citerior on the northeast coast of Spain, we have no sources that report about such missionary work.[24]

---

[23]See Jerome Murphy-O'Connor, *Paul: A Critical Life* (Oxford: Oxford University Press, 1996), pp. 359-61.

[24]The first explicit reference to Christians in Spain comes from Irenaeus the bishop of Lyon, without

Crete (64-65?). A comment in Paul's letter to Titus suggests a period of missionary activity on the island of Crete: "This is why I left you in Crete, so that you might put what remained into order, and appoint elders in every town as I directed you" (Tit 1:5). We do not know who established the churches on the island of Crete which were in existence at the time Paul wrote to Titus. Jewish pilgrims from Crete were present in Jerusalem in A.D. 30 on the Feast of Pentecost when Peter started to preach the gospel in Jerusalem (Acts 2:11). It is possible that some of these pilgrims came to faith on this occasion and brought the gospel back to Crete.

Conclusion

In his missionary work, Paul moved to geographically adjacent areas, moving from east to west. Since he was concerned for the salvation of the Jewish people, and since Jews lived in the cities of the Roman provinces, Paul focused on cities. Since he was called to focus his ministry in particular on Gentiles, he engaged in missionary work in cities because they are major population centers, centers of communication and of education, places where people speak Greek. Paul preached the gospel in synagogues, in the courtyard of the Jerusalem Temple, in front of a pagan temple, in marketplaces, lecture halls, workshops, and in private homes.[25] He explained the gospel to anyone who was willing to listen, whether they were Jews or Gentiles, men or women, free or slaves, members of the local elite or the disenfranchised.[26] Paul's missionary work was motivated by the burning desire to "win as many as possible" to faith in Jesus Christ, whether Jews or Gentiles (1 Cor 9:19-21 NIV).

---

any reference to Paul's missionary work (*Haer.* 1.10.2).

[25]Acts 9:20; 13:5, 14; 14:1; 16:12-13; 17:1, 10, 17; 18:1, 4, 18; and 19:8 explictly state the various synagogues where Paul spoke; Acts 21:27–22:21, speaking in the Temple courtyard on the occasion of his arrest; Acts 14:13-18, with reference to Lystra and the temple of Zeus which was located outside the city; Acts 17:17, in which the present tense of the verb indicates that preaching the gospel in the marketplace was Paul's regular practice; Acts 19:9, referring to the lecture hall (Greek *scholē*) of a certain Tyrannus, who may have been a philosopher who lectured in the classroom that Paul was able to rent, or the owner of the building; see Acts 18:3 for the leather workshop of Aquila and Priscilla in which Paul worked; and Acts 20:20, mentioned with reference to Paul's missionary work in Ephesus.

[26]Rom 1:14-16; 1 Cor 1:26-29; 9:20-23; 12:13; Gal 3:28; Col 3:11.

3

PAUL'S GOSPEL

♦ ♦ ♦

Robert L. Plummer

Ｉf one were to look at a list of current evangelical book titles (*What Is the Gospel?* or *The Naked Gospel* or *Gospel Wakefulness*, for example), one might conclude that a significant rediscovery of the gospel is in progress.[1] In addition, numerous recently founded organizations, blogs and conferences frequently employ the word "gospel" in their titles.[2] Even with this plethora of gospel language, there seems to be an ongoing fog surrounding what it means to have a life and ministry defined by the gospel of Jesus Christ. One well-established pastor confided in me, "I'm still trying to figure out what it means to preach a gospel-centered sermon."

A century ago, in his influential book *Missionary Methods: St. Paul's or Ours?* Roland Allen argues that one of the main principles undergirding the apostle Paul's entire ministry was his focus on the gospel. Allen writes,

> *St Paul was a preacher of the gospel, not of a law*. His Epistles are full of this. He reiterates it again and again. It was not simply that he was a preacher of the Gospel in contradistinction to the preachers of the Jewish law, he was a preacher of Gospel as opposed to the system of law. He lived

---

[1]E.g., Greg Gilbert, *What Is the Gospel?* (Wheaton, Ill.: Crossway, 2010); Andrew Farley, *The Naked Gospel* (Grand Rapids: Zondervan, 2009); Jared C. Wilson, *Gospel Wakefulness* (Wheaton, Ill.: Crossway, 2011).

[2]E.g., www.thegospelcoalition.org, or the Together for the Gospel conference (see http://t4g.org/).

in a dispensation of Gospel as opposed to the system of law. He administered a Gospel, not a law. His method was a method of Gospel, not a method of law. This is the most distinctive mark of Pauline Christianity. This is what separates his doctrine from all other systems of religion.[3]

Statistics support Allen's bold assertion. Paul uses some form of the word "gospel" seventy-seven times in his thirteen canonical letters.[4] Even where the word "gospel" (*euangelion*), "proclaim the gospel" (*euangelizō*) or other "gospel words" (e.g., *euangelistēs*, evangelist) are absent from Paul's writing, the concept remains prominent. For Paul, his divine commission to bring the salvation of God to a fallen world was nothing other than his defense and proclamation of the gospel (Rom 1:14-17).

THE GOSPEL ACCORDING TO PAUL

If the gospel is the indispensible defining element of Paul's apostolic ministry, it is essential that we truly know what he means by "gospel" or "proclaiming the gospel." For this investigation, perhaps it is best to listen to Paul's teaching on the gospel from one key passage, with brief forays into other related texts.

In 1 Corinthians 15:1-8, Paul gives one of the clearest definitions of the gospel found in his letters. The text reads,

> Now I would remind you, brothers, of the gospel I preached to you, which you received, in which you stand, and by which you are being saved, if you hold fast to the word I preached to you—unless you believed in vain. For I delivered to you as of first importance what I also received: that Christ died for our sins in accordance with the Scriptures, that he was buried, that he was raised on the third day in accordance with the Scriptures, and that he appeared to Cephas, then to the twelve. Then he appeared to more than five hundred brothers at one time, most of whom are still alive, though some have fallen asleep. Then he appeared to James, then to all the apostles. Last of all, as to one untimely born, he appeared also to me.

We will now look at eight truths about the gospel in this text by Paul.

---

[3]Roland Allen, *Missionary Methods: St. Paul's or Ours?* 2nd ed. (Grand Rapids: Eerdmans, 1962), p. 148 (emphasis in the 1962 edition). The book was first published in 1912.
[4]BibleWorks search on words that begin with εὐαγ- in the thirteen Pauline epistles.

Christian leaders must constantly remind themselves and others of the gospel. In 1 Corinthians, Paul is writing to a congregation with whom he had lived and ministered for about eighteen months (Acts 18:11). He has already written them a previous letter (1 Cor 5:9). One might think that at this point the Corinthians would be ready to "move beyond" the gospel to more advanced teachings on the Christian life. In fact, Paul says the opposite is true. Because the Corinthians have failed to grasp the gospel, their community is plagued with numerous relational and ethical problems. The Corinthians are factional (1 Cor 3:3-4), immoral (1 Cor 5:1), inebriated (1 Cor 11:21), irreverent (1 Cor 11:21), jealous (1 Cor 12:15), unloving (1 Cor 13:1-3) and theologically misinformed (1 Cor 15:12). We might be tempted to think that the Corinthians needed a unity ministry, a sex and marriage ministry, an alcoholic recovery ministry and so on, but Paul knows that such fractured, superficial fixes would fail to deal with the root issue of the Corinthians' problems. All of the community's troubles flow from their failure to understand the gospel and live in light of it. The Corinthians do not need to move beyond the gospel; they need to be "reminded" of the gospel which Paul preached to them (1 Cor 15:1).[5] The Corinthians' failure to remember the gospel is not an incidental oversight (like forgetting to pick up a gallon of milk on the way home from work), but an immoral forgetting—a straying from the truth about who God is, who we are and what God has done to save us.

Martin Luther recognized both the centrality of the gospel and the need for Christian leaders to maintain that central focus before the people they lead. Luther wrote, "Most necessary it is, therefore, that we should know this article [i.e., the gospel] well, teach it unto others, and beat it into their heads continually."[6]

In the altarpiece at St. Mary's Church in Wittenberg, painter Lucas Cranach captured this Lutheran (and biblical) emphasis on the gospel. In the altar painting, Luther stands in the pulpit in the front of the church.

---

[5]1 Cor 15:1 reads, Γνωρίζω δὲ ὑμῖν, ἀδελφοί, τὸ εὐαγγέλιον. Literally, Paul wants to "make known" the gospel to the Corinthian Christians. Of course, since the gospel has not changed and Paul is making it known again, the ESV translation rightly translates γνωρίζω as "remind" here.

[6]Martin Luther, *A Commentary on St. Paul's Epistle to the Galatians* (Cambridge, U.K.: James Clarke & Co., 1953), p. 101. I was pointed to this quote by Daniel Montgomery, who derived it from Tim Keller.

One of his hands is on the Bible. (And, indeed, the content of the proclaimed gospel must always flow directly from God's revealed word.) Luther's other hand points to the body of Christ suspended on a cross between the preacher and congregation. The eyes of the congregation are turned not to Luther, but to Christ on the cross.

Paul wrote the Corinthians to "remind [them] of the gospel" (1 Cor 15:1). The application for modern-day missionaries is quite clear: whether in initial proclamation or through ongoing discipleship, a missionary must focus on the gospel of Christ. We never move beyond the atoning death of Christ. All ethics and "practical matters" of the Christian life must be rooted in the unchanging truth of Christ's life, death and resurrection.

The gospel must be both proclaimed and received for its saving benefits to be applied. Philip Melanchthon famously quipped, "To know Christ is to know his benefits."[7] In other words, we do not know Christ in the same way that we know our neighbors, whom we can see. Nor do we know Christ in the same way that we master geometry in school. We know Christ when we hear what he has done for us and respond in repentance and faith, receiving the eternal salvation of our souls.

Some Christian theologians have speculated that persons may have a postmortem opportunity to repent and believe the gospel.[8] Other prominent Christian thinkers have speculated that sincere adherents of other faiths may be saved through Christ's death, even though that application of Christ's saving work remains unconscious to them in this life.[9]

Paul's letters and the rest of Scripture are not in sympathy with such theological speculations. In 1 Corinthians 15, Paul says he has "proclaimed the gospel" to the Corinthians and that they have "received" the message (1 Cor 15:1-2). For Paul, the saving benefits of the gospel are not present unless that good news is both announced and received. Paul makes the necessity of hearing and speaking the gospel especially clear in Romans 10:9-15, where he writes,

---

[7] Philip Melanchthon, *Loci Communes*, in *Melanchthon and Bucer*, ed. Wilhelm Pauck, LCC 19 (Philadelphia: Westminster Press, 1969), pp. 21-22.

[8] E.g., Clark H. Pinnock, *A Wideness in God's Mercy: The Finality of Jesus Christ in a World of Religions* (Grand Rapids: Zondervan, 1992), pp. 168-75.

[9] E.g., John Sanders, *No Other Name: An Investigation into the Destiny of the Unevangelized* (Grand Rapids: Eerdmans, 1992). See esp. pp. 215-80. For a thorough critique of inclusivism, see the fine essays in *Faith Comes by Hearing: A Response to Inclusivism*, ed. Christopher W. Morgan and Robert A. Peterson (Downers Grove, Ill.: InterVarsity Press, 2008).

If you confess with your mouth that Jesus is Lord and believe in your heart that God raised him from the dead, you will be saved. For with the heart one believes and is justified, and with the mouth one confesses and is saved. For the Scripture says, "Everyone who believes in him will not be put to shame." For there is no distinction between Jew and Greek; for the same Lord is Lord of all, bestowing his riches on all who call on him. For "everyone who calls on the name of the Lord will be saved." How then will they call on him in whom they have not believed? And how are they to believe in him of whom they have never heard? And how are they to hear without someone preaching? And how are they to preach unless they are sent? As it is written, "How beautiful are the feet of those who preach the good news!"

Jesus declares that others will know his followers by their love (Jn 13:35), yet a passive, nonverbal witness is an insufficient, truncated expression of the gospel. God has ordained his saving message to spread through the written or spoken words of human emissaries. In 1 Corinthians 15, Christians are reminded that they are not faithful missionaries unless they are making God's saving message known through spoken or written words. And, though the results ultimately rest with God, they cannot consider themselves successful missionaries unless their gospel words are received with expressions of repentance and faith.[10]

The gospel is a new dynamic realm in which we stand. Paul not only says the gospel has been received by the Corinthians but that it is something "in which" they now "stand" (1 Cor 15:1). This is an unusual way of speaking of a message. After watching the U.S. president's State of the Union address on TV, would you turn to the person next to you and say, "I stand in that message"? Would you walk out of church Sunday morning and comment to your spouse, "Let's stand in that sermon"? Paul's description of the gospel as a realm in which the Corinthian Christians now stand reveals that the gospel is more than simply a set of true propositions (though certainly not less). Elsewhere in Paul's letters he speaks of the gospel as growing and bearing fruit (Col 1:6). Paul describes the gospel as making a triumphant

---

[10]Of course, missionaries can go for long periods of time without seeing fruit, but the very fact that missionaries are dissatisfied with a lack of response shows that the ultimate joy and success of a missionary endeavor is to see nonbelievers respond in repentance and faith.

march, in whose way he does not want to stand (1 Cor 9:12). The gospel arrives (like a traveler) to a congregation (1 Cor 14:36; 1 Thess 1:5).

Paul thinks of the gospel as a dynamic entity that grows, prospers, rings forth, comes, advances and saves. Paul can personify the gospel in this way because the gospel is a powerful word from God. In Romans 1:16, Paul says, "I am not ashamed of the gospel, for it is the power of God for salvation to everyone who believes." The gospel is a dynamic entity because it is not ultimately a human word but a divine word. God's words do not simply observe reality, but create the reality of which they speak. In continuity with Paul's thought, we see many examples of the dynamic nature of God's word in the Old Testament. For example, in Genesis 1, God speaks and the world comes into existence. Throughout the historical and prophetic books, "the word of the Lord" comes to the prophets and moves them to proclamation (Hos 1:1; cf. 1 Sam 10:10; Ezek 2:2). The word is like a fire in their bones (Jer 20:9). About his word, the Lord declares, "Is not my word like a fire . . . and like a hammer that breaks the rock in pieces?" (Jer 23:29). God says elsewhere, "For as the rain and the snow come down from heaven and do not return there but water the earth, making it bring forth and sprout, giving seed to the sower and bread to the eater, so shall my word be that goes out from my mouth; it shall not return to me empty, but it shall accomplish that which I purpose, and shall succeed in the thing for which I sent it" (Is 55:10-11).

Paul did not think up the gospel himself, nor did he receive it from any human source (Gal 1:12). Paul received his gospel directly from the Lord (Gal 1:12, cf. Acts 9:5). Because the gospel was God's saving word to humanity, Paul could speak of it as a powerful entity, progressing through the world and accomplishing God's task of gathering a redeemed people for himself. Likewise, when this gospel came to rest in a new community, Paul confidently spoke of the way that this dynamic entity would continue to spread (1 Thess 1:6-8; 2:13; 2 Thess 3:1).[11] The gospel that progresses through the apostle Paul will continue to progress through those converts in whom it has come to dwell. This truth is arguably Paul's main basis for confidence that the gospel will continue to spread through his congregations. Insofar as the dynamic word of the Lord truly indwells the members of a local congre-

---

[11]See Robert L. Plummer, *Paul's Understanding of the Church's Mission: Did the Apostle Paul Expect the Early Christian Communities to Evangelize?* PBM (Milton Keynes, U.K.: Paternoster, 2008), pp. 59-64.

gation, that saving word will transform its hearers and continue to progress through them.

In a work that commemorates the contribution of Roland Allen, it is fitting to compare our conclusions on this point with Allen's reflections. In asking why Christian converts should share the gospel with non-Christian outsiders, Allen says that a "certain natural instinct" or "instinctive force" led early Christians to proclaim the gospel. Citing the proverbial difficulty of keeping a secret, Allen claims that new believers felt compelled to share the newly found joy they had discovered in Christ. Archytas of Tarentum's observation, as quoted by Cicero, provides an illustration for Allen of this psychological phenomenon: "If a man should ascend alone into heaven and behold clearly the structure of the universe and the beauty of the stars, there would be no pleasure for him in the awe-inspiring sight, which would have filled him with delight if he had not had someone to whom he could describe what he had seen."[12]

So, at this point at least, Allen grounds the necessity and compulsion of evangelism in the constraint of experience. In other words, the Christian message brings such an amazing experience to the Christian convert that he is unable to remain silent about it—just as one speaks compellingly and spontaneously about other joyful experiences in one's life. ("I just won the Publisher's Clearing House Sweepstakes!")[13] Allen also grounds the certainty of a missionary church in the presence and work of the Holy Spirit. Allen writes,

> One other effect of St Paul's training is very clear. His converts became missionaries. It seems strange to us that there should be no exhortations to missionary zeal in the Epistles of St Paul. There is one sentence of approval, "From you sounded out the word of the Lord," [1 Thess 1:8] but there is no insistence upon the command of Christ to preach the gospel. Yet, Dr. Friedländer is certainly right when he says, "While the Jews re-

---

[12]Roland Allen, *The Spontaneous Expansion of the Church and the Causes which Hinder It*, 3rd ed. (London: World Dominion, 1956), p. 12; Cicero, *De amicitia* 23.88, trans. William Armistead Falconer under the title *Laelius On Friendship*, LCL 154 (Cambridge, Mass.: Harvard University Press; London: William Heinemann, 1923), p. 195. Because of its greater readability, I have chosen Falconer's translation over Allen's. This footnote and the majority of the paragraph above are taken directly from my *Paul's Understanding of the Church's Mission*, p. 10.

[13]Actually, I did not. Please do not contact me about sharing my new wealth with you.

garded the conversion of unbelievers as, at the most, a meritorious work, for the Christians the spread of the doctrine of salvation was the highest and most sacred duty."[14] The Christians of the Four Provinces were certainly zealous in propagating the faith, and apparently needed no exhortation on the subject. This surprises us; we are not always accustomed to find our converts so zealous. Yet it is not really surprising. Christians receive the Spirit of Jesus, and the Spirit of Jesus is the missionary spirit, the Spirit of Him Who came into the world to bring back lost souls to the Father. Naturally when they receive that Spirit they begin to seek to bring back others, even as He did.[15]

It is true that believers in the New Testament seem constrained to speak of their life-changing experiences. The apostles Peter and John boldly tell the Sanhedrin, "As for us, we cannot help speaking about what we have seen and heard" (Acts 4:20 NIV). Also, Allen is right to give the Holy Spirit a prominent role in missionary reflection. A prominent pneumatic motif is certainly present in Acts, where the entire book is rightly understood as the Holy Spirit propelling the church throughout the world in witness to the gospel of Jesus Christ. Scholars widely recognize that the thematic statement in Acts 1:8 ("But you will receive power when the Holy Spirit has come upon you, and you will be my witnesses in Jerusalem and in all Judea and Samaria, and to the end of the earth") is fleshed out through literary framing brackets that emphasize the work of the Spirit and the concomitant spread and reception of the gospel message (Acts 1:2; 6:7, 8; 9:31, 32-35; 12:24; 13:2; 16:4, 6; 19:20, 21; 28:31).

Although Allen's assertions are both biblical and in agreement with Christian experience, it is appropriate to ask if there is a more distinctive *Pauline* view on the subject. Imagine that we asked Paul, "Should I preach

---

[14]Ludwig Friedländer (1824–1909) also writes, "The example of the first apostles continually inspired an ever-increasing number of imitators, who, in accordance with the teaching of the gospel, distributed what they had amongst the poor, and set out to carry the word of God from one people to another, and whose zeal never wearied nor abated even in the midst of the greatest dangers and difficulties" (*Roman Life and Manners Under the Early Empire*, trans. Leonard A. Magnus, J. H. Freese and A. B. Gough, 7th ed., 4 vols. [London: George Routledge & Sons; New York: E. P. Dutton, 1908–1913], 3:186). Friedländer's *Sittengeschichte Roms* was originally published from 1865–1871.

[15]Allen, *Missionary Methods*, p. 93. The unusual capitalization is Allen's own and typical of all his works. In his later volume, *The Spontaneous Expansion of the Church* (1927), Allen restates his case along similar lines (Allen, *Spontaneous Expansion of the Church*, pp. 8–9).

the gospel to others? And, if so, why?" What would he say?

Perhaps surprisingly, Paul usually seems to assume the missionary presence of his congregations rather than command it. Indeed, in many of Paul's letters, the addressed congregations or individuals are suffering for their faith (e.g., Gal 6:12; Phil 1:29-30; 1 Thess 2:14-16; 3:3-4; 2 Tim 1:8; 2:3; 3:12). Christians who are suffering because of their faith are clearly in no need of being told to make that faith known! In a few places, Paul does explicitly approve or enjoin the missionary activity of ordinary Christians (Eph 6:15; Phil 1:14-18; 2:16; 1 Thess 1:8; Tit 2:10). And, most significantly, Paul speaks of both himself and his congregations as on a course determined by God's dynamic saving word (Col 1:5-7; 1 Thess 1:8; 2:13-16; 2 Tim 2:8-9). So, according to Paul, why should ordinary Christians preach the gospel? Because they have been swept up into the triumphant advance of God's saving Word. It is as if Paul's congregations have fallen into the river of the gospel's flooding advance. The idea of not being carried downstream is unthinkable. Allowing a distinctively Pauline influence on our understanding of the biblical model of the believer's missionary motivation should emphasize the dynamic presence of the gospel, while not neglecting the pneumatic themes or explicit commands in Paul's letters.

The gospel announces the only way to be saved from God's righteous judgment. Paul says that the Corinthians "are being saved" by this gospel (1 Cor 15:2). In so doing, Paul declares that the Corinthians' adherence to this gospel is rescuing them from the eschatological wrath of God. That is, they are saved from eternal condemnation. They are saved by Jesus, the sin-bearer, from having to pay for their own sins.

Paul does not present this salvation as one path among many viable options. Paul believes that there is "one God, and there is one mediator between God and men, the man Christ Jesus" (1 Tim 2:5). Such exclusivist assertions should not be surprising from an apostle who claimed to be commissioned directly by Jesus, who said, "I am the way, and the truth, and the life. No one comes to the Father except through me" (Jn 14:6). Peter similarly declared, "Salvation is found in no one else, for there is no other name under heaven given to mankind by which we must be saved" (Acts 4:12 NIV).[16]

---

[16]Because they both preached the same gospel, Simon Peter extended to Paul "the right hand of fellowship" (Gal 2:9 NIV).

Perseverance in the gospel is necessary for salvation. There is no "plan B" if the Corinthian Christians embrace a life of sin and abandon Christ. Paul says that they are saved "if [they] hold fast to the word [he] preached to [them]—unless [they] believed in vain" (1 Cor 15:2). Genuine Christians disagree as to whether the Bible teaches that believers can lose their salvation (Arminianism) or believers are unable to lose their salvation (Calvinism). Regardless of what position theologians take on this important issue, almost all agree that the Bible offers no words of comfort for persons who deny Christ and live unrepentantly in sin.[17] Paul's gospel is no "easy believism." Paul does not offer "fire insurance" for the day of judgment. His gospel, while announcing a free gift, demands repentance from sin and faith in the Lord Jesus Christ. This repentance and faith are two undividable elements of the same conversion experience—turning away from sin and turning to Christ. Jesus said, "If anyone would come after me, let him deny himself and take up his cross and follow me" (Mt 16:24). While an unmitigated demand, the gospel is also an unmerited gift because the ability to repent and believe is itself a gift from God (Eph 2:8-10; Phil 2:12-13). As Augustine (A.D. 354–430) famously said, "God gives what God demands."[18]

The gospel is confirmed by authorized eyewitnesses to Christ's resurrection. Paul tells the Corinthian Christians, "For I delivered to you as of first importance *what I also received:* that Christ died for our sins according to the Scriptures . . ." (1 Cor 15:3, my emphasis). Elsewhere Paul is adamant that he received his apostleship and gospel directly from Jesus. Here, however, he seems to extend "the right hand of fellowship" (Gal 2:9) to other apostles by seemingly quoting from an early confessional formula in the church. Here we have "the original apostles' creed."

This language of "receiving" and "delivering" is important and reminds us that Christians are, at their best, not innovators but faithful transmitters. We transmit a message that describes the central event of all human history—the death and resurrection of Christ.

Beginning in the next verse (1 Cor 15:5), Paul lists the divinely authorized eyewitnesses through whom come all later Christian confessions. We

---

[17] The only dissenters to this view might be persons associated with the Grace Theological Society.

[18] Augustine, *Confessions*, 10.37 (my paraphrase), in *Nicene and Post-Nicene Fathers*, First Series, ed. Philip Schaff (reprint, Peabody, Mass.: Hendrickson, 2004) 1:159.

have a faith based on reliable, divinely authorized eyewitnesses.[19] While for apologetic purposes, Paul notes that Christ appeared to more than five hundred people at once. Paul is careful to distinguish those who are "apostles" from this broader group of eyewitnesses. These apostles are Christ's distinct emissaries whose preaching was written down, producing our canonical New Testament.

The gospel is what God did in history to save lost humanity through his Son, Messiah Jesus. Paul uses a double introductory formula for the gospel in 1 Corinthians 15. He writes, "Now I would remind you, brothers, of the gospel . . ." (1 Cor 15:1). And in verse 3, he says, "For I delivered to you as of first importance what I also received . . ." (1 Cor 15:3). This double introduction builds up and focuses rhetorical emphasis on Paul's statement of the gospel: "Christ died for our sins in accordance with the Scriptures, that he was buried, that he was raised on the third day in accordance with the Scriptures, [and] that he appeared . . ." (1 Cor 15:3-4). What is perhaps most striking in this Pauline statement of the gospel is how it differs from many modern gospel summaries that focus almost exclusively on the benefits of the gospel to its recipients. Instead, Paul states factually what God did in history through sending his Son. This giving over of God's Son to death was not, in the first measure, a means to maximize human potential or even fulfill humanity's longings. Jesus' death was "for our sins." The root problem in the world is humanity's rebellion against God and our resulting separation from him. Jesus deals with this sin (this rebellion and its effects) by dying a rebel's death in our place to save us.

The gospel is a fulfillment of God's prior saving promises. Paul reports that "Christ died for our *sins in accordance with the Scriptures*" and that he "was raised on the third day *in accordance with the Scriptures*" (1 Cor 15:3-4, emphasis added). Paul did not think that the Christian gospel was an innovation; it was rather the completion of a long story of God intervening in the world to reconcile his wayward image-bearers to himself. The only reliable and adequate record we have of these pre-Christ (B.C.) divine interventions is the one God has given us in the Scriptures—the thirty-nine books of the Old Testament. Scholars debate which of the many Old Tes-

---

[19]See Richard Bauckham, *Jesus and the Eyewitnesses: The Gospels as Eyewitness Testimony* (Grand Rapids: Eerdmans, 2008).

tament messianic promises Paul might have had in mind at this point. The reality is that Paul does not tell us, so we cannot be sure, but there are many possibilities (e.g., Ps 22; 110; Is 53; Mic 5).

CONCLUSION

In the exposition of 1 Corinthians 15:1-8 above, we have explored Paul's multi-faceted understanding of the gospel. The gospel is a propositional statement of what God has done, but it is also a dynamic power. It is a realm in which believers come to dwell, while also being the eyewitness testimony of authorized representatives. The gospel is the fulfillment of God's prior saving promises and the activity of God in history to save lost humanity through the atoning death of his Son. This gospel must be announced, received and remembered. It is the only way of salvation, and perseverance in it is necessary for deliverance from God's eschatological judgment. Indeed, while the gospel is so simple that young children can believe it, it is so profound and multidimensional that Christians spend the rest of their lives trying to grasp and live out its implications.

One hundred years ago, Roland Allen declared, "[Paul's] method was a method of Gospel, not a method of law. This is the most distinctive mark of Pauline Christianity." There could be no greater compliment than Christians of a future day looking back on our generation and saying, "Their method was a method of Gospel, not a method of law. This is the most distinctive mark of twenty-first century evangelical Christianity." May God make it true in our day.

4

PAUL'S ECCLESIOLOGY

♦♦♦

Benjamin L. Merkle

The apostle Paul was the greatest missionary and church planter the world has ever seen.[1] But what made Paul so successful? How was he able to plant churches in such a relatively short period of time? What can we learn from his church planting strategy? Answers to these questions are found primarily in Paul's theology of the church and the strategy that he developed based on that theology. In this chapter we will examine Paul's theology of the church by considering (1) its organization, (2) its ordinances and (3) its officers.

ITS ORGANIZATION

What exactly did Paul set out to do when he entered a new city? What type of church was Paul intending to plant? How would this church be organized? To answer these questions, we must first establish the meaning of the term "church," the nature of the church, and the members of the church.

The meaning of "church." The word *church* in modern English Bibles is a translation of the Greek term *ekklēsia*. This term does not describe a place, a

---

[1]Roland Allen writes, "In a very few years, he built the Church on so firm a basis that it could live and grow in faith and in practice, that it could work out its own problems, and overcome all dangers and hindrances both from within and without" (*Missionary Methods: St. Paul's or Ours?* 2nd ed. [Grand Rapids: Eerdmans, 1962], p. 7).

building or a denomination but rather an assembly of people. As a matter of fact, *ekklēsia* can refer to a secular gathering of people (Acts 19:32, 39, 41) or to the Old Testament people of God (Acts 7:38; Heb 2:12). The main idea associated with this term is that of people who are gathered together. For this reason, some early Bible translators, including William Tyndale, translated *ekklēsia* as *congregation* instead of as *church* so as to avoid misunderstanding. But because the KJV used the term *church*, *ekklēsia* is rarely translated as *congregation* or *assembly* in modern Bible translations—though these terms better communicate the meaning of *ekklēsia* in our modern context.

It is well known that the term *ekklēsia* can be used to represent two realities: (1) a local congregation and (2) the universal church (i.e., "the community of all true believers for all time"[2]). Most of the uses of *ekklēsia* are references to the local church. Paul uses the term *ekklēsia* sixty-two times in the New Testament and at least fifty of those uses refer to the local congregations.[3] Indeed, most of Paul's letters are written to local churches of a city or region.[4]

Paul uses many images or metaphors to describe the church. Perhaps the most common images are the church as the people of God (Rom 9:25-26; 2 Cor 6:16; Titus 2:14), the body of Christ (Rom 12:5; 1 Cor 12:12-17, 27; Eph 1:22-23; 4:4-6, 15-16; Col 1:18; 2:19), the bride of Christ (2 Cor 11:2; Eph 5:25-32), the temple of the Holy Spirit (1 Cor 3:16-17; 6:16, 19; Eph 2:21-22) and the family or household of God (Gal 6:10; Eph 2:19; 1 Tim 3:5, 12, 15; 5:1-2).[5] Other images found in Paul include a building (1 Cor 3:9; Eph 2:21; 1 Tim 3:15), an olive tree (Rom 11:17-24), a field or crops (1 Cor 3:6-9), and a body (1 Cor 10:17; 2 Cor 6:18). These images demonstrate the richness of the concept of *church* and we must therefore be careful to consider them all. None of these images should dominate to the exclusion or minimization of the others.

---

[2]Wayne Grudem, *Systematic Theology: An Introduction to Biblical Doctrine* (Grand Rapids: Zondervan, 1994), p. 853.

[3]For occurrences of *ekklēsia* that refer to the universal church, see Mt 16:18; 1 Cor 15:9; Eph 1:22; 3:10, 21; 5:23, 24, 25, 27, 29, 32; Col 1:18, 24. Some may also list Acts 20:28 and 1 Tim 3:15.

[4]Rom 16:5; 1 Cor 1:2; 2 Cor 1:1; Gal 1:2; Col 4:15-16; 1 Thess 1:1; 2 Thess 1:1; Philem 1:2.

[5]See Paul S. Minear, *Images of the Church in the New Testament* (Philadelphia: Westminster, 1960); Daniel. L. Akin, ed., *A Theology for the Church* (Nashville: B&H, 2007), pp. 772-75; Grudem, *Systematic Theology*, pp. 858-59; Millard J. Erickson, *Christian Theology*, 2nd ed. (Grand Rapids: Baker, 1998), pp. 1044-51.

The nature of the church. New Testament churches met together for a specific purpose. Paul urges his readers that whatever they do, they should "do all to the glory of God" (1 Cor 10:31). Therefore, the church exists to glorify God. Everything the church does should be done with the purpose of glorifying God and exalting Christ. At the same time, however, Paul emphasizes the need for believers to be edified because he knew that when believers were edified or built up, then God receives glory (1 Cor 12). There are at least five main ways this purpose is accomplished. First, the church glorifies God through worship which involves reading and preaching God's word (1 Cor 1:23-24; Col 4:6; 1 Tim 4:13; 2 Tim 4:2), praying (1 Tim 2:8), singing (Eph 5:19; Col 3:16-17), taking a collection (1 Cor 16:2; 2 Cor 9:6-12) and celebrating the Lord's Supper (1 Cor 11:17-34). Second, the church glorifies God through fellowship, which includes bearing one another's burdens (Gal 6:2; also see Acts 2:42; Heb 10:24-25). Third, the church glorifies God through discipleship, which includes equipping all believers (Eph 4:11-12) and training new leaders (2 Tim 2:2). Fourth, the church glorifies God through service, which includes using one's spiritual gifts (1 Tim 4:14). Finally, the church glorifies God through evangelism and missions. Jesus gave his disciples the Great Commission (Mt 28:19-20) and Paul expected the churches he planted to share the good news with others.

Because the church is the people of God and not an organization, this reality greatly affects what the missionary is seeking to establish. Paul understood this distinction with absolute clarity, emphasizing those spiritual elements mentioned above. Allen insists that importing external elements (such as buildings, foreign books and foreign ornaments of worship) gives the impression that Christianity is an institution instead of a relationship. He warns, "Christianity is not an institution, but a principle of life. By importing an institution we tend to obscure the truly spiritual character of our work. We take the externals first and so we make it easy for new converts to put the external in place of the internal."[6] Paul was not seeking to establish a building or seeking to import elements into the worship service that were not essential and could not be easily maintained or reproduced.[7]

---

[6]Allen, *Missionary Methods*, p. 55-56.
[7]Allen rightly notes that "no organization should be introduced which the people cannot understand and maintain" (ibid., p. 161).

It was Paul's goal not merely to win converts, but to plant churches in every city in which he ministered. Paul indicates several times that such congregations typically met in homes for their worship services (Rom 16:5; 1 Cor 16:19; Col 4:15; Philem 1:2).[8] Although Paul emphasizes the unity of the body of Christ, we also have evidence that each congregation was independently led. That is, the New Testament seems to favor a self-governing model of the church. In the early church, many important decisions—such as selecting leaders (Acts 1:23; 6:2-3), sending missionaries (Acts 13:3; 14:27), determining theological positions (Acts 15:22), deciding church discipline (Mt 18:17) and performing excommunication (1 Cor 5:2)—were the responsibilities of the local congregation. Additional support is found in the fact that Paul's letters to churches were addressed to entire congregations and not just to office-holders of the church (Rom 1:7; 1 Cor 1:2; 2 Cor 1:1; Gal 1:2; Eph 1:1; Phil 1:1; Col 1:2; 1 Thess 1:1; 2 Thess 1:1).

Interestingly, Allen, although an Anglican, strongly affirms the independence or autonomy of the local church. He admits that it is wrong to see the Jerusalem church as the "final court before which every act of disobedience must be tried."[9] He later states that Paul "refused to set up any central administrative authority from which the whole Church was to receive directions in the conduct of local affairs."[10] For example, in relation to financial independence he writes, "Every province, every church, was financially independent. The Galatians are exhorted to support their teachers [Gal 6:6]. Every church is instructed to maintain its poor. There is not a hint from beginning to end of the Acts and Epistles of any one church depending upon another, with the single exception of the collection for the poor saints at Jerusalem."[11]

The members of the church. The members of Christ's universal church are those who are truly regenerate (i.e., born again). God knows those who

---

[8] See Eckhard J. Schnabel, *Early Christian Mission* (Downers Grove, Ill.: InterVarsity Press, 2004) 2:1301-06, 1584-85.

[9] Allen, *Missionary Methods,* p. 130. Allen further comments, "That is the Roman system, a system which has so dominated the modern world that even those who repudiate the papal claim for themselves yet cannot resist the temptation to adopt it in principle when they establish missions among other peoples" (p. 130).

[10] Ibid., p. 131.

[11] Ibid., p. 51. He admits that Anglicans have a fear of "congregationalism," which he defines as "the claim of individual congregations to act as if they were alone in the world, independently of all other Christians" (p. 60 n. 1).

are his and their names are written in the book of life (Phil 4:3; 2 Tim 2:19). Many local congregations, however, include unregenerate members. And yet, the church should do what it can to ensure that those who become members are genuinely Christians. Membership should be limited to those who profess faith in Christ, have been baptized and live a life that is consistent with their profession. Of course, the church will sometimes mistakenly allow some to become members who are self-deceived or, worse, are really wolves in sheep's clothing (which is why provisions for church discipline are given). But the church leadership has a responsibility to protect the purity of the Bride of Christ. The leaders of the church should do what they can to protect the church, allowing only those who are truly regenerate to become members of the church. The imagery of the church as the people of God assumes that the members belong to God through their faith in His Son, Jesus Christ.[12]

What is to be done when it is discovered that unbelievers have become members of the local church? This process is termed *church discipline* and is something that Paul writes about on several occasions (1 Cor 5:1-13; 2 Thess 3:14; 1 Tim 1:19-20). Church discipline is the process by which someone who has committed a serious sin (or is living in sin) is confronted by other believers in an effort to correct this problem and restore fellowship. In Galatians 6:1 Paul states, "Brothers, if anyone is caught in any transgression, you who are spiritual should restore him in a spirit of gentleness." Those who refuse to repent and be restored are eventually excommunicated from the congregation. That is, they are removed from membership and considered as unbelievers (see Mt 18:15-20). This final step of church discipline is described by Paul as being "handed over to Satan" and is done for the purpose of restoration and reconciliation (1 Tim 1:20; cf. 1 Cor 5:5).

Paul's understanding of the church was quite simple. He viewed the church as the gathered people of God who trust in the risen Christ and meet together with the express purpose of worshiping the triune God and

---

[12]For an excellent discussion on the necessity of regenerate church membership, see John S. Hammett, *Biblical Foundations for Baptist Churches: A Contemporary Ecclesiology* (Grand Rapids: Kregel, 2005), pp. 81-131, and John S. Hammett, "Regenerate Church Membership," in *Restoring Integrity in Baptist Churches*, ed. T. White, J. G. Duesing and M. B. Yarnell (Grand Rapids: Kregel, 2008), pp. 21-43. Also see John S. Hammett and Benjamin L. Merkle, eds., *Those Who Must Give an Account: A Study of Church Membership and Church Discipline* (Nashville: B&H, 2012).

edifying one another. Those elements that carried cultural baggage were dispensed with and priority was given to the gospel. Congregations were united by this purpose but functioned independently of one another, allowing each congregation to flourish with its own local leadership. Members of the churches consisted of baptized believers who professed Jesus as Lord and Savior. Because Paul understood that occasionally unregenerate members slip into the church, he taught his congregations to practice church discipline.

Its Ordinances

Jesus commanded his church to practice two ordinances, both of which are found in the churches that Paul planted: baptism and the Lord's Supper. We have evidence from Acts that the early church regularly practiced these two ordinances.[13] Allen comments, "There is not a shadow of evidence to support the notion that these sacraments were considered optional in the early Church. In the writings of St Paul it is taken for granted that every Christian has been baptized and that all meet habitually at the Table of the Lord."[14]

Baptism. Baptism is the initiatory rite whereby those who give a credible profession of faith in Jesus Christ are immersed or dipped into water. According to Paul, it is a sign or symbol of a believer's union with Christ in his death, burial and resurrection: "Do you not know that all of us who have been baptized into Christ Jesus were baptized into his death? We were buried therefore with him by baptism into death, in order that, just as Christ was raised from the dead by the glory of the Father, we too might walk in newness of life" (Rom 6:3-4). Also, "In him also you were circumcised with a circumcision made without hands, by putting off the body of the flesh, by the circumcision of Christ, having been buried with him in baptism, in which you were also raised with him through faith in the powerful working

---

[13] For example, the verb "to baptize" (βαπτίζω) occurs 21 times and the noun "baptism" (βάπτισμα) occurs 6 times in Acts. The Lord's Supper is usually referred to as the "breaking of bread" (see Acts 2:42, 46; 20:7, 11; 27:35). For support that the phrase "breaking of bread" is a reference to the Lord's Supper, see I. Howard Marshall, *Acts,* TNTC 5 (Leicester: InterVarsity; Grand Rapids: Eerdmans, 1980), p. 8; John B. Polhill, *Acts,* NAC 26 (Nashville: Broadman, 1992), p. 119; Ben Witherington, *The Acts of the Apostles: A Socio-Rhetorical Commentary* (Grand Rapids: Eerdmans, 1998), pp. 160-61.

[14] Allen, *Missionary Methods*, p. 89. He later adds, "The Sacraments unquestionably were administered in the churches founded by St Paul" (p. 103).

of God, who raised him from the dead" (Col 2:11-12).

Jesus gave his disciples the command to baptize new converts (Mt 28:19), and here Paul gives us the theology of baptism: it is a picture of the believer's death to sin and his new life in Christ. Although these texts are not speaking of water baptism per se, it is unnatural to separate water baptism from conversion. In the earlier church persons were normally baptized the same day they were converted.[15] Restricting the meaning of this text to Spirit baptism introduces a dichotomy that would have been foreign to the first-century church.

Baptism not only signifies union with Christ, it is also a sign of unity with other believers. Paul teaches that there is "one Lord, one faith, one baptism" (Eph 4:5). He also states, "For in one Spirit we were all baptized into one body—Jews or Greeks, slaves or free—and all were made to drink of one Spirit" (1 Cor 12:13). This verse emphasizes the participation of all believers in baptism, demonstrating the importance of this rite. Again, this text is probably not speaking of water baptism but of a conversion, when the believer is immersed in the Spirit. Water baptism, however, is closely related to this Spirit baptism as a sign of union with Christ and unity with other believers. It is an outward symbol of an inward reality. The unity of believers is signified by their one baptism. Baptism is shared in common by all those who are united to Christ by faith (Gal 3:27).

Baptism is the visible initiation into the Christian community.[16] After publicly confessing his sins and believing in Jesus as Lord and Savior, a new convert was immediately baptized. Paul indicates that he did not normally baptize all of the new converts but left that to others. In Corinth, Paul baptized the first converts (Crispus, Gaius and the household of Stephanas) but emphasizes that he did not baptize any others (1 Cor 1:14-16). Presumably these first converts, some of whom we know became leaders in the church (1 Cor 16:15), baptized the others. This also indicates

---

[15]In the New Testament conversion includes (1) repentance, (2) faith, (3) confession, (4) receiving the Holy Spirit, and (5) baptism. Of these five (which normally happened at the same time or on the same day in the New Testament), baptism was typically viewed as the final step (See Robert H. Stein, "Baptism in Luke-Acts," in *Believers Baptism: Sign of the New Covenant in Christ*, ed. Thomas R. Schreiner and Shawn D. Wright [Nashville: B&H, 2006], pp. 33-66).

[16]Allen states that people "were admitted by their baptism into a very visible society" (*Missionary Methods*, p. 76).

that Paul was also not in charge of deciding whether a candidate was worthy to be baptized. This decision was left to the local church leaders. Allen suggests that this is "one of the most important elements of [Paul's] success" because it encouraged mutual responsibility.[17] The local leaders knew the people more intimately than an outsider and would have to live with the decision they made.

Another important issue related to baptism is the time of baptism. When is a new convert ready for baptism? As stated above, in the early church, baptism normally occurred on the same day as conversion. There was not a long time of teaching and testing beforehand. If baptism is a symbol of death and resurrection with Christ and entrance into the body of Christ, it makes sense that baptism should be done as close to conversion as possible. Thus, in the early church, teaching followed baptism (cf. Mt 28:19-20).[18] Allen notes that by making converts wait until they have enough knowledge of Christian doctrine and are living according to their profession, we are teaching them that baptism is not really important and that they can attain righteousness in their own strength. He writes,

> We have taught them that union with Christ is the source of strength, we have taught them that baptism is the sacrament of unity, and then we have told them that they must prove their sincerity by practising virtue in their own strength before they can be admitted to the sacrament by which they are to receive strength to be virtuous. In other words, we have taught them that the one great need of men is Christ, and that without Christ men cannot attain to righteousness, and then that they must attain to righteousness by themselves in order to receive Christ.[19]

The Lord's Supper. Although it is assumed that all of the churches that Paul planted celebrated the Lord's Supper, we only have specific evidence from the church at Corinth—and that is because they were having problems during the celebration of this ordinance.[20] Jesus instituted the Lord's Supper

---

[17] Ibid., p. 98.
[18] Allen insists that "teaching followed, it did not precede, baptism. For baptism, apparently very little knowledge of Christian truth was required as an indispensable condition" (ibid., p. 95).
[19] Ibid., p. 97.
[20] It must be remembered that Paul's letters were occasional or situational so that what is written in each letter reflects the particular situation in each church. Simply because an issue is not mentioned does not mean it is unimportant but that there was no reason to mention it.

on the night he was betrayed (Mt 26:26-29; Mk 14:22-25; Lk 22:19-22) and Paul repeats this tradition to the Corinthian believers:

> For I received from the Lord what I also delivered to you, that the Lord Jesus on the night when he was betrayed took bread, and when he had given thanks, he broke it, and said, "This is my body which is for you. Do this in remembrance of me." In the same way also he took the cup, after supper, saying, "This cup is the new covenant in my blood. Do this, as often as you drink it, in remembrance of me." For as often as you eat this bread and drink the cup, you proclaim the Lord's death until he comes. (1 Cor 11:23-26)

From these verses the central meaning of the Lord's Supper is evident—it is a reminder of the gospel. The bread represents Christ's body that was broken for the church and the wine represents his blood that was poured out for the church. The evidence from Acts indicates that this celebration was practiced weekly (Acts 20:7, 11; 1 Cor 11:18, 20). Paul prefaces his teaching concerning the Lord's Supper with the phrase, "when you come together as a church" (1 Cor 11:18). Thus, this symbolic ordinance was practiced in the context of the corporate gathering. Paul also teaches that the Lord's Supper was a testimony to the unity of the body of Christ. By participating in the bread and the wine, believers are also participating in the body and blood of Christ. Paul states, "Because there is one bread, we who are many are one body, for we all partake of the one bread" (1 Cor 10:17).

From the evidence of the New Testament we learn the following concerning the Lord's Supper in the early church: (1) It is a symbolic proclamation of the gospel of Jesus and believer's unity; (2) It was a main element of the worship services; (3) It was practiced weekly; (4) It was practiced corporately; and (5) It was restricted to those who professed faith in Christ and were baptized.

Its Officers

When Paul planted churches, he did not simply instruct his converts to gather together without giving them instruction and guidance regarding church leaders. Although he clearly teaches that every believer is gifted by the Holy Spirit and is important to the body (1 Cor 12:7, 11, 14-26), not all are given the same authority in the church. Some, because of their gifts and maturity are given leadership and authority in the church that is not given to others. The two church offices that Paul identifies are that of elder/overseer and deacon.[21]

Elders or overseers. The terms *elder* (*presbyteros*) and *overseer* (*episkopos*) are two different titles that refer to the same office.[22] There are a number of factors that support this position. First, the terms *elder* and *overseer* are used interchangeably (Acts 20:17, 28; Tit 1:5, 7; 1 Pet 5:1-2). Second, elders are never given separate qualifications. If elder and overseer are two separate offices, then it would seem reasonable to expect Paul to give the necessary qualifications for each office. Paul, however, only gives qualifications for overseers (1 Tim 3:1-7; Titus 1:7-9), although elders are also mentioned in 1 Timothy 5:17-25 and Titus 1:5. Third, because elders and overseers are given the same tasks of ruling/leading (Acts 20:28; 1 Tim 3:4-5; 5:17) and teaching (1 Tim 3:2; 5:17; Tit 1:9), they should be viewed as representing the same office. Fourth, the elders and overseers are never listed as separate offices. This usage suggests that the three-tiered ecclesiastical system that later developed in many churches is foreign to the New Testament.

Although the title *pastor* is commonly used in our modern church context, it is used only one time in the New Testament as a reference for a church leader. In Ephesians 4:11 Paul writes, "Christ himself gave the apostles, the prophets, the evangelists, the pastors and teachers" (NIV). The term *pastor* is coupled with the term *teacher*, which together denote one order of ministry.[23]

What then is the relationship between the office of pastor and that of the elder/overseer? Does the term *pastor* represent a separate and distinct office to that of the elder or overseer? There are at least two reasons this term represents the same office. First, elders/overseers are given the same tasks as

---

[21] We will not discuss apostles, prophets, or evangelists because these offices (or gifts) are not technically considered *church* offices since they minister outside the local church or are not confined to one specific church.

[22] See Benjamin L. Merkle, *The Elder and Overseer: One Office in the Early Church,* Studies in Biblical Literature 57 (New York: Peter Lang, 2003); Benjamin L. Merkle, *40 Questions About Elders and Deacons* (Grand Rapids: Kregel, 2008), pp. 54-58, 76-83; Benjamin L. Merkle, *Why Elders? A Biblical and Practical Guide for Church Members* (Grand Rapids: Kregel, 2009), pp. 17-28.

[23] The Greek construction favors interpreting this phrase as one office: the pastor/teacher. There is not one office of pastor and a separate office of teacher.

pastors: shepherding (Acts 20:17, 28; Eph 4:11; 1 Pet 5:1-3) and teaching
(1 Tim 3:2; 5:17; Tit 1:9). Second, as we mentioned earlier, the term *pastor* is
only found once in the New Testament as a designation of a church leader.
If the office of pastor is separate from the elder/overseer, what are the qualifications needed for those who hold this office? Paul gives us qualifications
for the elder/overseer but never for the pastor. Perhaps the reason for this
omission is because in giving the qualifications for the elder/overseer, he is
giving the qualifications for those who can also be called "pastor."

The number of leaders. The concept of shared leadership is a common
theme in the Bible. In the Old Testament, leadership was shared by the
elders of Israel.[24] In the New Testament, Jesus chose twelve apostles to lead
the church. In addition, the early church appointed seven men to assist the
apostles by caring for the church's widows (Acts 6:1-6). This pattern of plurality was continued with the churches that Paul planted:[25]

- Paul and Barnabas planted churches in the cities of Antioch, Iconium, Lystra,
  and Derbe and "appointed *elders* for them in every church" (Acts 14:23).

- At the end of his third missionary journey, Paul summoned "the *elders* of
  the church to come to him" (Acts 20:17).

- When Paul writes to the church at Philippi, he specifically greets the
  "*overseers* and deacons" (Phil 1:1).

- Paul writes to Timothy, "Let the *elders* who rule well be considered
  worthy of double honor, especially those who labor in preaching and
  teaching" (1 Tim 5:17).

- Paul directed Titus to "appoint *elders* in every town" (Tit 1:5).[26]

There are also other terms used to describe the plurality of leaders in the
church. For example, in his first letter to the church at Thessalonica, Paul exhorts the believers "to respect *those* who labor among you and are over you in
the Lord and admonish you" (1 Thess 5:12, emphasis mine). Although the
term *elders* is not used, it is clear that those to whom Paul is referring were the
spiritual leaders of the congregation, performing elder-like functions.[27]

---

[24]See, e.g., Ex 3:18; 12:21; Deut 19:12; 21:3; 22:15; 1 Sam 8:4; 2 Sam 5:3; 17:4, 15; Ezra 5:5 6:7, 14.
[25]Emphasis is added to the following verse citations.
[26]Also see Acts 11:30; 15:4, 22-23; Jas 5:14; 1 Pet 5:1.
[27]Also see 1 Cor 16:15-16; Heb 13:7, 17, 24.

The New Testament evidence indicates that it was the norm for every church to be led by a plurality of elders. There is no example in the New Testament of one elder or pastor leading a congregation as the sole or primary leader. There were a plurality of elders at the churches in Jerusalem (Acts 11:30), Antioch of Pisidia, Lystra, Iconium and Derbe (Acts 14:23), Ephesus (Acts 20:17; 1 Tim 5:17), Philippi (Phil 1:1), the cities of Crete (Tit 1:5), the churches in the dispersion to which James wrote (James 1:1), the Roman provinces of Pontus, Galatia, Cappadocia, Asia and Bithynia (1 Peter 1:1), and possibly the church(es) to which Hebrews was written (Heb 13:7, 17, 24).

The authority of elders. Paul did not pastor the churches he planted but gave that responsibility to the local leaders. As soon as possible, usually after about six months to a year, Paul appointed leaders (elders) in the newly planted churches. These new leaders were given responsibility for the spiritual oversight of the congregation (see 1 Cor 16:15-16; 1 Thess 5:12; 1 Tim 5:17). Thus, although the congregations as a whole made important decisions (see Mt 18:17; Acts 1:23; 6:2-3; 13:3; 14:27; 15:22; 1 Cor 5:2), the daily leadership and authority of the church was given to the elders.

The very functions or duties of the elders communicate that their office carries with it a certain amount of authority. As teachers, they are charged with the task of authoritatively proclaiming God's word (1 Tim 3:2; 5:17; Tit 1:9). As shepherds, the elders are given the task of leading God's people (Acts 20:28; Eph 4:11; 1 Peter 5:2). As representatives, they speak and act on behalf of the entire congregation (Acts 11:30; 20:17).

The authority of the elders comes from God and not the congregation. Although the congregation affirms their calling and authority, it is an authority with a divine origin. Paul tells the Ephesian elders that the Holy Spirit made them overseers (Acts 20:28). They were called and given authority by God and not by man. In the letter to the Ephesians, Paul states that Christ has given gifts to the church, including pastor-teachers (Eph 4:11). Therefore, the authority of an elder does not come from the congregation, but from Christ himself.

It must be pointed out, however, that the elders' authority is not absolute. Jesus Christ and his word have ultimate authority in the church. Everything should be done under his authority because he is "the head of the body, the church" (Col 1:18). The elders derive their authority from the word of God, and when they stray from that word, they abandon their God-given authority (Acts 17:11; Gal 1:8). The authority that the elders possess is not so much found in their office, but in the duties they perform (and the Christlike character they display). That is, the elders are not to be obeyed simply because they are elders. Rather, they are to be obeyed because they have the responsibility of shepherding and teaching the congregation (1 Thess 5:13). But if their shepherding and teaching stray from Scripture, their authority as shepherds and teachers is no longer binding on the congregation.

The authority of elders is balanced by the authority of the congregation as a whole. Thus, key decisions in the church should not be given only to the elders but should be brought before the entire congregation. Because the church is a body (and not merely a head or feet), all in the church are important and should be allowed to be a part of major decisions.

Deacons. The office of deacon is a separate and distinct office to that of the elder/overseer/pastor. The word *deacon* is a translation of the Greek term *diakonos*, which normally means "servant." Only context can determine if the term is being used generally to mean "servant" or more technically as a designation of a church officer. The Greek term is used twenty-nine times in the New Testament, but only three or four of those occurrences refer to an office-holder (Rom 16:1[?]; Phil 1:1; 1 Tim 3:8, 12). The origin of the deacon is not known for certain, but many scholars suggest that the seven chosen in Acts 6 provide the prototype of New Testament deacons. In this passage, the apostles decided it was best for the church to appoint seven men who could help with the daily distribution of food for the widows so that the apostles could devote themselves "to prayer and to the ministry of the word" (Acts 6:4).

The New Testament does not offer much information concerning the role of deacons. The requirements given in 1 Timothy 3:8-12 focus on the deacon's character and family life. The most noticeable distinction between elders and deacons is that deacons do not need to be "able to teach" (1 Tim 3:2). Deacons are called to "hold" to the faith with a clear conscience, but they are not called to "teach" that faith (1 Tim 3:9). This suggests that the deacons do not have an official teaching role in the church. This does not mean that deacons cannot teach in any capacity, but simply that they are not called to teach or preach as a matter of responsibility related to their office as deacon. It should also be noted that deacons, as their very name indicates, do not rule or lead the congregation but have a service-oriented ministry. Although the Bible does not clearly indicate the function of deacons, based on the pattern established in Acts 6 with the apostles and the Seven, it seems best to view the deacons as servants who do whatever is necessary to allow the elders to accomplish their God-given calling of shepherding and teaching the church. Just as the apostles delegated administrative responsibilities to the Seven, so the elders are to delegate responsibilities to the deacons so that the elders can focus their efforts on the ministry of the word and prayer (Acts 6:4). As a result, each local church is free to define the tasks of deacons based on their particular needs.

There is no indication in Acts that Paul appointed deacons in the churches. During Paul's first missionary journey, he and Barnabas appointed elders in the church of Asia Minor (Acts 14:23). Yet nowhere does Luke indicate that deacons were appointed. While this omission does not prove that deacons did not exist in the churches at that time, the fact that they are not mentioned indicates that they were not as important to the progress of the gospel in the mind of Luke. Later, Paul commands Titus to appoint elders in every city on the island of Crete (Tit 1:5) but says nothing of deacons. This information suggests that although deacons are important to the life and health of the church, they were only appointed after elders were established and the need for deacons became evident.

Conclusions about church leadership. There are several important concluding comments we can make regarding the leadership of the churches that Paul planted.

Paul's churches had multiple leaders. As was demonstrated above, it was the pattern of Paul's churches to be led by a plurality of leaders. These leaders were sometimes called "elders," "overseers" or "pastors." The key element here is not precisely what the leaders were called, but that there was always a plurality. On his first missionary journey, Paul planted multiple churches in Asia Minor as he went through the various cities. As he doubled-back on his return trip, we read that he "appointed elders for them in every church" (Acts 14:23). Thus, as soon as leadership was established in these churches, it was established on principle that each church should be governed by more than one leader. Based on this pattern, it is best for church planters not to find one, strong, visionary leader and give that person all of the leadership responsibility. Instead, from the very beginning if possible, leadership should be given to a number of qualified disciples who can lead together. Allen's analysis of the data is correct: "St Paul was not content with ordaining one elder for each church. In every place he ordained several. This ensured that all authority should not be concentrated in the hands of one man."[28]

Paul's churches had accountable leaders. If having a plurality of elders that share equal authority is God's design, there will be many benefits by following the biblical pattern. Although having a plurality of elders does not guarantee the church leadership will not encounter problems or conflict, it does at least provide several safeguards against some problems and difficulties that a single-pastor church often faces—especially in the area of biblical accountability. Biblical accountability is needed for at least two reasons. First, it helps protect a pastor from error. Pastors often possess a lot of authority in their churches—too much authority with too little accountability. Such authority can cause one to believe that he is more important than others and thus become proud. Other pastors given autocratic authority may act in ways that are insensitive or unscriptural but be blinded to their faults. Second, biblical accountability is needed to help foster maturity and godliness among the elders. The author of Hebrews highlights the need for accountability when he writes, "Exhort one another every day . . . that none of you may be hardened by the deceitfulness of sin" (Heb 3:13). The more mature elders can help train the younger ones in how to be an effective shepherd.

Paul's churches had paid or unpaid leaders. The idea that only full-time, paid pastors can lead the church is not found in the Scriptures. In fact, such a view can lead to an unhealthy church. Having both paid/staff and unpaid/nonstaff elders allows for a church to have more leaders than a comparable church with only paid elders/pastors. According to the Bible, there is no requirement that a leader must be paid to be an elder or pastor. And yet, it is the responsibility of the church to pay an elder for his work if he needs to be financially supported. Paul argued that both he (1 Cor

---

[28]Allen, *Missionary Methods*, p. 104.

9:8-10) and elders (1 Tim 5:18) had the right to be paid for their work (cf. Mt 10:10; Lk 10:7).[29] Elders who spend their days shepherding and teaching the church ought to be not only respected for their duties, but should also be financially compensated (also see Gal 6:6). This does not mean, however, that all (or any) of the elders must be paid for their work or that only those who work full time for the church can rightfully be called "elders" or "pastors." Paul, as an apostle and missionary, certainly had the right to be supported by the churches he established and in which he labored. And yet, for sake of the gospel, he chose not to claim his rights. Instead, he chose to work with his own hands (1 Cor 4:12). Just like Paul, there are many elders who are self-supported in the sense that they draw a salary from outside the church. They spend much of their free time in helping to shepherd the congregation but are not paid for their labors. Some churches have difficulty financially supporting one or more elders. By having elders who do not receive monetary compensation for their work, the church is able to include more elders without the extra burden of supporting them financially. This situation allows the elders to shepherd the congregation more effectively (by having more elders) and allows for more rapid church planting to occur (by having unpaid elders).

Paul's churches had qualified leaders. In the early church, leadership belonged to those who were biblically qualified. When reading the qualifications for an elder/overseer (see 1 Tim 3:1-7; Tit 1:5-9) or deacon (1 Tim 3:8-13), one is immediately struck by the relative simplicity of the qualifications. In fact, the qualifications needed for an elder are the basic characteristics that are expected of all Christians. There is no mention of being full-time or paid. There is no formal training required.[30] The focus of the qualifications is on who a person is more than what a person does. It should also be noted

---

[29]Allen suggests that the right to financial support belonged exclusively to "wandering evangelists and prophets, not to settled local clergy" (ibid., p. 50 n. 1). He maintains that Paul's words to the elders of Ephesus "directs them to follow his example and to support themselves" (ibid.). Paul tells the elders, "I coveted no one's silver or gold or apparel. You yourselves know that these hands ministered to my necessities and to those who were with me" (Acts 20:33-34). But in this text, Paul is not commanding what the elders must do, but is simply recalling what he himself did while among them. Furthermore, in 1 Tim 5:17-18 Paul clearly establishes the right for elders to be paid for their hard work.

[30]Allen remarks, "They were not necessarily highly educated men" (*Missionary Methods,* p. 101).

that leaders were chosen from the congregation itself. There was no committee set up to consider the qualifications of Christians from outside the
congregation. As Allen notes, "Paul ordained as elders members of the
church to which they belonged."[31] They were selected because they met the
qualifications. They were men of high moral character, of good reputation
and respected by the congregation.

Paul's churches had reproducing leaders. According to Paul, leaders are
given to the church "to equip the saints for the work of the ministry" (Eph
4:12). The role of the elder as teacher is important not just for the health of
the church in the present, but also for the growth of the church in the
future. As a result, it is not enough for the elders to simply be teachers, they
must also be purposefully equipping the next generation of elders to minister alongside them or to plant new churches. Paul tells Timothy, "What
you have heard from me in the presence of many witnesses entrust to
faithful men who will be able to teach others also" (2 Tim 2:2). As Paul's
faithful coworker, Timothy was entrusted with the task of passing on the
pure gospel as preached by Paul. He had been equipped by Paul and was
now to become an equipper. Thus, he was to entrust what he had learned
to "faithful men," which is probably another way of describing the elders of
the church. But this task of equipping does not stop with the elders. They
are also to become equippers "who will be able to teach others also." It is
the task of the elders to identify others who will be faithful to carry on the
gospel message.

CONCLUSION

Paul's method of being obedient to the Great Commission was to plant
churches and not simply to win converts. Because he is regarded as the
church's greatest church planter, it is crucial for us to examine Paul's
theology of the church and the strategy he employed based on that theology.
What we find is that Paul planted churches that were gospel-centered. The
preaching focused on Christ (1 Cor 1:23; 2:2). The fellowship was in Christ
(1 Cor 1:9). The service was for Christ (Eph 6:7). The ordinances were about
Christ (Rom 6:3-5; 1 Cor 11:24-26). And the leaders of the church shep-

---

[31]Ibid., p. 100. He later adds, "The elders were really *of* the church to which they ministered" (ibid.).

herded under Christ (Eph 1:22; Col 1:18). Paul did not have a complex strategy, but he did have a Christ-centered one. Getting Paul's ecclesiology right will enable us to get his methodology right as well.

5

PAUL'S MISSION AS THE
MISSION OF THE CHURCH

♦ ♦ ♦

Christoph W. Stenschke

Paul the missionary is often seen as a solitary figure who worked on his own, independently of churches. However, a close look at the book of Acts— where Paul commands center stage from the second half onward—and at his extant letters indicates that Paul's mission was embedded in several early Christian churches, supported by these churches in various ways and extended through the ministry of churches.

In his influential study *Missionary Methods: St. Paul's or Ours?* of 1912, Roland Allen referred to the churches' involvement in Paul's own mission and the missionary enterprise more generally on several occasions, but he did not argue this case in detail.[1] For example, Allen noted that Paul "intended his congregation to become at once a centre of light. . . . There is no particular virtue in . . . establishing a church in an important place unless the church established in the important place is a church possessed of sufficient life to be a source of light to the whole country round" or, in similar

---

[1] The first edition was published in 1912. I use the edition published by World Dominion Press, London, in 1960. For an excellent summary and critical assessment of Allen's study, see H. Christiansen, *Missionieren wie Paulus? Roland Allens missionstheologische Rezeption des Paulus als Kritik an der neuzeitlichen Missionsbewegung*, Missionswissenschaftliche Forschungen NF 24 (Neuendettelsau: Erlanger Verlag für Mission und Ökumene, 2008).

words, "St Paul did not go about as a missionary preacher merely to convert individuals: he went to establish churches from which the light might radiate throughout the whole country round."[2] Elsewhere Allen observed, "One other effect of St Paul's training is very clear. His converts became missionaries. . . . The Christians of the Four Provinces were certainly zealous in propagating the faith, and apparently needed no exhortation on the subject. . . . [T]his was not really surprising. Christians receive the Spirit of Jesus, and the Spirit of Jesus is a missionary spirit, the Spirit of Him who came into the world to bring back lost souls to the Father."[3] For Allen, part of the true character of the church is that the church is self-propagating.[4]

This article follows Allen's observations and examines whether there is evidence for Allen's observations and claims. It argues that Paul's mission was inextricably linked to churches and that it can and should be understood as the mission of the church(es). We shall first look at the evidence in Acts and in Paul's letters for the active involvement of churches in Paul's own mission in the northeastern quarter of the ancient Mediterranean world of the first century A.D. Then we shall ask whether, and to what extent, Paul expected the churches to not only support his own missionary endeavor, but also to be actively involved themselves in spreading the gospel through their behavior and verbal witness in their places of residence and spheres of influence.

THE MISSION OF PAUL AS THE MISSION OF EARLY CHRISTIAN CHURCHES
The portrayal of Paul's mission in the book of Acts. Our concern is with

Luke's description of Paul's mission.[5] However, long before Paul *the missionary* appears on the scene in Acts 13, the mission to Jews and Gentiles is well on its way and is described in one way or another as the mission of the church.[6]

---

[2]Roland Allen, *Missionary Methods: St. Paul's or Ours?* (London: World Dominion, 1960), pp. 13, 81, respectively.

[3]Ibid., p. 93.

[4]Ibid., p. 94.

[5]See I. H. Marshall, "Luke's Portrait of the Pauline Mission," in *The Gospel to the Nations: Perspectives on Paul's Mission,* ed. P. Bolt and M. Thompson (Downers Grove, Ill.: InterVarsity Press, 2000), pp. 99-113. For an able defense of the essential historicity of Acts with regard to mission see E. J. Schnabel, *Early Christian Mission* (Downers Grove, Ill.: InterVarsity Press, 2004) 1:12-35.

[6]Before the first missionary journey of Acts 13-14, Paul had preached the gospel in the synagogues

Although the twelve apostles, representing Israel regathered and restored, dominate the first few chapters, there is no reason to believe that
witness to the gospel was limited to them. The other disciples who had
come with Jesus from Galilee (like the apostles, some of them had been
commissioned by Jesus before Easter; cf. Lk 9:1-6; 10:1-12) and who had
experienced the miracle of Pentecost together with the Twelve (Acts 1:14-
15), would also have been active. The first Christians to share the gospel
outside of Jerusalem of whom we know were Diaspora Jews who started
the early Christian mission as refugees from Jerusalem (Acts 8:4). One of
them, Philip the evangelist, took the gospel to Samaria (Acts 8:5-25). The
church in Jerusalem followed his ministry with keen interest and sent
Peter and John to Samaria. By Acts 9:2 there were Christians in Damascus;
by Acts 9 Peter travelled throughout Judea and visited Christians in Joppa
and Lydda (Acts 9:32-43). Acts 9:31 mentions that there were churches in
"all Judea and Galilee and Samaria." When Peter headed for Caesarea to
meet Cornelius, other Jewish Christians, who later baptized the first
Gentile believers and served as witnesses of God's intervention, accompanied him. When Peter returned to Jerusalem, some believers there again
took a critical yet lively interest in his mission and its implications for his
Jewish identity (Acts 11:2-3). Later the persecuted Diaspora Christians of
Jerusalem took the gospel to Phoenicia and Cyprus and Antioch (Acts
11:19). In Antioch, some of them preached the Lord Jesus to Gentiles also.
Mission was not solely the work of the apostles but involved other Christians. The Christians of Jerusalem sent Barnabas to Antioch to see what
God was doing there (Acts 11:22-24) because they were interested in the
activities of their (former) members.

Barnabas brought Paul to Antioch and included him in the mission or
the churches of Jerusalem and of Antioch (Acts 11:25f). For the so-called
first missionary journey, Paul was commissioned together with Barnabas by
the Holy Spirit and the Antiochene church (Acts 13:1-3; "they had been
commended to the grace of God for the work," cf. Acts 14:26).[7] Their activ-

---

of Damascus (Acts 9:20-22) and to Jews in Jerusalem (Acts 9:28-29). In Antioch, Paul appears as
a teacher of the church (Acts 11:26). Gal 1–2 suggests further mission involvement between Acts
9:30 and Acts 11:25-26. Acts 15:23 points to Paul's missionary activities in Syria and Cilicia prior
to his coming to Antioch.

[7]For Paul's mission in Acts, see Eckhard J. Schnabel, *Paul the Missionary: Realities, Strategies and*

ities can be understood as an extension of the church. In this sense, as messengers of the Antiochene church, Paul and Barnabas are called *apostles* in Acts 14:4, 14. They returned to Antioch, gathered the church about them and reported all that God had done among them (Acts 14:27), and served the church there for a longer period of time.

Some of the Christians in Jerusalem continued to show a lively interest in the developments in Antioch and went there to demand the circumcision of the Gentile believers (Acts 15). In this way the further course of the mission and the question as to under what conditions Gentiles may partake in God's salvation for Israel was raised. Eventually these issues were discussed in Jerusalem. Paul and Barnabas attended the meeting and reported the signs and wonders that God had wrought among the Gentiles.[8] The gathering approved of the law-free mission for the Gentiles of the Antiochene church (i.e., how it was put in practice in Antioch and through the missionaries from Antioch in other places). The decision taken in Jerusalem was accepted as binding. Paul and Barnabas, together with (other) Jewish Christians of Jerusalem, returned to Antioch and communicated by word of mouth and in writing the decision taken in Jerusalem.[9] Paul and Barnabas remained deeply involved in the church of Antioch.

The Christians of Antioch commended Paul and Silas to the grace of God for their second missionary journey. Later they returned to Jerusalem and to Antioch and spent some time there (Acts 18:22-23). For the third journey, Paul again set out from Antioch.

When Paul returned to Jerusalem at the end of the third journey, he was accompanied by a number of representatives from the churches of several areas and cities in which he (and others!) had planted churches and where he ministered for longer periods (Acts 20:4). His final visit to the church in Jerusalem, which Paul initially persecuted and which included him in its mission work in Antioch (and through Antioch, elsewhere), was anchored in these churches and in the churches that he visited on the way (Acts 21:1-16).

Methods (Downers Grove, Ill.: InterVarsity Press, 2008), and Eckhard J. Schnabel, *Early Christian Mission* (Downers Grove, Ill.: InterVarsity Press, 2004), 2:923-1485.

[8]On their way to Jerusalem "they passed through both Phoenicia and Samaria, describing in detail the conversion of the Gentiles, and brought great joy to all the brothers" (Acts 15:3).

[9]The decree greets Gentile Christians in Antioch, Syria and Cilicia. Did these people come to faith during Paul's stay in Tarsus?

While there were some Jewish Christians in Jerusalem who were suspicious about Paul's ministry to Jews in the Diaspora, the Christian leaders of Jerusalem gave Paul a whole-hearted welcome and set their seal of approval on his mission work (Acts 21:17-20). Strangely, Paul ended up in Roman captivity as he set out to prove his own allegiance to Judaism to his fellow Jewish Christians in Jerusalem (Acts 21:20-36).

Paul the prisoner continued his mission in the constraints of captivity and, during his time in prison, was in contact with the different churches (Acts 27:3; 28:14-30).

In addition to this close link between Paul's mission and the churches of Jerusalem and Antioch, two further observations may be added to Luke's portrait of Paul's mission.

The mission prior to Paul and Paul's own mission led to the establishment of other churches. These churches shared in the mission work in their own locations by providing missionaries with hospitality (cf. Lydia in Acts 16:15 or Titus Justus in Corinth, Acts 18:7)[10] or by providing the missionaries with what they needed to move on and to proceed with their work elsewhere (the Greek verb *propempō*, "being sent on one's way" or "to accompany," implies such provision, see Acts 15:3; 20:38; 21:5).[11] Presumably they continued to spread the gospel after Paul and his coworkers had left the area. Timothy, one of the Christians in Lystra (where a church was founded early on; Acts 14:21), later joined the second missionary journey as a coworker of Paul (Acts 16:1-4; does the fact that his name is not mentioned in Acts 14:21 imply that he came to faith *after* Paul's departure through the witness of others?). Others who appear in the team probably also came from churches (Erastus, Acts 19:22; possibly also Luke himself).

Paul was not the only early Christian missionary. Luke's account also mentions other Christian missionaries who were not directly linked with one congregation (for example, Aquila, Priscilla and Apollos appear in Corinth) and who worked with Paul for a certain period of time. However, they were also members of churches. Aquila and Priscilla presumably be-

[10]For the significance of hospitality in Acts, see A. E. Arterbury, *Entertaining Angels: Early Christian Hospitality in its Mediterranean Setting*, NTM (Sheffield: Sheffield Phoenix Press, 2005).

[11]See J. P. Dickson, *Mission-Commitment in Ancient Judaism and in the Pauline Communities: The Shape, Extent and Background of Early Christian Mission*, WUNT 159 (Tübingen: Mohr Siebeck, 2003), pp. 194-201.

longed to one of the Roman congregations and, as Jewish Christians, had to leave Rome (Acts 18:1-3).

In past research on Luke-Acts, Luke's portrayal of Paul has been criticized as either biased or as a distortion of the actual course of events. Allegedly, Luke wrote to bridge the gap between Paul and Peter or Pauline and Petrine Christianity and to construct a harmonized picture.[12] However, more recent assessment of the historical reliability of Acts has been far more positive and provided solid evidence for this reappraisal. Luke's purpose for writing Luke-Acts required the reliability of his presentation. If Luke wanted to provide certainty for Theophilus and other readers about the things in which they had been instructed (Lk 1:4), he needed to "get his facts right" if he wanted to achieve his objective. The readers can be assured that the gospel preached to them by Paul and/or his coworkers is reliable.

While Luke obviously omits some aspects of Paul's life (some of them we know through his letters) and at the same time puts an emphasis on Paul (more than on any other human figure), there is no reason to doubt the essential reliability of his presentation of Paul's mission as the mission of the churches of Jerusalem and Antioch and of the churches founded by Paul. It is in these churches that Paul's mission was so deeply embedded.

Given our observations of Paul's strong links with these churches, it may seem odd that we do not know of or hear of letters of Paul to the churches of Jerusalem and Antioch. Other than several brief references to the saints of Jerusalem and one reference to the Christians of Antioch in Galatians 2:11-14, neither church plays a role in Paul's extant letters. This may be due to the fact that Paul went to both churches regularly to report on his mission, which meant that there was no need for him to write to these churches. Also, of course, there were mature Christian leaders in both churches who had come to faith before Paul. If any problems arose, they could deal with them. Paul may also have applied the principle mentioned in Romans 15:20-21 to existing churches. When Paul addressed an existing church outside his sphere of influence, as in his letter to the Romans, Paul appears to do so rather hesitantly (Rom 15:14-16).[13]

---

[12]For a survey of research, see W. W. Gasque, *A History of the Interpretation of the Acts of the Apostles* (Peabody, Mass.: Hendrickson, 1989).

[13]This does not apply to Colossians, because the church there seems to have been founded by one of Paul's coworkers; cf. Col 1:7; 2:1; 4:12.

The portrayal of Paul's mission in his letters. All of Paul's letters are closely linked to his mission and cannot be understood apart from this context.[14] Paul wrote these letters to address issues that arose from his mission work—that is, when he could not address these churches in person or through one of his coworkers.

Paul's letters contain a number of clues about how churches and individuals were actually involved in Paul's mission work and about how Paul expected them to become involved.[15] Here we follow the excellent presentation of this topic in John Dickson's study *Mission-Commitment in Ancient Judaism and in the Pauline Communities*.[16] Dickson sets out with a survey of mission and missionaries in ancient Judaism and describes the mission-commitment among the Jewish faithful. He then studies the structure of Pauline mission and the significance of evangelists and their relationship to local churches. Dickson next outlines several areas of mission-commitment in which the churches ("congregational involvement in the advance of the gospel") supported Paul's mission.[17] Dickson discusses financial assistance and prayer; other expectations were the provision of coworkers and moral support for himself and his colleagues.[18]

The financial maintenance of missionaries.[19] Paul expected the churches to provide for the people whom they had sent out on the task of mission,

---

[14]Schnabel, *Early Christian Mission,* 2:123-54, offers a summary of "The missionary task according to Paul's letters"; see also C. Stenschke, "Das Neue Testament als Dokumentensammlung urchristlicher Mission: Alter Hut oder neue Perspektive?" *Jahrbuch für evangelikale Theologie* 19 (2005): 167-90.

[15]We do not distinguish between churches and individual Christians, as they appear as members of churches. Our purpose here is not to examine how Paul understood his own mission or how he went about it; for such an examination, see Schnabel, *Early Christian Mission* 2 and P. Bolt and M. Thompson, eds., *The Gospel to the Nations: Perspectives on Paul's Mission* (Downers Grove, Ill.: InterVarsity Press, 2000).

[16]Dickson, *Mission-Commitment,* pp. 178-227.

[17]Ibid., p. 212.

[18]For a detailed presentation and evaluation of Dickson's monograph, see my review article in the *European Journal of Theology* 15 (2006): 125-34.

[19]Cf. J. M. Everts, "Financial Support," *DPL*, pp. 295-300. Allen, *Missionary Methods,* pp. 49-61 argued that Paul had three principles regarding finances: "He did not seek financial help for himself; he took no financial help to those to whom he preached; he did not administer local church funds" (p. 49). On the first principle Allen elaborates that "He received money; but not from those to whom he was preaching. He refused to do anything from which it might appear that he came to receive, that his object was to make money" (p. 51). An excellent survey of finances in Paul's mission and of his financial policies is C. R. Little, *Mission in the Way of Paul: Biblical Mission for the Church in the Twenty-First Century,* Studies in Biblical Literature 80 (New York: Peter Lang, 2005).

during the time they served as coworkers with Paul himself or elsewhere. Paul also expected the churches to fund his own mission work, which in many cases could not be separated from the mission work of his co-workers. Demanding extended hospitality and finances for further traveling, he writes to the Corinthians: "and perhaps I will stay with you or even spend the winter, so that you may help me on my journey, wherever I go" (1 Cor 16:6). In 2 Corinthians 1:16 he announces, "I wanted to visit you on my way to Macedonia, and to come back to you from Macedonia and have you send me on my way to Judea." Paul expected such support for his ministry elsewhere. For example, he hoped that the Romans would help him with support on his journey to Spain (Rom 15:24).

In 1 Thessalonians 2:1-9 and 2 Thessalonians 3:8-9, Paul mentions his right to material support, a right that he did not make use of. An extended discussion of this can be found in 1 Corinthians 9:1-18. Paul did not make use of this right during his ministry *in Corinth*, although "the Lord commanded that those who proclaim the gospel should get their living by the gospel" (1 Cor 9:14). When he worked elsewhere, he expected support—even from the Corinthians.

Paul made similar demands for his coworker Timothy: "So let no one despise him. Help him on his way in peace, that he may return to me, for I am expecting him with the brothers" (1 Cor 16:11; see below on Tit 3:13).

Occasional financial missionary gifts. The second point is closely related to the first. The prime example of such gifts is a sum of money, sent by the church in Philippi to Paul. Paul acknowledges its receipt and expresses his gratitude in some detail in Philippians 4:10-20.[20] He reminds the Philippians that when he left Macedonia "no church entered into partnership with me in giving and receiving, except you only" (Phil 4:15; possibly "no other" only applies to the churches of Macedonia). Even when Paul worked in Thessalonica—and when the Thessalonian beneficiaries of this ministry should actually have supported him—it was the Philippians who again sent Paul money (Phil 4:16).[21] Paul writes, "I have received full payment, and more. I

---

[20]For detailed discussion, see Dickson, *Mission-Commitment*, pp. 201-12.
[21]Paul's stay in Thessalonica was short; see his reflection in 1 Thess 2:1-9. While Paul was there, Jason provided hospitality (Acts 17:5-6). The account also illustrates that such provision could be dangerous for the host.

am well supplied, having received from Epaphroditus the gifts you sent, a fragrant offering, a sacrifice acceptable and pleasing to God" (Phil 4:18).

That this is the only example of this type of gift is due to Paul's reluctance to receive support from other churches. Such support might have led to a misunderstanding concerning Paul's motivation for preaching the gospel or, possibly, these gifts had "strings" attached to them (see above regarding the situation in Thessalonica and Corinth).

Closely related to Paul's mission was his collection for the poor saints in Jerusalem (cf. Rom 15:25-31; 1 Cor 16:1-4; 2 Cor 8–9).[22] Paul expected the churches he had founded to contribute generously to this expression of the Gentile Christians' indebtedness to the Jewish believers and went to great lengths to convince them of the need for, and worthiness of, such giving.[23]

The provision of coworkers.[24] It is noteworthy that Paul apparently intended to come to Rome by himself. There are certainly no indications to the contrary in his letter to the Christians at Rome. In Romans 15:24, he mentions his plans of visiting the Roman Christians on his way to Spain (cf. also Rom 1:8-15) and expresses his hope "to be helped on my journey there by you, once I have enjoyed your company for a while." Obviously Paul expected financial support from the Romans for the journey. He also will have expected their prayers for the westward journey, as he asks for their prayers for this impending journey to Jerusalem (Rom 15:30-31). However, it is probable that Paul also hoped to find some coworkers in Rome.[25] Possibly he had in mind some of the people whom he mentioned in his detailed and affectionate list of greetings (Rom 16:3-15). His coworkers up to that moment were needed in the churches in the East, to complete the mission there. Many of the Christians then in Rome would have spoken Latin (which Paul

---

[22]Cf. S. McKnight, "Collection for the Saints," *DPL*, pp. 143-47; J. M. Everts, "Financial Support," *DPL*, pp. 295-300.

[23]For a recent summary see D. J. Downs, *The Offering of the Gentiles: Paul's Collection for Jerusalem and its Chronological, Cultural and Cultic Contexts*, WUNT II.248 (Tübingen: Mohr Siebeck, 2008).

[24]Dickson treats the sending of missionaries under the provision of financial assistance. It does imply and involve finances, but there is more to it. For the coworkers of Paul, see E. E. Ellis, "Coworkers, Paul and His," *DPL*, pp. 183-89.

[25]In his recent commentary on Romans, R. Jewett has interpreted the whole letter in view of Paul's intention of establishing an apostolic partnership with the Romans; *Romans: A Commentary*, Herm (Minneapolis: Fortress Press, 2006).

and others in his company were probably unable to speak and write) and might have had more experience in contexts where the Christian mission could not begin in the Jewish synagogue. This wish for coworkers might also explain why Paul planned a longer stay in Rome.

What Paul applied to Titus would also have applied to the churches, since Paul's letter to Titus is not private correspondence (cf. "Grace be with you *all,*" Tit 3:15, emphasis added): "Do your best to speed Zenas the lawyer and Apollos on their way; see that they lack nothing" (Tit 3:13).[26]

Prayer on behalf of unbelievers.[27] Paul assures the Romans that he prays for unbelieving Jews: "my heart's desire and prayer to God for them is that they may be saved" (Romans 10:1). Paul urges "that supplications, prayers, intercessions, and thanksgivings be made for all people, for kings and all who are in high positions, that we may lead a peaceful and quiet life, godly and dignified in every way. . . . I desire then that in every place the men should pray" (1 Tim 2:1, 8).

Prayer for Paul and his coworkers. In the final instructions in the letter, the Thessalonians are charged, "Brothers, pray for us" (1 Thess 5:25). This is repeated in 2 Thessalonians 3:1: "Finally, brothers, pray for us, that the word of the Lord may speed ahead and be honored, as happened among you, and that we may be delivered from wicked and evil men." The Ephesians are to pray for all the saints, "and also for me, that words may be given to me in opening my mouth boldly to proclaim the mystery of the gospel . . . that I may declare it boldly, as I ought to speak" (Eph 6:19). The Colossians are admonished, "pray also for us, that God may open to us a door for the word, to declare the mystery of Christ . . . that I may make it clear, which is how I ought to speak" (Col 4:3-4; cf. Acts 14:27; 1 Cor 16:9; 2 Cor 2:12). Paul's catalogue of suffering in 2 Corinthians 11:23-29 lists some of the strains and dangers involved in mission work—all of which required prayer.[28] Paul asked the Roman Christians to strive together with him in their prayers to

---

[26]It is noteworthy that Paul writes in this context: "And let our people learn to devote themselves to good works, so as to help cases of urgent need, and not be unfruitful" (Tit 3:14).

[27]For a summary of Paul's requests for prayer see W. B. Hunter, "Prayer," *DPL*, p. 726; see also D. A. Carson, "Paul's Mission and Prayer," in *The Gospel to the Nations,* ed. P. Bolt and M. Thompson (Downers Grove, Ill.: InterVarsity Press, 2000), pp. 175-84.

[28]For a summary, see B. W. Winter, "Dangers and Difficulties for the Pauline Mission," in *The Gospel to the Nations,* ed. P. Bolt and M. Thompson (Downers Grove, Ill.: InterVarsity Press, 2000), pp. 285-95.

God on Paul's behalf as he traveled to Jerusalem (Rom 15:30-32).

However, Paul not only requested prayer for his ministry, he also generously prays for the churches. For example, to the Philippians, Paul wrote, "I thank my God in all my remembrance of you, always in every prayer of mine for you all making my prayer with joy" (Phil 1:3-4).[29]

"Refreshed in your company" (Rom 15:32). Paul also expected encouragement and spiritual blessings from churches. It was not a case of the churches providing finances, people, and prayer and Paul providing spiritual blessings in exchange to them or to others (cf. Rom 1:11-15; 15:29). For Paul it worked both ways; he also wanted to be spiritually refreshed by the churches. After having completed his task in the east and before venturing west towards Spain, Paul wrote to the Romans: "For I long to see you, that I may impart to you some spiritual gift to strengthen you—that is, that *we may be mutually encouraged by each other's faith, both yours and mine*" (Rom 1:11-12, emphasis added); "once I have enjoyed your company for a while" (Rom 15:24); "that . . . I may come to you with joy and *be refreshed in your company*" (Rom 15:32, emphasis added). This support of the mission work was limited neither to the Roman Christians nor to Paul. The "partnership in the gospel from the first day until now," which Paul had with the Philippians, was not limited to finances and prayer (Phil 1:5).

In addition to his extant letters (they give an indication of at least three further letters; cf. 1 Cor 5:9, 2 Cor 2:4, 9; Col 4:16), Paul's coworkers formed a strong link between Paul, his mission and the churches. Some of this encouragement would have come to Paul and other missionary colleagues through them. Paul's letters also suggest that in addition to his own ministry and that of his coworkers, other Christian leaders were active in "his" churches and in evangelism. For example, the Corinthians also knew of Apollos' and of Peter's ministry (cf. 1 Cor 9:5; 12:28-29, 15:7). Paul mentioned fellow Christians who were encouraged to speak more fearlessly because of his example (Phil 1:14-18): "Paul is not concerned about the motives of the preachers, still less about their identity; all that he wants to see is Christ being preached, no matter by whom."[30]

---

[29]For Paul's intercession for the churches, see Hunter, "Prayer," p. 728.

[30]I. H. Marshall, "Who Were the Evangelists?" in *The Mission of the Early Church to Jews and Gentiles*, ed. J. Adna and H. Kvalbein, WUNT 127 (Tübingen: Mohr Siebeck, 2000), p. 259 (see also pp. 251-63).

The Extension of Paul's Mission in the Mission of the Churches

Paul's expectation of congregational involvement in evangelism. A number of studies have addressed the issue of whether Paul was content with the significant involvement of the churches in supporting his mission (see the section immediately preceding this for a summary) or whether he expected the churches he had founded (and others) to be actively involved themselves in spreading the gospel. A number of older studies suggested that—as far as we know—Paul had no such expectations (or only limited expectations).[31] At first glance their case seems convincing: when today's church leaders want to encourage for mission or evangelism, they usually refer to the Great Commission of Matthew 28 or other non-Pauline texts. There is only one verse in Paul's letters that can be understood as a direct charge to be actively involved in mission (Phil 2:16, see below).[32] This apparent lack is all the more striking given that Paul and his letters cannot be understood apart from early Christian mission. However, several more recent studies have convincingly argued that Paul had such expectations and that he voiced them.[33]

Ethical living. Before we examine the evidence for what might be called *congregational verbal evangelism*, we should note that Paul also emphasizes the importance of ethical living for Christian witness. Both issues are inseparably linked. Dickson describes these pleas as calls to "mission-commitment" through "social integration, ethical apologetic, public worship and verbal apologetic."[34]

Despite all calls to personal holiness and warnings to disassociate from immoral people professing to be believers, *Christians are not to withdraw from*

---

[31]For a brief summary of the debate, see Marshall, "Evangelists," pp. 252-56. For a detailed survey see R. L. Plummer, *Paul's Understanding of the Church's Mission: Did the Apostle Paul Expect the Early Christian Communities to Evangelize?* PBM (Milton Keynes, U.K.: Paternoster, 2006), pp. 1-42. After the survey of research Plummer examines "The church's mission in the Pauline letters: a theological basis for apostolic continuity," pp. 43-70.

[32]Allen, *Missionary Methods*, p. 93 noted: "There is one *sentence of approval*, 'From you sounded out the word of the Lord', but there is no insistence upon the command of Christ to preach the Gospel" (italics added). In the same context Allen writes, "Paul's converts became missionaries."

[33]For a summary of the evidence, see Schnabel, *Early Christian Mission,* 2:1451-72 and the studies presented here in more detail.

[34]Dickson, *Mission-Commitment*, pp. 228-308; these aspects express "congregational commitment to local mission" (p. 308).

the world, but are to mix with the unbelievers around them (1 Cor 5:9-10).[35]
The Corinthians are not to isolate themselves, but are to use the evangelistic
opportunities which local banquets provide (1 Cor 10:31–11:1): they are to
eat or drink, or whatever they do, for the glory of God, giving no offense to
Jews, Greeks or Christians. They should please everyone in everything they
do, not seeking their own advantage, but that of many, that they may be
saved. In this they are to imitate Paul.

*Christians are to have a good appearance before non-Christians (1 Thess
4:12: "so that you may walk properly before outsiders").* They are to display
gracious, sound judgment (Phil 4:5, "Let your reasonableness be known to
everyone") and they are to walk wisely toward outsiders (Col 4:5; cf. also Tit
2:2-10; 3:1-8) who observe their conduct. Christian slaves are called to "in
everything . . . adorn the doctrine of God our Savior" (Tit 2:10). All Christians are to be ready for every good work, to speak evil of no one, to avoid
quarrelling, to be gentle, and to show perfect courtesy towards all people
(Tit 3:1). They are to devote themselves to good works: "These things are
excellent and profitable for people" (Tit 3:8).

*At least some of Christian worship is to be public and is to be at least indi-
rectly evangelistic (1 Cor 14:23-25).* Paul assumes that some unbelievers
attend church meetings with a degree of regularity. The unbelievers who
experience what is described in 1 Corinthians 14:24-25 ("he is convicted by
all, he is called to account by all, the secrets of his heart are disclosed, and
so, falling on his face, he will worship God and declare that God is really
among you") will surely be led to repentance and to saving faith.[36]

*Christians are to be able to answer with gracious speech, seasoned with salt,
questions regarding their behavior and faith (Col 4:6).* Much of this behavior

---

[35]Allen, *Missionary Methods*, p. 119, noted that Paul "made it possible for converts to continue to
work at their trades as members of a heathen guild or society. . . . They were present, but they did
not partake." Allen comments on the consequences when the mission paradigm of his own day
chose a different route, "The Christians cannot so leaven society when they are, as it were, outside
it, as they can when they are really in it, living in the same life, sharing the same toil, the same
gains, the same losses, as their heathen fellows; they and their religion are peculiarly the care of
the foreign missionary, they are looked upon as having separated themselves from the life of the
nation; their religion does not appear to belong to their people" (p. 120).

[36]See a detailed discussion in Plummer, *Paul's Understanding*, pp. 94-96. He writes, "In this passage,
Paul presupposes the Corinthians' desire for non-Christians to be convicted of sin and turn to the
Lord in faith. To accomplish this desire, Paul explains, communication within the church meeting
should be intelligible to a visiting non-believer" (pp. 94-95).

of the Christians will have led to opportunities for verbal witness to the gospel, as 1 Peter 3:15 suggests: "Always being prepared to make a defense to anyone who asks for a reason of the hope that is in you; yet do it with gentleness and respect."

Proclamation of the gospel. Let us now turn to the evidence that Paul expected the churches also to actively proclaim the gospel.[37]

Paul suggests actions that have the salvation of others in mind. Paul twice urges the Corinthians to become imitators of him (1 Cor 4:16; 11:1).[38] The imitative behavior that Paul desires from his congregations includes imitation of his missionary concern and activities.

Paul also speaks of the missionary task of the believer married to an unbeliever; this task probably entails exemplary conduct aimed at the eschatological salvation of the unbelieving spouse (1 Cor 7:12-16). Says Plummer, "The apostle exhorts a believing spouse to live at peace with a non-believing spouse. The ultimate goal of this irenic behavior is not temporal harmony, but eschatological salvation. . . . In this conjugal relationship, as in other relationships, the evangelistic concern of the believer is assumed. Paul does not write, '[Believing] wife, you must desire, pray and actively work for your husband's salvation.' Such active concern is assumed. . . . While including attractive behavior of the spouse, Paul's instructions in 7:12-16 cannot be relegated to simply the 'passive' category of missionary activity."[39]

Paul considers his readers ambassadors of Christ. Rather than being limited to Paul and his missionary colleagues, the first person plural in 2 Corinthians 5:18–6:2 probably includes the Corinthians in Paul's statement as being Christ's ambassadors: "the language itself clearly indicates that those who have been reconciled themselves become agents of reconciliation."[40]

In 1 Thessalonians 1:8 the word *exēcheō* should be understood as follows: "from you *has sounded forth* the Word of the Lord not only in Macedonia

---

[37]For a convenient summary, see Marshall, "Evangelists," pp. 258-63.

[38]See a detailed argument of this case in Plummer, *Paul's Understanding*, pp. 81-92 and P. T. O'Brien, *Gospel and Mission in the Writings of Paul: An Exegetical and Theological Analysis* (Carlisle, U.K.: Paternoster, 1995), pp. 83-107.

[39]See a detailed discussion in Plummer, *Paul's Understanding*, pp. 93-94, and C. Stenschke, "Married Women and the Spread of Early Christianity," *Neotestamentica* 43 (2009): 176-78, 181-83. Plummer, *Paul's Understanding*, pp. 95-96 offers further circumstantial evidence that indicates that the Corinthians imitated Paul in his missionary concern.

[40]Marshall, "Evangelists," p. 260.

and Achaia, but everywhere else your faith in God has gone forth, so that
we have no need to say anything" (author's translation). "Accordingly, we
have evidence of a mission developed from Thessalonica, which Paul relates
with enthusiasm and implied approval."[41] Schnabel observes, "In 1 Thessalonians 3:12, Paul prays that the love of the believers in Thessalonica 'for one
another and for all' might increase. He reminds them that they should not
allow the new community and fellowship that they enjoy as new converts to
be solidified as a 'closed group' that insulates itself against society, a behavior that would prevent others from hearing the news of Jesus."[42]

Regarding Philippians, Schnabel also notes, "Paul thanks the Christians
in Philippi for their 'sharing in the gospel' (Phil 1:5). The phrase 'in the gospel'
(*eis to euangelion*) describes an active participation of the church in Philippi
in his own missionary work. They cooperated in preaching the gospel not
only through their financial support for Paul (Phil 4:15f) and through their
prayers (Phil 1:19), but also in terms of passing on the news of Jesus."[43]

Also, in Philippians 2:14-17 the Greek word *epechontes* can be understood as "holding forth" rather than the traditional rendering of the expression with "holding fast."[44] Thus the Christians are charged to hold forth
the word of life, i.e., to present the word and to shine as lights in the midst
of a crooked and twisted generation (Phil 2:15). James Ware writes, "As such
Philippians 2:16 is very significant, for while Paul nowhere else in his letters
gives an explicit command to his churches to spread the gospel, his exhortation to the Philippians to do so reveals that Paul did envision his churches
as having an active mission to those outside. . . . Paul did not understand his
apostolic mission as fulfilled in the establishment of firmly founded communities, but in the independent spread of the Gospel from the communities he founded."[45]

In addition to the significance of this single expression, Ware has argued

---

[41]Ibid., p. 259. Schnabel, *Paul the Missionary*, p. 244 agrees: "This description has been interpreted
in the sense that Paul sketches a picture of active preaching by the Thessalonians in Macedonia
and Achaia and beyond."

[42]Schnabel, *Paul the Missionary*, p. 244.

[43]Ibid., p. 245.

[44]For a detailed discussion of this word see Marshall, "Evangelists," p. 260 and J. P. Ware, *The Mission of the Church in Paul's Letter to the Philippians in the Context of Ancient Judaism*, NTS 120
(Boston: Brill, 2005), pp. 256-70.

[45]Ware, *Mission*, p. 284.

in detail for the "Mission of the Church in Philippians 2:12-18," discussing the work of God and of the Philippians (Phil 2:12-13), the relationship of eschatology and mission (Phil 2:14-15), the relation between the mission of the church and the mission of Paul (Phil 2:16-18), the priestly activity of the Philippians (Phil 2:17-18), and Paul's apostolic self-description in the latter half of Philippians 2:16.[46] Ware concludes,

> In 2:12-18, Paul spells out the consequences of the preceding Christ hymn by exhorting the Philippians to proclaim the gospel. Paul's exhortation to the Philippians in 2:12 to work out their own salvation does not introduce a new command but functions to sum up and climax Paul's entire appeal in 1:12–2:11. Echoing themes and motifs carefully developed throughout the epistle, the command functions within this wider context of the letter as an exhortation to the Philippians to boldly spread the gospel despite the threat of suffering and persecution. . . . Paul's portrayal of the Philippians as lights among the gentiles reflects the widespread use of light imagery in ancient Judaism to depict the eschatological conversion of the nations. In applying these traditions to the Philippians, Paul portrays the church in Philippi as the eschatological Diaspora of God set in the midst of both Jews and gentiles and bringing them the light of God's salvation.[47]

Mark J. Keown has recently argued an even more comprehensive case for all of Philippians as exhorting the readers to congregational evangelism.[48]

Paul views the churches as gifted for spreading the gospel. The gifts of the Spirit to the church for its ministry include that of evangelism (Eph 4:11). Paul expected that individual Christians would receive this gift and use it. Says Schnabel, "The *charismata* that the Holy Spirit gives to the church for 'building up the body of Christ' (Eph 4:12) include the task of proclaiming the news of Jesus. The orientation of this task toward the nurture of the church does not diminish the primary meaning of the word: evangelists, particularly if they are not at the same time 'shepherds' and teachers, pro-

---

[46]Ibid., pp. 237-84; see my review in *NovT* 51 (2009): 404-7. Ware rightly understands Philippians 2:12-18 in view of the progress of the gospel in Philippians 1:12-18 (treated on pp. 163-99) and in view of suffering and mission in Philippians 1:1-2:11 (pp. 201-36).

[47]Ware, *Mission*, p. 283.

[48]*Congregational Evangelism in Philippians: The Centrality of an Appeal for Gospel Proclamation to the Fabric of Philippians*, Paternoster Biblical Monographs (Carlisle, U.K.: Paternoster, 2008); see my forthcoming review in *Missionalia*. For Plummer's survey of Paul's instructions to the Philippians to proclaim the gospel, see Plummer, *Paul's Understanding*, pp. 72-77.

claim the gospel of Jesus Christ *also* and perhaps primarily before people who have not yet heard the gospel or who have not yet come to faith in Jesus Christ."[49] This gift does not exonerate others from the call to active witness.

The extended military metaphor in Ephesians 6:11-17 includes the charge to wear shoes, "having put on the readiness given by the gospel of peace" (Eph 6:15). Plummer rightly asks: "What, then does it mean to have one's feet fitted with 'the readiness of the gospel of peace'? What is one ready or prepared to do? How does the gospel relate to this readiness?"[50] Observing that Paul alludes to Isaiah 52:7 and Nahum 1:15-2:3 (LXX 2:1-4), Plummer argues that Paul has preaching the gospel in mind: "Both texts present God as victor over enemy powers. God is the one who brought peace and blessings, which must be joyfully proclaimed. . . . The combination of these OT texts with Paul's current concerns may help explain what influenced Paul to speak so explicitly at this point about the church's readiness to proclaim the gospel."[51] Therefore the NRSV rightly translates: "As shoes for your feet put on whatever will make you ready to proclaim the gospel of peace." Two further elements in the immediate context confirm this reading: the charge to wield the sword of the Spirit (which is the word of God) probably also has evangelistic connotations, and the readers are called upon in Ephesians 6:18-20 to pray for the fearless proclamation of the gospel: "In the two other instances where Paul requests prayer for his evangelistic mission, the apostle also mentions a missionary role for the congregations which he addresses (Col 4:2-6; 2 Thess 2:16f; 3:1f). Paul seems unwilling to request prayer for his gospel preaching without noting the missionary work of his churches."[52]

---

[49]Schnabel, *Paul the Missionary,* p. 245 (emphasis in original).

[50]Plummer, *Paul's Understanding,* pp. 78f; see also Schnabel's treatment of the passage (*Paul the Missionary,* pp. 246-47).

[51]Plummer, *Paul's Understanding,* p. 80.

[52]Ibid. Concerning the Pastoral Epistles, Schnabel, *Paul the Missionary,* p. 247-48 refers to 1 Tim 3:7 ("The 'good reputation' (*martyria*) of the elders determines the witness (*martyria*) of the church. Both the elders and the congregation are committed to the obligation to represent, display and communicate the will of God who wants to save sinners," p. 247), 2 Tim 4:5 ("The leaders of the congregations are called upon to proclaim the gospel, evidently before people who have not yet heard the message of Jesus Christ. The congregations are not to wait for traveling missionaries who pass through. Rather, they are to make sure that people hear the gospel," p. 247), Tit 2:3-5 ("The exhortation to the 'older women' . . . may be motivated by missionary concerns. . . . Their behavior should not discredit the evangelistic efforts of the church but promote them," pp. 247-48) and Tit 2:9-10 ("The credibility of the gospel, which is preached in connection with the mis-

For Roland Allen, the missionary involvement of Paul's churches "was not really surprising. Christians receive the Spirit of Jesus, and the Spirit of Jesus is a missionary spirit, the Spirit of Him who came into the world to bring back lost souls to the Father."[53] None of the more recent studies of congregational evangelism include this pneumatological argument. Like many of Allen's observations, this is a case that deserves to be argued in more detail.

Paul sees the churches as continuing the work of evangelists other than himself. Both Plummer and Marshall gather further "*incidental* evidence that Paul expected the churches to spread the Gospel in the apostolic pattern" and that he was aware of an ongoing mission through Christians other than himself.[54] Marshall, for example, notes that the "comings and goings of the apostles and their co-workers will have led to a blurring of the distinction between congregation and the missionaries."[55]

Marshall concludes his survey of the evidence: "The cumulative effect of these points is to demonstrate that early congregations and individual believers did have an evangelistic function that appears to have developed spontaneously."[56] Or, in Plummer's words, "There can be no doubt that Paul instructs and approves of his churches actively proclaiming the gospel. In Philippians, Ephesians and 1 Corinthians, we have examined texts in which Paul commands the churches to declare the gospel, to be prepared to do so, or to imitate him in the way that he strives for the salvation of non-Christians."[57]

Conclusion

Our survey has shown that the mission of Paul should be understood as deeply embedded in churches in a number of ways. According to the book

---

sionary activities of the local church, would be discredited if they display a rebellious attitude. The Christian slaves are encouraged 'to make the gospel as attractive as possible for those around them,'" p. 248).

[53]Allen, *Missionary Methods*, p. 93.

[54]This is Plummer's chapter heading, *Paul's Understanding*, pp. 107-39 (italics added); Marshall, "Evangelists," p. 258-59.

[55]Marshall, "Evangelists," p. 261.

[56]Ibid., p. 262; see also Schnabel, *Paul the Missionary*, p. 244: "There is sufficient evidence to conclude that Paul's teaching included the encouragement of the believers to share their faith in Jesus Christ with other people."

[57]Plummer, *Paul's Understanding*, p. 96. Plummer then surveys "Paul's commands to witness passively" (pp. 96-105).

of Acts, the mission of Paul was closely linked with the churches to which he belonged and who commissioned him and the churches he founded. His mission is to be understood as the mission of the church(es).

Paul's letters indicate that he expected the churches to actively support his *translocal mission*. This support included the financial maintenance of missionaries, occasional financial missionary gifts, the provision of co-workers, prayer on behalf of unbelievers, prayer for Paul and his coworkers, and the provision of spiritual refreshment to missionaries.

Paul also expected the churches he addressed to be actively involved themselves in *local evangelism*. Robert Plummer's question "Did the apostle Paul expect the early Christian communities to evangelize?" is to be answered in the affirmative. Paul expected them to spread the gospel through their exemplary behavior at home, at church and elsewhere in their day-to-day living and through verbal communication of the gospel in different situations.

Roland Allen noted this close link between Paul's mission and the churches and the missionary involvement of his churches, although he did not argue the case in detail. The material presented here (and the scholars whose work is also collected) supports Allen's case: there is evidence that Paul "intended his congregations to become at once a centre of light." His churches were "possessed of sufficient life to be a source of light to the whole country round."[58] Allen's claims that Paul's "converts became missionaries" and that "The Christians of the Four Provinces were certainly zealous in propagating the faith" can be substantiated.[59] While some congregations "apparently needed no exhortation on the subject," the Corinthians, Philippians, Ephesians and Thessalonians needed some encouragement and prodding in the right direction as far as their involvement in mission work was concerned.[60]

Paul intended the churches he founded to be "self-propagating."[61] However, one should add that the churches were intended to be self-propagating

---

[58] Allen, *Missionary Methods*, p. 13.

[59] Ibid., p. 93.

[60] Ibid. Allen's comment about the lack of need for exhortation is a rather precarious argument from silence!

[61] Ibid., p. 94. The spread of the church in the postapostolic age confirms that this was actually the case; see the survey by R. Hvalvik, "The Expansion of the Church in the pre-Constantinian Era," in *The Mission of the Early Church to Jews and Gentiles* , ed. J. Adna and H. Kvalbein, WUNT 127 (Tübingen: Mohr Siebeck, 2000), pp. 265-87.

in conjunction with other churches (Allen rightly emphasized the unity of the church[es]), and in cooperation with the missionaries they had sent or others working in different places. [62]

Following Luke's portrayal, Paul's own statements and Allen's analysis of Paul's mission, we may conclude that, as far as the mission of the church in the twenty first century is concerned, if our mission is to reflect Paul's mission, it must be embedded in churches. Churches, if they are to reflect Paul's theology and practice, need to be involved in mission in several ways: they are called to support mission in other places by prayer, by providing for people and by contributing funds. Local churches are called not only to support mission and evangelism elsewhere in various ways, but also to be actively engaged in evangelism through word and deed in their own surroundings. That Paul had to address these issues indicates that even in the early days of Christianity—often glorified through hindsight—such involvement was not self-evident and needed prompting and encouragement. This calling of the church needs to be reintegrated into New Testament theology and present day ecclesiology. In many parts of the world—for a number of reasons—the continuation and/or the rediscovery of the mission of the church will be the only way in which the church can fulfill its calling to make disciples of the nations.

Mission as the mission of the church has to overcome challenges in our day and age that are similar to the challenges the churches of the first century A.D. faced. Three of many possible such issues deserve mention.

First, as in New Testament times, involvement in mission elsewhere and locally may provoke resistance and persecution on the part of those who reject the gospel. How Christians themselves respond to these challenges will, in itself, underline their witness.[63]

Second, mission as the mission of the church involves sacrifice: a church might "lose" (it seems!) its best people to tasks elsewhere or to local evangelism. These people are then not (or not fully) available for the church's ministry to its own members. In addition, churches are called to

---

[62]Allen, *Missionary Methods*, pp. 126-38.

[63]On mission and suffering, see Plummer, *Paul's Understanding*, pp. 121-38 and S. Hafemann, "The Role of Suffering in the Mission of Paul," in *The Mission of the Early Church to Jews and Gentiles*, ed. J. Adna and H. Kvalbein, WUNT 127 (Tübingen: Mohr Siebeck, 2000), pp. 165-84.

invest some of their means in mission work elsewhere and to support it with their prayers.

Third, churches are called to rediscover their role of providing spiritual refreshment for their own missionaries and missionaries from other churches.

If mission is to be understood and practiced as the mission of the church, each congregation has the opportunity to not only address its own needs and matters, but also to partake in God's vision and mission for this world until the day comes when Christ triumphantly gathers his saints "from east and west, and from north and south, and [they] recline at [his] table in the kingdom of God" (Lk 13:29).

6

PAUL'S THEOLOGY OF SUFFERING

♦ ♦ ♦

Don N. Howell Jr.

DESTINED FOR SUFFERING

From the outset, suffering was a keynote of Paul's Christian experience. Apprehended by the one whose followers he had come to Damascus to arrest, the transformation began with the words that followed—"I am Jesus, whom you are persecuting" (Acts 9:5). Saul came to understand that the crucified, accursed Nazarene, heretofore viewed as a false prophet and blasphemer, was the risen and exalted Lord whose death on the cross bore the curse of death for lawbreakers as their sinless substitute (Gal 3:13).[1] But there was more. Jesus identified himself with the sufferings of his witnesses—to persecute them was to persecute him. In his earthly ministry Jesus had repeatedly bound his disciples to himself in a fellowship of sacrifice and hardship (Mt 5:11-12; 10:17-25; 24:9-14; Jn 15:18-25; 16:33). While his sufferings as the Isaianic servant of the Lord were redemptive, those of his people would be representative and testimonial. When an obscure disciple named Ananias approached Saul to restore his sight, he also communicated the divine calling to proclaim the saving name of Jesus to the Gentiles and to Israel, a calling of which the context would be suffering: "I will show him

---

[1]Martin Hengel, *The Pre-Christian Paul*, trans. John Bowden (Philadelphia: Trinity Press International, 1991), pp. 64, 83-84.

how much he must suffer for the sake of my name" (Acts 9:16). This pro-
nouncement means that the apostle Paul will take on the posture of Isaiah's
suffering servant, not like the messianic Servant whose vicarious sacrifice is
unique and unrepeatable, but in the sense of a witness whose sufferings bear
the image of the Servant-Lord whose person and work he proclaims to the
Gentiles (Is 42:1, 6-7; 49:6; Acts 13:46-47; 22:21; 26:15-18).[2]

Luke's record in Acts portrays the ministry of Paul as constantly attended
by suffering as he prosecutes his evangelistic mission, "first to the Jew, then
to the Gentile" (Rom 1:16 NIV). Most of the hostility to his preaching pro-
ceeds from Jewish quarters due to religious prejudice (Damascus [Acts
9:23-25]; Pisidian Antioch [Acts 13:45-46]; Iconium [Acts 14:4-5]; Lystra
[Acts 14:19]; Thessalonica [Acts 17:4-9]; Berea [Acts 17:13]; Corinth [Acts
18:6, 12-13]; Greece [Acts 20:3]; Jerusalem and Caesarea [Acts 21:27-36;
22:22-23; 23:2-4, 12-15; 25:9-12, 16-19; 26:21]; Rome [Acts 28:23-28]), though
at times the threatened monetary interests of Gentile opponents propel the
attacks (Philippi [Acts 16:19-24]; Ephesus [Acts 19:23-41]). But in all of these
setbacks Paul is not taken by surprise, for he reminds the persecuted
churches in Galatia that they "must go through many hardships to enter the
kingdom of God" (Acts 14:22 NIV).[3] In fact, he embraces suffering, and even
death, as the divinely determined setting of his life's work—to testify concerning God's grace in the gospel of his Son (Acts 20:23-24; cf. Acts 21:13).

Roland Allen identified "the most distinctive mark of Pauline Christianity" as the apostle's commitment, not to a set of religious ideals or ethical
principles, but to the life-giving gospel of Christ crucified and risen, a commitment proven by his willingness to suffer for its pure proclamation:

Christ came to give that life, and St Paul came as the minister of Christ, to

---

[2]When years later Paul exhorts the Philippian believers to emulate the humility of the preincarnate
Christ (Phil 2:5), he chooses the term δοῦλος for the posture that Christ assumed in his incarna-
tion (Phil 2:7), the very term that has been (along with ἀπόστολος) his favorite self-designation
(Rom 1:1; Gal 1:10; 2 Cor 4:5; Phil 1:1; Tit 1:1), as well as the proper designation for his coworkers
(Phil 1:1; Col 1:7; 4:7, 12; 2 Tim 2:24). While παῖς is the definitive Christological term for the messianic Servant in the early apostolic preaching (Acts 3:13, 26; 4:27, 30), δοῦλος is the term of
choice in the Carmen Christi (Phil 2:6-11), a hymn that supports the command to imitate the
mind of Christ (Phil 2:5). Do not these two terms together point to two dimensions of the work of
the suffering Servant: (1) the exclusivity of his vicarious sacrifice παῖς and yet (2) his attitude of
self-sacrificial abandonment to the divine purposes that demands imitation δοῦλος?
[3]The impersonal verb δεῖ ("must" or "is necessary"), both here and in Acts 9:16, refers to the divinely orchestrated destiny being worked out in the sufferings of Paul and the churches.

lead men to Christ who is the life, that in Him they might find life. His gospel was a gospel of power. So he taught, and for that all his life was one long martyrdom. If he would have admitted for a moment that his work was to introduce a higher law, a new system, he would have made peace with the Judaizers and he would have been at one with all contemporary reformers; but the Gospel would have perished in his hands. In his own words he would have fallen away from grace; Christ would have profited him nothing. That he refused to do and for that he suffered.[4]

We must turn to Paul's epistles for an exposition of his full-orbed theology of suffering.

ENABLED IN SUFFERING

The epistles of Paul are replete with the language of hardship.[5] One of the great interpretive hurdles for the twenty-first-century Western commentator (less of a hurdle for those who write out of a contemporary setting of persecution) is to capture the full force of language written to churches whose normal life setting was that of personal harassment, societal marginalization, and material loss. The secret of Paul's resilience, and that of the churches he planted, was a confidence in the divine purposes being worked out through their sufferings.

Paul expounds a theology of Christian suffering that encompasses three overlapping and complementary purposes. First, his sufferings are endured for the *edification* of the church, the body of Christ. His ministry as a pioneer church planter begins with proclamation of the gospel to unreached areas. In Thessalonica, where he encountered severe opposition from the leaders of the Jewish community (Acts 17:5, 13; cf. 1 Thess 2:14-16), Paul reminds the church that such trials were the ordained path of God both for

---

[4]Roland Allen, *Missionary Methods: St. Paul's or Ours?* 2nd ed. (Grand Rapids: Eerdmans, 1962), p. 148.

[5]The major terms are: (1) πάσχω, συμπάσχω and πάθημα, the general term for suffering of Paul and the churches (16 times in this sense); (2) θλίβω and θλίψις, tribulation, affliction or distress (29 times in this sense); (3) διώκω and διωγμός, persecution (16 times in this sense, including Paul's former persecuting activity [1 Cor 15:9; Gal 1:13, 23; Phil 3:6]); (4) (συγ)κακοπαθέω, bear ill treatment, endure affliction (with) (4 times in 2 Timothy). Many other related terms occur in Paul's catalogs of sufferings: Rom 8:35 (7 items); 1 Cor 4:11-13 (11 items); 2 Cor 4:8-9 (4 contrastive pairs); 2 Cor 6:4-5 (18 terms for hardships of various kinds); 2 Cor 11:23-29 (27 experiences of hardship listed, especially various kinds of dangers [κίνδυνος: 8 times in 2 Cor 11:26; cf. 1 Cor 15:40]); 2 Cor 12:10 (5 items listed).

him and for them (1 Thess 3:3-4). Such has also been the case in Galatia (Gal 3:4) and Philippi (1 Thess 2:2). The promotion of the kingdom of God—that is, his dynamic and transformational reign over those who embrace Jesus as Lord—is the design of the believers' persecutions and afflictions endured by faith (2 Thess 1:4-5). In his final written correspondence, the second letter to Timothy, written shortly before his death, Paul locates his sufferings and those of his trusted pastoral envoy in the context of the gospel. It is for the sake of the gospel that both he and Timothy must endure hardship (2 Tim 1:8, 12; 2:3, 9; 4:5). Though his time of temporal deliverance in such troubles is drawing to a close (2 Tim 3:10-12), he anticipates eternal reward in the heavenly kingdom (2 Tim 4:7-8, 16-18). His ministry to the church in Philippi (Phil 2:17) and his approaching death (2 Tim 4:6) are described under the sacrificial imagery of a drink offering poured out to God.

He counts as his most precious legacy the people won to Christ and the churches planted across five Roman provinces from Syria to Achaia (Rom 15:16; Gal 4:19; Phil 4:1; 1 Thess 2:19-20). If the believers are standing firm in the Lord, his trials are nothing more than a minor nuisance because of his joy and gratitude over their spiritual progress (1 Thess 3:6-10). His distresses, then, are designed for the comfort of the church, so that, by observing the fortitude of their beloved apostle, the believers will learn to endure patiently the sufferings that likewise bind them to Christ (2 Cor 1:5-7; Eph 3:13). Paul writes to the church in Colossae that he is enabled to joyfully endure his physical sufferings on their behalf because they "fill up . . . what is still lacking in regard to Christ's afflictions, for the sake of his body, which is the church" (Col 1:24 NIV). We can forthrightly dismiss any idea that there is something insufficient in the redemptive sufferings of Christ that the apostle must somehow supply. The undiminished deity of Jesus (Col 1:15-19; 2:9-10) and the fully efficacious benefits of his death on the cross (Col 1:20-22; 2:11-15) are two points of emphasis in this epistle written to correct a defective Christology troubling the church. The meaning of the enigmatic language of Colossians 1:24 seems to be that Paul acts as a shield or buffer to absorb some of the appointed number of blows aimed at the body of Christ.[6]

---

[6]Peter T. O'Brien, *Colossians, Philemon*, WBC 44 (Waco, Tex.: Word, 1982), pp. 78-81. This interpretation takes the language at face value: ἀνταναπληρῶ τὰ ὑστερήματα denotes in some sense the "filling to the full" of "things that are lacking." But it is the identification of Christ with his

This understanding of the language fits the flow of Paul's logic here. God has designed suffering to confirm the churches' solidarity with her Lord as she proclaims the gospel of the crucified and risen Christ to the Gentile world (Col 1:25-27). Paul sees his appointed role not only as pioneer, but also as perfecter, laboring with all his God-given energy to present the believers mature in Christ (Col 1:28-29). Paul stands in as protector and defender of the young, vulnerable churches. He receives in their stead a portion of the hardships and persecutions which otherwise might cause the people of God to be disheartened. All the sufferings that Paul endures are for the edification of the churches, both their building and their building up.

Second, the suffering of the apostle, and by extension that of the churches, certifies their *identification* with Jesus, the suffering Servant. Suffering brings the apostle into a participation in the humiliation experienced by Jesus which, by breaking down all levels of trust in human resources, releases the power of the risen Lord to become operative in his life (2 Cor 1:5; 4:7-12). Further, the sufferings of Paul, and of all believers, are a defining mark of being an heir of the coming kingdom and are thus the ordained preparatory stage for that glorious future inheritance (2 Cor 4:16-18; Rom 8:17-18). Here we see the apostle's eschatological dualism, which integrates the three phases of the timeline of salvation: the past (Christ's death and resurrection) has secured the future (kingdom glory), which in turn is to condition the present (transformed character and empowered living).[7] Paul's theology of suffering is not a self-deprecating delight in personal pain for its own sake. Rather, harsh realities such as physical ailments, aggressive opponents, malicious verbal attacks, and even physical assaults crush every

---

body (rather than in terms of his Passion), which is the church (specified in the final clause), that is the sphere of the afflictions that must be filled up. The Jewish apocalyptic teaching regarding the "woes of the Messiah" which must reach their appointed measure before the consummation of the kingdom is, plausibly, the background of this expression. For another interpretation, which also has a good contextual fit but which, in this writer's view, deals less successfully with the terminology (e.g., ἀνταναπληρόω means to "extend" the gospel to the Gentile world), see Thomas R. Schreiner, *Paul: Apostle of God's Glory in Christ* (Downers Grove, Ill.: InterVarsity Press, 2001), pp. 100-102.

[7] James D. G. Dunn, *The Theology of the Apostle Paul* (Grand Rapids: Eerdmans, 1998), pp. 482-87. Dunn points out that in a number of the Pauline texts which speak of the believer's identification with Christ's death and resurrection (Rom 6:5; Gal 2:19; 6:14), the apostle employs the perfect tense (completed action of the past event with a state that continues to the present). "Between the 'with him' of the already ('buried with him') and the 'with him' of the not yet ('raised with him'), there is the 'with him' of the in-between times ('suffer with him')" (p. 485).

fiber of self-reliance, so that he becomes a useful vessel through which God's triumphant power can flow (2 Cor 12:7-10). Further, his hardships bring him into a deeper fellowship with the Lord who suffered in his place; to know, in his personal experience, Christ's sufferings is to know his resurrection power (Phil 3:10). These coordinate areas of identification with Christ, namely, his death and resurrection, promote the sanctification of God's people and prepare them for the glory of Christ's unmediated presence in the kingdom of God to be ushered in at the final resurrection (Phil 3:11). In the final section, we will highlight how suffering, endured in faith, refined the character of Paul.

Third, the apostle's hardships are marks of *authentication* as a true servant of Christ. His physical sufferings brand him as one who belongs to Jesus (Gal 6:17) and distinguish him from the Judaizing infiltrators in Galatia.[8] The latter sought to avoid persecution from their fellow Jews by proclaiming a legalistic message more palatable than Paul's offensive doctrine of salvation through faith alone in the finished work of the crucified Messiah (Gal 6:12; cf. Gal 2:21; 3:13; 5:11-12). To a church divided by personality-centered factions, Paul reminds the Corinthians that he, Apollos and Cephas are but servants of Christ and stewards of the gospel who will render an account of their stewardship (1 Cor 4:1-5). To authenticate his true servants, God has put the apostles on display like prisoners of war who march in chains to the place of execution behind their conquerors (1 Cor 4:9). This "spectacle" serves as a testimony to the entire universe of people and angels that these are servants of the Servant (1 Cor 4:9-10 NIV).[9] The solidarity is found not in the common experiences of physical deprivation and brutal treatment alone (1 Cor 4:11-12), but also in how the apostles emulate the Lord's nonretaliatory posture when he suffered (1 Cor 4:12-13). In two extended catalogs of trials, Paul provides the Corinthian church with a set of criteria by which it can determine whose claims to authentic servanthood are credible (2 Cor 6:3-10; 11:23-33). The first catalog, a portrait of godly conduct in a context of trouble, establishes the credibility of his claim to be the true servant of God (2 Cor

---

[8]The term στίγμα was used of the branding of animals to certify ownership. Judged from the near context (Gal 5:11-12; 6:12-15), Paul is likely contrasting his "marks" (from beatings and tortures [Acts 14:19; 2 Cor 6:5; 11:23-25]) that authenticate him as a servant of the gospel of grace with the marks of circumcision that confirm the Judaizers as slaves of the law (*EDNT*, 3:276-77).

[9]Richard B. Hays, *First Corinthians*, Int (Louisville: John Knox, 1997), pp. 71-72.

3:4). The second catalog is offered as a foolish boast (2 Cor 11:16-18, 21) to counteract the patently ridiculous claim of the "super-apostles" (2 Cor 11:5; 12:11) to be servants of Christ (2 Cor 11:23). If you want to recognize true servants, Paul says, observe the level of their sacrificial imitation of the suffering Servant. Paul's résumé lists no academic degrees, published works or human accolades, only imprisonments (2 Cor 11:23), tortures (2 Cor 11:23-25), dangers (2 Cor 11:25-26), physical deprivations (2 Cor 11:27), internal pressures (2 Cor 11:28) and heartaches (2 Cor 11:29).

To conclude, Paul's sufferings *authenticate* him as God's servant, *identify* him with the crucified and risen Christ and *edify* the church. One who aspires to lead, that is, to impact others for the kingdom of God, must imitate Paul, who himself imitates Christ (1 Cor 11:1).[10]

REFINED BY SUFFERING

Paul views his sufferings, for the church, with Christ and as a servant, through the lens of God's providential goodness. Both his hardships and those endured by the churches are God's tool to refine and polish "jars of clay" (2 Cor 4:7) into holy vessels useful to the Master (2 Tim 2:21). Suffering, if embraced by faith as a painful but gracious gift from a loving Father (Rom 8:28-29, 35-39), draws one deeper into a transforming fellowship with the Lord Jesus (Phil 3:10), producing a refined character filled with buoyant hope (Rom 5:3-5).[11] This is why the apostle can view suffering for the sake of Christ, like saving faith itself, as God's good gift to his people

---

[10]The NIV renders 1 Cor 11:1, "Follow my example, as I follow the example of Christ." This is a less than desirable rendering since "to follow" (ἀκολουθέω) is the characteristic term used by Jesus to set forth his unique authority and to call his followers to committed discipleship under that authority (Mt 4:20, 22; 8:19, 22, 23; 9:9; 10:38; 16:24; 19:21, 27-28). Paul only uses this term once, of the spiritual rock that "accompanied" (NIV) Israel in the wilderness (1 Cor 10:4). He prefers the language of imitation (ὁ μιμήτης in 1 Cor 11:1; cf. 1 Cor 4:16; Eph 5:1; 1 Thess 1:6; 2:14). Precisely speaking, then, Paul does not summon the churches to "follow" his leadership, for Christ alone is their leader, whereas he is a servant commissioned to enhance their allegiance to Christ (2 Cor 1:24; 4:5; 6:4).

[11]The Greek term in Rom 5:4 is δοκιμή and all seven of its New Testament occurrences are in Paul's writings. This noun can mean one of three things: (1) a "test" or "trial," the outcome of which is uncertain (2 Cor 2:9; 8:2); (2) the demonstrable "proof" that what one claims is in fact true (2 Cor 9:13; 13:3); and (3) "proven character" that has been refined through hardship (Rom 5:4 [twice]; Phil 2:22). In the last text Paul praises Timothy to the Philippians for his "proven character," which has been refined over the past twelve years in the rough and tumble of missionary work as his most trusted associate.

and one that signifies their sonship (Rom 8:16-17; Phil 1:28-30). Here we highlight *four features* of Paul's character produced in the crucible of hardship that molded the indefatigable pioneer evangelist into a tender and nurturing parent to the fledgling churches (1 Thess 2:6-12).

Humility. Paul becomes a model of his own injunction to the Romans: "Do not think of yourself more highly than you ought, but rather think of yourself with sober judgment" (Rom 12:3 NIV). One can trace a sense of unworthiness as his hardships break and conform Paul into the image of his suffering Lord (Phil 3:10). He progresses downward, in his own estimation, from the least of the apostles (1 Cor 15:9), to the least of all saints (Eph 3:8), to the chief of sinners (1 Tim 1:15). Especially in his correspondence to the church in Corinth, a continuously seething caldron of relational disturbances that tested the limits of his patience, does the apostle willingly admit his inadequacies and expose his insecurities. Paul states that he first arrived in Corinth "in weakness and in fear and much trembling" (1 Cor 2:3). He had been forced to leave the promising work in Macedonia due to persecution both from secular and religious quarters (Acts 16:38-40; 17:5-9, 13-15). Upon his arrival in Athens, he met with a limited, and possibly discouraging, response to his evangelistic efforts (Acts 17:32-33). He then came to the capital of the province of Achaia, a large multiethnic city full of idols and gross immorality, yet with a culture fascinated by itinerant teachers who espoused Greek wisdom and delivered impressive orations. Paul deliberately refrained from imitating the rhetorical style of these sophists and set forth the gospel with clarity and in dependence on the Holy Spirit (1 Cor 1:17; 2:4-5). He warns the church that knowledge in and of itself, unless conditioned by love, puffs one up with a distorted view of one's importance (1 Cor 8:1-2). The Corinthians' fascination with human wisdom and oratorical style helps account for the personality-centered factions that developed in the church (1 Cor 1:10-17). Paul is shocked most by the group that claims allegiance to him; he intentionally distances himself from all attempts to elevate him beyond his appointed role as a servant and steward of the gospel (1 Cor 1:12-13; 3:4-9, 21-23; 4:1-2, 6-7).

Vulnerability. When he addresses the area of moral temptation, Paul is conscious of his vulnerability to fall into sin (1 Cor 10:12-13). He therefore exercises rigorous self-discipline lest he himself become "disqualified" for eschatological reward (1 Cor 9:26-27).[12] Paul's deep sense of self-distrust is similarly expressed in Philippians 3:10-11. He makes the experiential knowledge of Christ's resurrection power and continual conformity to his sufferings his singular pursuit, "and so, somehow, attaining to the resurrection from the dead" (Phil 3:11 NIV).[13] This text should not be understood to call into question Paul's assurance of final salvation, which he boldly articulates in many places (e.g., Rom 8:28-30; 2 Cor 5:6-10; Phil 1:20-24; 1 Thess 4:17-18; 2 Tim 1:12). Nor, however, should Paul's language be emptied of its force. He recognizes his own capacity for sin and unbelief, and maintains a conscious dependence on God's strength to enable him to persevere in faith, which is a precondition for eschatological salvation.[14] After nearly three decades of front line sacrificial ministry, we find Paul still following hard after Christ, refusing to be handicapped by past failures and deeply aware that he has not attained to spiritual perfection (Phil 3:12-14). Such determination, undergirded by divine grace (Phil 2:12-13), flows from his fellowship with Christ's sufferings coupled with reliance on the power of Christ's resurrection.

Dependence. The second epistle to the Corinthians discloses an apostle who actually delights in his weaknesses because human limitations afford God's power the opportunity to rest upon his ministry. The pressures Paul faced in Ephesus reached a level where he "despaired of life itself" and "felt . . . the sentence of death" (2 Cor 1:8-9).[15] This near-death experience broke him of self-reliance and made him God-dependent (2 Cor 1:9). Now the

---

[12]This is the rendering of the NIV, NASB and ESV of the term ἀδόκιμος in 1 Cor 9:27. Paul is referring not to his final salvation (perhaps implied in AV: "castaway"), but to the testing of his apostleship. He fears, through the lack of rigorous self-discipline, forfeiting the divine approval through failure to fulfill his apostolic commission as faithful steward of the gospel to the Gentiles. See Judith M. Gundry Volf, *Paul and Perseverance: Staying In and Falling Away* (Louisville: Westminster Press, 1990), pp. 233-37.

[13]The much anticipated experience of resurrection is expressed with several elements of contingency (Phil 3:11): the conditional particle "if" (εἴ), compounded with the indefinite adverb "somehow" (NIV) or "by any means possible" (ESV) (πως), governs an aorist subjunctive (mood of probability) verb (καταντήσω).

[14]Moises Silva, *Philippians* (Chicago: Moody Press, 1988), pp. 191-93, comments with balance and insight on this text.

[15]Margaret E. Thrall, *A Critical and Exegetical Commentary on the Second Epistle to the Corinthians,* ICC (Edinburgh: T & T Clark, 1994), 1:117-19, concludes that this expression, "sentence of death," denotes not a formal death sentence handed down by a judicial court, but to a "mortally perilous situation" that moved the apostle to rely not upon himself but exclusively on God.

trials of Ephesus are behind him.[16] As Paul writes this letter from Macedonia, Paul is filled with gratitude at what God has been producing in his
life through suffering. What level of confidence he has as a privileged minister of the new covenant comes from the God who makes him competent
(2 Cor 3:4-6). He is, as it were, nothing more than a clay jar, unattractive and
of little intrinsic value, yet smudged with the divine fingerprints and filled
with the divine power (2 Cor 4:7). He witnesses an aging body that is gradually wasting away, but refuses to lose heart because God's mercy has assigned him this apostolic mission and has pledged a glorious eternity (2 Cor
4:1, 16-18). The unknown physical malady that he calls "a thorn in my flesh"
(2 Cor 12:7 NIV) is interpreted as God's way of preventing him from becoming conceited over a unique revelatory experience granted to him (2
Cor 12:1-6).[17] The Lord's refusal to answer his earnest and importunate plea
for its removal carries with it a promise: "My grace is sufficient for you, for
my power is made perfect in weakness" (2 Cor 12:9). Thus Paul will "boast"
in his physical infirmities, unlike the supremely confident "super-apostles"
who took pride in oratory and knowledge (2 Cor 11:5-6; 12:11), because his
weakness drives him to fuller reliance on God's strength (2 Cor 12:9-10; cf.
2 Cor 11:30).

Magnanimity. Paul's sober self-assessment, tempered through hardships,
prevents him from treating others harshly and liberates him to be gracious
with others, especially those who fail and even those who cause him grief.
He instructs the Galatians that when a believer falls into sin and subse-

---

[16]Paul spent approximately three years in Ephesus during his third missionary journey (Acts 19:10;
20:31). During these years he engaged in widespread evangelism in the province of Asia (Acts
19:8-10), saw God's power triumph over animistic superstitions (Acts 19:11-20), and collided
forcibly with the vested interests of the silversmiths serving the cult of Artemis (Acts 19:23-41).
Other passages scattered in Acts and the Corinthian correspondence (the two extant letters written from Ephesus [1 Cor 16:5-9] and Macedonia [2 Cor 2:13; 7:5] respectively) specify a variety
of trials he faced while prosecuting his mission: plots from the Jews (Acts 20:18-20); manifold
hardships and persecutions (1 Cor 4:11-13); dying daily while glorying in Christ (1 Cor 15:31);
a contest with "wild beasts," probably a metaphorical expression for the ferocity of his opponents
(1 Cor 15:32); a great open door for evangelism, accompanied by many opposing him (1 Cor
16:8-9); and the just mentioned "sentence of death" (2 Cor 1:9).

[17]Thrall, *Second Corinthians*, 2:809-18, provides a detailed excursus on the main attempts that have
been offered in the history of interpretation to identify this σκόλοψ τῇ σαρκί. She concludes that
it was a recurrent malady such as migraines or malarial fever that produced acute pain, but which
alternated with extended periods of relief during which he could energetically carry out his evangelistic and pastoral ministry.

quently repents, the mature believers must remember their own susceptibility to temptation and restore such a one in the spirit of meekness (Gal 6:1). He counsels the Thessalonians to exercise patient pastoral care of all the brothers, even when such care requires strict admonition (1 Thess 5:14). When a believer stubbornly persists in idleness, the remedy should take on the character of household discipline of a brother, rather than condemnation of an enemy (2 Thess 3:14-15). Paul reveals his generosity of spirit when he urges the Corinthians to forgive and comfort a sorrowing individual who has been duly chastened by the congregation (2 Cor 2:5-11). This probably refers to the ringleader who maliciously attacked Paul at the time of his "painful visit" to Corinth (2 Cor 2:1). In the severe letter that followed (not extant), he demanded that the church punish the offender (2 Cor 2:3-4, 9). But now is the time for restoration. They should affirm their love for him lest this individual become swallowed up by excessive grief and lest a spirit of unforgiveness provide Satan the opportunity to exploit the situation to great harm (2 Cor 2:7-8, 10-11). When Paul was placed under house arrest in Rome, certain brothers saw this as an opportunity to usurp his position of authority. They began to preach Christ while filled with envy, rivalry and selfish ambition. In fact, their actions were even designed to increase the pain of his imprisonment by pulling the loyalty of the churches to them and away from Paul (Phil 1:15-17). But whatever the motives, whether in sincere exposition of the truth or as a pretext for self-promotion, Paul rejoiced that Christ was being proclaimed (Phil 1:18). Here is a leader who does not view himself as indispensable, but whose chief concern is the fulfillment of the evangelistic mission, whether through him or through others.

Paul and the Church on Mission

Suffering was from beginning to end the understood context of Paul's life and ministry as the apostle to the Gentiles (Acts 9:16). What sets Paul apart as a leader is the extent to which he was willing to sacrifice physical comforts, personal security and normative life expectations, such as family and a potentially lucrative career (1 Cor 9:3-15), to fulfill his calling to establish churches among the Gentiles. His encounter with the risen Lord as he approached Damascus reversed his life direction. Each of his autobiographical memoirs focuses on the radical transformation wrought in his heart by the grace of the Lord Jesus Christ (Gal 1:15-16; 2:15-16; Phil 3:4-11; 1 Tim 1:12-17). In his letters we discover a man whose growing appreciation of God's redeeming grace, preeminently expressed in the humiliation of his Son (Phil 2:6-9), produces a deepening humility, refreshing transparency and mellowing sweetness. The result is a facilitative pattern of leadership that is never dictatorial, but always seeks to propel others to spiritual fruitfulness (2 Cor 1:24).[18] Such a commitment brings him persecution, hardship and eventually a martyr's death. But suffering is to Paul a friend, not a foe, for it refines his character, fortifies the churches, binds him to Christ and credentials his ministry.

Paul urged believers to, literally, "be imitators of me, as I am of Christ" (1 Cor 11:1; see footnote 10). His cruciform pattern of proclaiming Jesus Christ is a paradigm for the church to imitate. In these early years of the twenty-first century, three great religiocultural bastions remain largely resistant to the missionary endeavor, the peoples that embrace Buddhism (esp. Japan, Thailand, Taiwan, Tibet), Hinduism (esp. northern India) and Islam. To penetrate the hearts of those bound to these deeply rooted belief systems will require the costliest of sacrifices of Christ's servants, just as it ultimately cost Paul his earthly life. But God's people, both those who go and those who send and support them, can be assured that through their meager sufferings, Christ will fulfill his promise to build his church (edification), draw them into a deeper fellowship with himself (identification), certify the authenticity of their servant status (authentication) and refine their characters into conformity with his own (transformation).

---

[18]It is this facilitative, rather than paternalistic or coercive, pattern of ministry, grounded in a profound confidence in the presence of the Holy Spirit in all believers individually and in the freshly planted congregations corporately, that the missionary-statesman Roland Allen summoned the church to recapture. See Don N. Howell Jr., "Confidence in the Spirit as the Governing Ethos of the Pauline Mission," *TJ* 17 (1996): 203-21.

7

PAUL AND SPIRITUAL WARFARE

♦ ♦ ♦

Craig Keener

Many have linked spiritual warfare with missions.[1] Whether this link is accurate or not depends to a great extent on what we mean by *spiritual warfare*.[2] If by *spiritual warfare* we mean particular prayer practices such as "casting down" heavenly powers, we have little biblical warrant. If, however, we mean by *spiritual warfare* what the image means in the New Testament, missions and the Christian life *are* spiritual warfare. This spiritual battle includes but is not limited to prayer.

Though writing prior to the common use of the phrase *spiritual warfare*, Roland Allen similarly recognized the essential role of God's divine intervention in the advance of the gospel. Allen writes, "It is faith [in God's working] which we need today. We need to subordinate our methods, our systems, ourselves to that faith. We often speak as if we had to do simply with weak and sinful men. We say that we cannot trust our converts to do this or that, that we cannot commit the truth to men destitute of this or that par-

---

[1] The emphasis here must be *spiritual* warfare; the New Testament does not use the warfare metaphor against people.

[2] For one discussion, see "Appendix: Statement on spiritual warfare: A Working Group Report," in *Deliver Us from Evil: An Uneasy Frontier in Christian Mission*, ed. A. Scott Moreau, Tokunboh Adeyemo, David G. Burnett, Bryant L. Myers and Hwa Yung (Monrovia, Calif.: Lausanne Committee for World Evangelization, 2002), pp. 309-12.

ticular form of education or training. We speak as if we had to do with mere men. We have not to do with mere men; we have to do with the Holy Ghost."[3]

One could treat the subject of spiritual warfare in greater detail or breadth, but to remain concise I will focus on two primary topics: the image of spiritual warfare in Paul's letters, especially Ephesians; and Paul's confrontations with the demonic in evangelistic settings, what missiologists often call "power encounters" (especially Acts 13:6-12; 16:16-18; and 19:11-20).

SPIRITUAL WARFARE IN PAUL'S LETTERS

Paul often portrayed the Christian life in terms of spiritual conflict. These conflict images are not limited to, but do include, the issue of conflict with superhuman powers. Even so, some modern approaches to spiritual warfare often miss crucial elements of Paul's teaching on the subject. The most commonly used text regarding spiritual warfare is Ephesians 6:10-20, which I address here in some detail.[4]

The background. Ancient thinkers often portrayed life or their work as a battle; in a world where virtually everyone knew about warfare, the image carried great weight. Thus everyone would understand when Paul speaks of fighting the good fight (1 Tim 1:18; 6:12; 2 Tim 4:7). They could portray destroying false ideologies as "tearing down strongholds" and the like.[5] When Paul speaks of destroying speculations and capturing thoughts for Christ (2 Cor 10:3-5), he may refer to challenging false ideologies (like those of his opponents in Corinth). Ancient philosophers also spoke of waging war against the passions, so when Paul speaks of conflict with passions in such language (Rom 7:23; cf. "peace" in Rom 8:6), his audience will understand him.[6] Indeed, on a deeper level, humanity is at enmity with God and can be reconciled in peace with him only through Christ (Rom 5:1, 10-11; Col 1:20-22).

While Greek usage made explicit warfare understandable to Paul's audience, Scripture had already provided the theology of superhuman con-

---

[3]Roland Allen, *Missionary Methods: St. Paul's or Ours?* 2nd ed. (Grand Rapids: Eerdmans, 1962), pp. 149-50.

[4]I take Ephesians to be a genuinely Pauline letter. See the argument in Harold W. Hoehner, *Ephesians: An Exegetical Commentary* (Grand Rapids: Baker, 2002), pp. 2-61, 114-30.

[5]See, e.g., Seneca *Lucil.* 109.8-9; Diogenes *Ep.* 10; and sources in Craig S. Keener, *1-2 Corinthians* (Cambridge: Cambridge University Press, 2005), p. 217.

[6]See e.g., Diogenes *Ep.* 5; 12; and sources in Craig S. Keener, *Romans* (Eugene, Ore.: Cascade, 2009), pp. 94-95.

flict, even if the details were not always clear. More recently, Jesus may have figuratively portrayed his disciples' ministry of deliverance from demons as Satan's fall from heaven (Lk 10:17-20).[7] But such conflicts already appeared in the Old Testament as well. Jacob struggled all night with an angel before facing Esau—a spiritual battle that preempted a physical one (Gen 32:9-31; Hos 12:4). While Joshua fought the Amalekites on a physical level, Moses was upholding his people spiritually, holding up the rod that symbolized God's power on their behalf (Ex 17:8-13). Joshua encountered the heavenly commander of the Lord's army (Josh 5:13-15), and it was presumably the heavenly host that brought Jericho's walls down when Israel shouted (Josh 6:20; certainly it was not simply a sonic boom!).

When David heard the sound of marching in the trees, he knew that God's army had gone before him, paving the way for his victory over the Philistines (2 Sam 5:24; 1 Chron 14:15). When Elisha's aide feared the human army that surrounded their city, Elisha prayed for his eyes to be opened, and he saw the heavenly army of fiery chariots and horses (2 Kgs 6:17; for the future, cf. 2 Thess 1:7; Rev 19:11-14). As the aide's spiritual eyes were opened, the enemy army's physical eyes were blinded and they were pacified without a fight (2 Kings 6:15-23). (Elisha's own mentor, Elijah, had been caught up to heaven in a heavenly chariot; 2 Kings 2:11.) When Judah's army worshiped God, he threw their enemies into confusion, so Judah did not have to engage in any physical battle (2 Chron 20:22-25); as in Ephesians 6, the spiritual battle takes priority.

Even when physical battles proved necessary, God sent his hornet to confuse the adversaries (Deut 7:20; Josh 24:12); this hornet may well serve figuratively for his angel leading Israel (Ex 23:28 with Ex 23:20, 23; 32:34; 33:2). The angel of the Lord could strike down even Israel, though on a purely human level the judgment could be accomplished by a plague (2 Sam 24:15-17). That is, what human beings experience as natural events are not incompatible with, and often work in tandem with, superhuman intelligent causes. (See Rev 12:7-9 for the heavenly warfare surrounding Jesus' passion and exaltation in the context.) Can anyone who takes the Bible seriously

---

[7]Cf. George Eldon Ladd, *The Gospel of the Kingdom* (Grand Rapids: Eerdmans, 1959), p. 50; Gerald F. Hawthorne, *The Presence & the Power: The Significance of the Holy Spirit in the Life and Ministry of Jesus* (Dallas: Word, 1991), pp. 149-50.

deny that the spiritual issues are paramount in carrying out our mission? It may be wise, on the human level, to use various techniques and strategies for evangelism and church growth that are often known to work, but it is God that causes the growth (1 Cor 3:7). If we want his blessing, we must defer to him the credit.

God's armor. Besides the weapons in 2 Corinthians 10:4 noted above, Paul probably mentions spiritual "armor" in Romans 13:12, and possibly Romans 6:13 and 2 Corinthians 6:7 (the Greek term in all these cases can also be used in a nonmilitary sense). Paul's most extensive development of the image, however, comes in 1 Thessalonians 5:6-8 and Ephesians 6:10-20. By comparing the lists in 1 Thessalonians 5:8 and Ephesians 6:14-17, we see that elements of the believer's armor can prove interchangeable from one letter to another. That is, Paul draws on the particular items in the familiar Roman soldier's equipment not to pair spiritual concepts with these items in a one to one correspondence, but to illustrate that we need to be spiritually equipped. Salvation or the hope of salvation is a helmet in both cases, but Paul has the breastplate of faith and love in one case, with a breastplate of righteousness and shield of faith in the other.

We should note that his images of spiritual warfare do not involve special formulas or secret techniques, but salvation, faith, love, righteousness and so on. Without having to rule out the "mystical" elements that some see in spiritual warfare at times (as in 2 Kings 6:17), Paul's images of spiritual warfare tend to be more practical than some imagine. Most involve protective armor, and we are protected by our right relationship with God and one another.

As is also often pointed out, God's warriors, like Roman soldiers, have protection only for the front and not the back. Soldiers who discarded their shields and fled made easy targets for pursuing enemies; Roman soldiers who marched side by side, advancing on the enemy, were considered virtually invincible.[8] Whereas soldiers wore some pieces of armor in other circumstances, they normally donned the helmet and breastplate only for battle. The armor depicted here, therefore, involves a spiritual warrior directly engaged in spir-

---

[8]See, e.g., Dionysius of Halicarnassus *Ant. Rom.* 9.9.9; 9.20.4; applied figuratively, Maximus of Tyre *Or.* 15.10. Retreat and flight were also both dishonorable (Polybius *Hist.* 6.37.12-13; Silius Italicus *Pun.* 10.7; Dio Chrysostom *Or.* 31.17) and severely punishable (Polybius *Hist.* 6.38.1-4; Dionysius *Ant. Rom.* 6.9.4).

itual war, with the assumption that this is the believer's normal state.

The triad of virtues envisioned in the armor of 1 Thessalonians 5:8 are a triad familiar in Paul's ethics: faith, hope and love (cf. 1 Cor 13:13; Gal 5:5-6; Col 1:4-5; 1 Thess 1:3). We will focus here, however, on the more extensive list in Ephesians 6:14-17. The expression, "armor of God" (Eph 6:11, 13) could refer simply to "armor from God" or "divine armor," but because some pieces of armor that Paul goes on to depict match items of God's own armor in Isaiah 59:17, Paul may also imply that spiritual warriors are carrying on God's own mission, functioning as his divinely protected representatives. What we can say for certain in Paul's context is that we dare not wage our battle in our own strength, but by depending on God (Eph 6:10). Western Christians have grown accustomed to depending on economic resources, technology, information and everything else but God; the way to advance the kingdom, however, is by humble recognition that God does the most important work and deserves the real credit.[9]

Because the first piece of armor mentioned guards the waist or loins (Eph 6:14), it refers to a "belt" or "girdle."[10] It may thus evoke the Roman soldier's leather apron beneath the armor or the metal belt that guarded his lower abdomen. God's warrior is protected partly by truth, which in the context of other virtues mentioned here may include integrity (cf. Eph 4:15, 25). For Paul, however, including in Ephesians, "truth" involves particularly the truth of the gospel, recognizing and living in the reality of God's claims as opposed to the world's falsehood (see Eph 1:13; 4:21, 24-25; 5:9; cf. Rom 1:18-19). Believers must live and speak consistently with God's reality.

Paul next mentions the "breastplate" (Eph 6:14), meant to protect the chest and usually made of leather with metal over it. God himself wears "righteousness as a breastplate" in Isaiah 59:17, so he can enact justice and

---

[9]Roland Allen writes, "What systems, forms, safeguards of every kind cannot do, He can do. When we believe in the Holy Ghost, we shall teach our converts to believe in Him, and when they believe in Him they will be able to face all difficulties and dangers. They will justify our faith. The Holy Ghost will justify our faith in Him. 'This is the Victory which overcometh the world, even our faith'" (*Missionary Methods*, p. 150).

[10]For soldiers' apparel, see G. L. Thompson, "Roman Military," *DNTB*, pp. 991-95 (here 993); James S. Jeffers, *The Greco-Roman World of the New Testament Era: Exploring the Background of Early Christianity* (Downers Grove, Ill.: InterVarsity Press, 1999), p. 175. Many additional details treated in this section are documented in standard Ephesians commentaries (e.g., Markus Barth, *Ephesians: Introduction, Translation and Commentary*, AB 34-34A [New York: Doubleday, 1974] and Andrew T. Lincoln, *Ephesians*, WBC 42 [Waco, Tex.: Word, 1990]).

righteousness in a world that has abandoned it (Is 59:14-16). Part of God's mission into which he has invited us as agents is to work for righteousness and justice, for God's honor and the right treatment of people made in his image. Given Paul's usual usage, however (including in Eph 4:24; 5:9), this "righteousness" is also part of the new standing and character God has given us in Christ. Only those with this status and heart before God will be pure agents of his righteousness in the world.

Soldiers also would wear sandals or half boots (Eph 6:15); this was necessary preparation for battle, so that one could advance against the enemy without needing to be distracted by what one might step on.[11] Paul applies the image to "the gospel [good news] of peace," clearly alluding to Isaiah 52:7, where heralds bring good news of divine deliverance and restoration for God's people. Readiness to carry the gospel is necessary for God's warriors to advance and, as we shall see, prepares us for the one offensive weapon that Paul will include: the gospel message (Eph 6:17).

Roman soldiers used rectangular shields about four feet high, covered with leather. Because such shields could be vulnerable to flaming arrows, soldiers could wet their shields before battles where such projectiles were expected. As the soldiers marched together in formation, the front row's shields covering their front and the second row's lifted shields guarding both rows from above, they were considered virtually invulnerable to projectiles that individuals hurled against them. Greeks and Romans sometimes thought of sexual temptation in terms of fire or wounds, but the meaning is undoubtedly broader than that; Scripture already used arrows as a metaphor for attacks from the wicked, including slander (Ps 11:2; 57:4; 58:6-7; 64:3; cf. 120:2-4; Prov 25:18). Given the normal case of the Roman soldier, however, Paul might assume something about our defense that we sometimes neglect: we dare not break ranks. We must march together, protecting one another.

The threat for Paul is not human, as for Roman armies, but "the evil one."[12] While Satan is powerful, however, Paul declares that the shield of

---

[11]For soldiers' footwear, see R. J. Forbes, *Studies in Ancient Technology* (Leiden: E. J. Brill, 1957) 5:60; Alexandra T. Croom, *Roman Clothing and Fashion* (Charleston, S.C.: Tempus, 2000), p. 63.

[12]One might read this title generically as "the evil person" (cf. possibly 2 Thess 3:3 with 3:2), but context makes explicit that the adversary is the devil (Eph 6:11), not human beings (Eph 6:12).

faith is sufficient to put out the fire on his arrows. Believers should not become fearful of Satan's attacks, but stand firm in faith. When readers think of "faith" today, because of the past two centuries of trends in philosophy we often think of a subjective feeling or of a mental ability to extinguish all doubt, both of which approaches put the focus on the believer's effort. In Jesus' teaching, however, the question is not how much faith one has (a mustard seed is enough), but in whom one has faith. In Paul's letters, Jesus and God the Father are the proper objects of faith. This is not a leap into the dark, as some generalized attitude of belief would be; this is a deliberate step into the light of God's reality. The protection afforded by faith comes not when we trust our faith, but when we trust God who is absolutely trustworthy and able to protect us.

Roman soldiers wore for battle bronze (or iron) helmets with long cheek pieces (Eph 6:17). The specific phrase, "helmet of salvation," echoes Isaiah 59:17, as in Ephesians 6:14. In the immediate context in Isaiah, this helmet referred to God acting to deliver the oppressed from the wicked (Is 59:15-16), but in the larger context of Isaiah the theme of salvation included God delivering his people and all who would turn to him among the nations (e.g., Is 46:13; 49:6; 51:5-8). The message of salvation and God's reign is also called "good news of peace" (Is 52:7; see also Eph 6:15). That context might suggest that we participate in bringing God's message of salvation; more directly, given Paul's usage in 1 Thessalonians 5:8, Paul means that we are protected by means of God's salvation.

The list climaxes, however, with the only offensive weapon in the soldier's equipment that Paul will list (Eph 6:17). This limitation is not because Roman soldiers carried only one weapon; in fact they carried more, a pike or lance (or two) as well as their sword and dagger. For believers, however, there is only one weapon—God's message—and it is logical that Paul chooses the image of the sword over the lance. The front row of an advancing legion carried heavy pikes that deterred attackers and could be thrust into them at fairly close range. Once close battle ensued, however, the heavy pikes became less practical than swords. (The sword here was the *gladius*, roughly 20-24 inches in length.) Paul envisions hand-to-hand combat, spiritual warfare not from afar at this point but at close range.

Paul declares that this one offensive weapon is the "sword of the Spirit,

which is the word of God." While God's word includes Scripture (which
Jesus deployed against Satan at his temptation), Paul usually uses this phrase
especially for the gospel (e.g., the same term in Rom 10:8, 17; the same idea
in Eph 1:13). Every other piece of equipment Paul mentions protects us; the
one piece that enables us to take back ground taken by the devil is the
gospel—evangelism. Too often the church lives off the benefits of past revivals, waging a merely defensive battle as the world surrounds and con-
stricts the church. The most strategic means God has provided us of re-
versing the direction of influence is for us to bring the good news of peace
and salvation to the world, through evangelism. Evangelism is the one element of spiritual warfare that takes back Satan's possessions. Without it,
spiritual warfare is incomplete. Likewise, we are kept safe by truth, righteousness and salvation.

Heralds of peace, bearing the sword of the Spirit, will not always be well-
received. People in antiquity understood that heralds were granted diplo-
matic immunity, and any mistreatment of an ambassador signaled an act of
war against the sender. Paul, however, is "an ambassador in chains" (Eph
6:20). Rome's earthly empire was not willing to submit to God's greater
kingdom. Yet past earthly empires, including Rome, now lie in the dust, and
God's kingdom spreads, as promised, among all peoples. Jesus will return,
and God's kingdom will prevail. In the meantime, it often spreads, not
through conquest, but through its agents' suffering, as in Paul's case.

Spiritual powers in Ephesians. Much of the church in Ephesus was converted from a background familiar with magic and spiritual power (Acts
19:18-20). Paul thus reminds believers in and around Ephesus that they have
been exalted with Christ above rulers and authorities in the heavenly realms
(Eph 1:20-22; 2:6). These are the sort of spiritual powers against whom spiritual warriors have their conflict in Ephesians 6:12.

Early Jewish sources used titles like these not only for earthly rulers
(which are not the point here) but for the spiritual powers that stood behind
them, including angels of the nations.[13] These heavenly powers probably
appear in the likeliest original reading of Deuteronomy 32:8, and most certainly and importantly in Daniel 10.[14] Here the "prince of Persia" and the

---

[13]Cf. *Jub.* 15:30-32; *1 En.* 89:59–90:19; later *1 En.* 40:9; 61:10.
[14]See here e.g., Tremper Longman, *Daniel*, NIVAC (Grand Rapids: Zondervan, 1999), pp. 250-51.

"prince of Greece" delay a divine messenger until Michael, Israel's prince, helped him (Dan 10:13, 20-21). In Daniel, these princes clearly relate to the political entities that they govern, but they are not identical with them.

For those with a background in the occult, it was important to know that Jesus' name was above every name that was invoked (Eph 1:21). This declaration is particularly important in Ephesus, where people repudiated their magic when they learned that Jesus' name worked only for those authorized by Jesus, not as a magical formula to be manipulated for gain (Acts 19:13-16)! Echoing Psalm 110:1, Paul announces that Christ has been enthroned above these hostile powers (Eph 1:20-21) and that believers have been exalted with him (Eph 2:6). Indeed, because we comprise Christ's body and these exalted powers are beneath his feet, they are beneath us as well (Eph 1:22-23).

Paul's point is not that believers can go around ordering these rulers to obey them, thereby shaping the destiny of nations. Our one biblical example of dealing with these powers involves persistent, patient prayer to God, not commands to the powers themselves (Dan 10:12-13). Rather, it means that they have no control over us. It was widely believed in this period that Fate controlled people's future, ruling them through the heavenly stars. Only some exalted deity or other figure could free people from this tyranny (and most of our extant examples of this idea are later than Paul). But for Paul, believers are exalted above the control of these spirits. In a letter reinforcing the unity of Jewish and Gentile believers (Eph 2:11-22), transcending "angels of the nations" who symbolized their division would be important.

Spiritual warfare in Ephesians. What Paul has in mind in describing exaltation above these spiritual powers is made clearer by his continuing comments. Believers now exalted with Christ were previously dead in sin, living by the values of the present age characterized by the world (Eph 2:1-2). This world is ruled by the prince with authority over the atmospheric realm, that is, the leader of the hostile rulers in the heavenly realms noted in Ephesians 1:20-22; this ruler is active among the disobedient (Eph 2:2).

Some of Paul's contemporaries acknowledged Satan's activity in the world, but conceptualized it differently. For example, the sect that wrote the Dead Sea Scrolls viewed every human action as determined either by the

Spirit of Truth (God's Spirit) or the spirit of error; as fixation on magic and demons became more widespread, some Jewish people came to believe even that one could not stick out one's hand without touching a thousand demons.[15] Paul's approach is, however, more sober. Paul argues that Satan works through human passions and the world system (Eph 2:2-3), apparently not micromanaging every sin but promulgating sinful patterns, ideas and temptations. In Western culture driven by marketing to consumers' desires, for example, Satan can extend his influence strategically through the entertainment industry. (Many Christians who do not have the mentality that we are at war with eternal stakes even spend more time watching television than reading their Bibles.) Satan also targets centers of philosophy, public opinion and so forth, making intellectually reasoned responses important as believers carry forward the gospel (cf. 2 Cor 10:3-5).

Paul's point is that Jesus has liberated his followers from Satan's grasp and from this lifestyle. To borrow popular idiom, Christians no longer have the right to say, "The devil made me do it." In this passage, then, the key element of spiritual warfare is recognizing what God has already done for us in Christ. Exalted above these spiritual powers, we no longer need fear them nor submit to their influence on our respective cultures. Western Christians need not practice syncretism with materialism, lust for comfort, skepticism about God and the supernatural, dependence on solely natural solutions and the like that pervade our culture. Christians in some other cultures need not be swayed by beliefs about ancestors, fear of spirits or the like. To the extent that Christians reflect unbiblical values in their cultures more than the kingdom, to that extent they are failing at spiritual warfare, whether because they fail to acknowledge Christ's victory or fail to recognize the seriousness of their situation.

In Ephesians 4:27, Paul warns believers against giving ground to the devil, in other words, against providing him opportunity. Context probably specifies what means of giving ground Paul has in mind: the Ephesians must avoid deception, anger, stealing and unhealthy speech, instead speaking truth, providing for the needy, speaking upbuilding words, forgiving and loving as in Christ's example (Eph 4:25–5:2).[16] That is, the way that believers

---

[15]1QS 3.19-21; *Test. Benj.* 6:1; *Num. Rab.* 11:5.
[16]Cf. here also Clinton E. Arnold, *Ephesians: Power and Magic. The Concept of Power in Ephesians*

avoid giving ground to the devil by maintaining godly relationships, preserving the unity of Christ's body (Eph 4:1-6, 13, 16; 5:21). Similarly, James speaks of resisting the devil (Jas 4:7) by resisting the world's values of greed and retaliation (Jas 3:15–4:4). The similar passage in 1 Peter 5:8-9 in context refers to resisting the devil by withstanding persecution, refusing to fall away from the faith.

After mentioning the armor of God, Paul invites Spirit-inspired prayer for all those set apart for God, including his own mission as a herald (Eph 6:18-20). Perhaps Paul continues to think of how Roman soldiers cover one another (though he is no longer listing pieces of armor), but whether that image is in view or not, believers' unity has been a matter of considerable emphasis in this letter (e.g., Eph 4:1-6). By prayer, covering one another and those working on the front lines of God's kingdom is part of spiritual warfare.

More generally, as noted earlier, bad relationships among Christ's servants yield ground to the devil (Eph 4:27); elsewhere in Paul's letters, failure to forgive succumbs to Satan's plots (2 Cor 2:11). Even in other contexts, forgiveness is linked with prayer (Mt 6:12-15; Mk 11:25). Christians cannot claim to depend on God to help them when they still want to take revenge into their own hands or hearts. Spiritual warfare, then, includes some very practical elements of relationships with one another. If a mission team is in disunity among its members, unwilling to live at peace with one another, they compromise God's blessing on their mission.

One should be clear about what spiritual warfare is not. I attended one "prayer meeting" where, instead of praying to God, the people (including my close friends who brought me) spent the entire time directly rebuking Satan and "casting down" spiritual powers. In antiquity, a number of Jewish people cursed the devil; others recognized that this approach was unwise. Scripture is clear that mocking the devil, or treating lightly the devil or delegated heavenly authorities, is wrong (2 Pet 2:10-11; Jude 8-9). Moreover, such a practice lacks clear biblical precedent for directly addressing heavenly powers. In all biblical cases of rebuking and casting out demons, the demons addressed were active on earth. In the case of heavenly princes in Daniel 10, Daniel prayed to God, who took care of the earthly powers. Satan was dis-

---

in Light of its Historical Setting, SNTSMS 63 (Cambridge: Cambridge University Press, 1989), pp. 65, 118.

placed from his role in heaven by Christ's victory (Jn 12:31-33; 16:11; Rev 12:5-10). Christians essentially wage a ground war with evil as they find it here; they trust God for the air cover.

This does not mean that believers should not be informed about spiritual issues relevant to the lands for which they are praying, so they may pray most intelligently. Prayer manuals like *Operation World* are among the most valuable tools for informing prayer for the nations; moreover, there is biblical precedent for believing that those who pray for workers are often sent as workers (Mt 9:37–10:1, 10).[17] But these important considerations do not justify using prayer time, which should address God, to address directly spiritual powers who are not likely listening and whom even believers are not normally divinely authorized to confront in that manner, except perhaps in rare cases of special prophetic inspiration.

Paul's Power Encounters in Acts

Looking to Paul's ministry in Acts, the image of warfare (common in Greek writers, hence intelligible to Paul's audience) is less obvious, but spiritual conflict itself is quite clear. Paul's letters address only some aspects of his ministry, particularly situations that arose through his interaction with the communities of believers to whom he was writing. Acts addresses a different side of his ministry, one that carries forward the sort of power encounters reported in the Gospels.[18]

Power encounters appear before Paul in Luke's work. He earlier reported Jesus' deliverance of those afflicted or controlled by demons. He also reported similar ministry for the Jerusalem apostles and recounted the confrontation with Simon the Samaritan sorcerer (Lk 4:33-36, 41; 6:18; 7:21; 8:2, 27-39; 9:1, 39-42; 10:17; 11:14; 13:11-13; Acts 5:16; 8:7-11, 18-24). Now he reports at least three of Paul's major confrontations; the first involves the Jewish magician Elymas Barjesus toward the very beginning of his mission from

---

[17]Patrick Johnstone and Jason Mandryk, *Operation World: 21ˢᵗ Century Edition* (Waynesboro, Ga.: Paternoster, 2001).

[18]On power encounters, see further the sources cited in Craig S. Keener, *Miracles: The Credibility of the New Testament Accounts*, 2 vols. (Grand Rapids: Baker Academic, 2011), pp. 843-52. Roland Allen writes, "Miracles were illustrations of the character of the new religion. They were sermons in act. They set forth in unmistakeable terms two of its fundamental doctrines, the doctrine of charity and the doctrine of salvation, of release from the bondage of sin and the power of the devil" (*Missionary Methods*, p. 45).

Antioch with Barnabas. Luke often emphasizes Jesus' representatives as better proclaimers of monotheism than their non-Christian Jewish detractors were (Acts 17:29-30; 19:26), noting Jewish magicians (as here in Acts 13:6, 8; also Acts 19:13-14; cf. Acts 8:9-11). Moved by God's Spirit, Paul pronounced judgment on the magician, leaving him with a temporary physical blindness that corresponded to his spiritual state.

Paul's ministry in Philippi is another step forward in his mission and again encounters opposition. Troas, from which he sailed for Philippi, was widely regarded as a traditional boundary between what the Greeks called Asia and what they called Europe; it was also the location of the two most famous Greek and Macedonian invasions of Asia in antiquity, namely the Trojan War and Alexander the Great's invasion of Persia. Paul's small mission, however, brought a message of peace from Asia to Europe and ultimately into the heart of the Roman Empire.[19] Paul's first stop there is in the Roman colony of Philippi, and from there until he leaves Macedonia he faces serious hostility.

In Philippi he encounters a slave girl who is doubly exploited: she is possessed by (literally) the "spirit of a pythoness," and her legal possessors exploit her for her "gift" (Acts 16:16, 19). The literal "pythoness" was the priestess of Apollo at Delphi, the most famous of all Greek oracular shrines; she is thus possessed by a powerful and perhaps respected prophetic spirit.[20] She announces that Paul and his colleagues are servants of the Most High God (a common name for Israel's God), announcing the way of salvation (Acts 16:17). Jesus had silenced the witness of demons to his identity (Lk 4:34-35), and Paul does the same, although he waits a few days. Perhaps he waits because he was not ready, or perhaps he waits simply because he recognized in advance the trouble that this exorcism could cause.

In any case, he orders the demon out, ending part of the young woman's exploitation (Acts 16:18), and the slaveholders, recognizing their loss of profit, drag Paul and Silas before the civic authorities. We should note that the missionaries' direct persecution here stems not from the demons per se

---

[19]See discussion in Craig S. Keener, "Between Asia and Europe: Postcolonial Mission in Acts 16:8-10," *Asian Journal of Pentecostal Studies* 11, no. 1-2 (2008): 3-15. I address all these Acts passages in greater detail in *Acts: An Exegetical Commentary*, 4 vols. (Grand Rapids: Baker Academic, 2012–).

[20]E.g., Apollodorus *Bib.* 1.4.1; Lucan *C.W.* 5.86-101.

but from human greed. When the success of the mission challenges vested economic interests, whether by delivering this slave girl or later by challenging the economic interests of those dependent on the Artemis cult (Acts 19:25-28), local hostility follows. In various settings, confrontations with spiritual power are necessary, but one should not suppose that victory in such confrontations always makes believers' lives simple; confronting and casting out demons does not exhaust the forms of evil they must face. Some other parts of the New Testament portray persecution and other sufferings in the language of warfare (Rev 11:7; 12:11; 13:7); whatever our various tests, however, believers are summoned to "overcome" (Rev 2:7, 11, 17, 26; 3:5, 12, 21; 12:11; 15:2; 21:7 NASB), language often used in battle or conflict settings.[21]

Paul's most prominent public ministry in Acts occurs in Ephesus, after years of experience in less publicly visible forums. There for some two years Paul spreads the Christian message through the accepted public role of a teacher (Acts 19:9; many would have viewed him as a philosopher). Meanwhile, however, miracles are also taking place, including many exorcisms; some of these take place even secondhand (Acts 19:11-12). Paul's success invited imitators: some popular non-Christian exorcists (in antiquity, exorcism often overlapped with magic) try to use the name of Jesus whom Paul preaches (Acts 19:13-14). People used various incantations and even malodorous substances to try to coax spirits to vacate their hosts; another method was to invoke more powerful spirits to expel lesser ones.

The magical exorcists discover, however, that Jesus' name is not simply a magical formula to be exploited; it bears an authority delegated only to those authorized to use it (Acts 19:15-16). Like the spirit in Acts 16:17, this demon recognizes who God's servants are (Acts 19:15). Whereas Jesus and his followers cast out demons by the finger of God, some other exorcists did not, and hence would accomplish little if any long-term good (Lk 11:19-20). In response to this distinction between Jesus' true servants and those whose magic was ineffective against true demons, many people in Ephesus, including some syncretistic Christian converts who had secretly kept one foot in a magical worldview, publicly repudiated their magic. By confessing their practices (Acts 19:18), they repudiated them. (Indeed, divulging spells was

---

[21]Cf. perhaps also insights in Richard J. Bauckham, *The Climax of Prophecy: Studies on the Book of Revelation* (Edinburgh: T & T Clark, 1993), pp. 216-18.

believed to deprive them of their efficacy.) Burning books (Acts 19:19) was also a conventional way of publicly repudiating their content.

IMPLICATIONS OF PAUL'S POWER ENCOUNTERS FOR MISSIONS TODAY

Today, Christians in many cultures often encounter situations like that of "those who had believed" in Ephesus, who publicly rejected their practices only once they saw God's superior power demonstrated (Acts 19:18). In some parts of the world, Christians continue to visit shamans and other traditional religious practitioners because their new faith seems to lack power to confront the problems that their old faith addressed. Elsewhere, however, local Christians reading Scripture have recognized that God's power is greater than that of its putative competitors and have learned to pray to God for their various needs, sometimes with striking results. Sometimes missionaries in the past resisted such insights because their Western lenses forced them to read past these examples in Scripture; in other cases, their interaction with local cultures helped them to readjust their lenses.[22] Missions today often involves partnering with local believers, often in teaching roles; but it also involves learning. Although the West dominated missions for several centuries, today Christian missionaries from various cultures can learn from one another's insights, recalling Paul's Asian mission to the West.

Power encounters are reported in subsequent missions history, including through Patrick in Ireland; Columba in Scotland; and Boniface in Germany; they are reported frequently in new evangelistic settings today as well.[23] In many parts of the world, believers are more aware of these intense spiritual battles than those in the West are.[24] In the twentieth century, for example,

---

[22]Roland Allen expects the Holy Spirit to authenticate and empower the advance of the gospel in his day, though not in miracles of the type mentioned in Acts. He writes, "We have powers sufficient to illustrate in act the character of our religion, its salvation and its love, if only we will use our powers to reveal the Spirit. One day we shall perhaps recover the early faith in miracles. Meanwhile, we cannot say that the absence of miracles puts an impassable gulf between the first century and today, or renders the apostolic method inapplicable to our missions. To say that were to set the form above the spirit" (*Missionary Methods,* p. 48).

[23]E.g., on Boniface's confrontation, see Stephen Neill, *A History of Christian Missions* (Harmondsworth, U.K.: Penguin, 1964), p. 75; Kenneth Scott Latourette, *A History of Christianity* (San Francisco: HarperSanFrancisco, 1975), 1:348.

[24]See, e.g., R. E. K. Mchami, "Demon Possession and Exorcism in Mark 1:21-28," *Africa Theological Journal* 24, no. 1 (2001): 17-37 (here 17); Felix Augustine Mensah, "The Spiritual Basis of Health

the earlier Chinese church leader Watchman Nee challenged some particularly theologically divisive Western critics with the observation that their theological debates would benefit them little in his country "if when the need arose you could not cast out a demon."[25] Granted, those who recognize the reality of superhuman evil beings are more apt to indulge in fearful speculation and may sometimes imagine such activity where it does not exist. Many circles also harden particular views about such spirits into theological traditions that differ from actual realities.

Nevertheless, many cases of spiritual activity cannot be explained on the purely materialistic terms that Westerners prefer.[26] Many of these are documented even in some academic literature, despite the prejudices against such beliefs in the academy today.[27] For example, the well-known New Testament scholar David Instone-Brewer reports encountering a spirit controlling a person who knew David's very thoughts.[28] I also am a personal witness to the reality of superhuman spiritual forces. My wife is from the Evangelical Church of Congo, and we, along with our family in Congo, have had to confront some of these spiritual forces in ways that I as a Western Christian was not initially prepared to confront and would not have believed had I not experienced them myself. Those involved with what locals considered witchcraft were—at least in these cases—dealing with real and

---

and Illness in Africa," in *Health Knowledge and Belief Systems in Africa*, ed. Toyin Falola and Matthew M. Heaton (Durham, N.C.: Carolina Academic Press, 2008), pp. 171-80 (here 176); cf. also John S. Mbiti, *African Religions and Philosophies* (Garden City, N.Y.: Doubleday, 1970), pp. 253-56.

[25]Angus Kinnear, *Against the Tide: The Story of Watchman Nee* (Wheaton, Ill.: Tyndale House, 1978), p. 152.

[26]See e.g., Paul G. Hiebert, "The Flaw of the Excluded Middle," *Missiology* 10, no. 1 (1982): 35-47 (here 43).

[27]E.g., Craig S. Keener, *Miracles,* pp. 788-856; idem, "Spirit Possession as a Cross-Cultural Experience," *Bulletin for Biblical Research* 20 (2010): 215-36; Paul Rhodes Eddy and Gregory A. Boyd, *The Jesus Legend: A Case for the Historical Reliability of the Synoptic Jesus Tradition* (Grand Rapids: Baker Academic, 2007), pp. 67-69; Stafford Betty, "The Growing Evidence for 'Demonic Possession': What Should Psychiatry's Response Be?" *JRelHealth* 44, no. 1 (2005): 13-30; M. Scott Peck, *Glimpses of the Devil: A Psychiatrist's Personal Accounts of Possession, Exorcism, and Redemption* (New York: Free Press, 2005); David W. Van Gelder, "A Case of Demon Possession," *JPastCare* 41, no. 2 (1987): 151-61; R. Kenneth McAll, "The Ministry of Deliverance," *ExpT* 86, no. 10 (1975): 296-98; see especially John Warwick Montgomery, ed., *Demon Possession: A Medical, Historical, Anthropological and Theological Symposium* (Minneapolis: Bethany House, 1976).

[28]David Instone-Brewer, "Jesus and the Psychiatrists," in *The Unseen World: Christian Reflections on Angels, Demons and the Heavenly Realm*, ed. Anthony N. S. Lane (Grand Rapids: Baker; Paternoster, 1996), pp. 133-48 (here 140-41).

dangerous powers that sometimes threatened our lives. I can also affirm, however, that God's power to protect his children is much greater than the power of these created entities.

Conclusion

Images of spiritual conflict in Paul's letters apply to a wide range of struggles, with false ideologies, with sin and with spiritual forces at work in the world to lead people away from God's truth and righteousness. For Paul, believers resist hostile spiritual forces by how they live and pray for one another; they take ground from those forces through evangelism. As we examine Paul's own missionary experience reported in Acts, we see that Paul also had to confront these forces on a more direct level in power encounters. These direct encounters with demonic forces did not by any means exhaust the evils Paul faced, but they were among them.

Part Two

Paul's Influence on Missions

♦ ♦ ♦

8

PAUL'S MISSIONS STRATEGY

♦ ♦ ♦

David J. Hesselgrave

The question has often been asked, "Did the apostle Paul have a missionary strategy?" Mission historian J. Herbert Kane answered that question in a very commonsense fashion. He said that it all depends on what is meant by the word *strategy*.[1] The same is true with reference to Roland Allen except that Allen employed the word *methods*. That's too bad because the word *methods* occasions misunderstandings and elicits the wrong questions. This unfortunate reality means that to evaluate Allen's contribution, one must deal with how the word *methods* can occasion misunderstandings and elicit the wrong questions. Once these matters are dealt with, one sees that Allen's assessment of Paul does in fact suggest attitudes and actions appropriate for reassessment by missionaries in any age.[2]

A SUMMONS TO *GENERATIONAL RESUBMISSION*

Allen's readers are faced with something of an anomaly. We know he is urging something important when he speaks of "St. Paul's Methods," but we do not readily understand exactly what he is urging.

---

[1] J. Herbert Kane, *Christian Missions in Biblical Perspective* (Grand Rapids: Baker, 1976), p. 73.
[2] Lesslie Newbigin, foreword in Roland Allen, *Missionary Methods: St. Paul's or Ours?* (Grand Rapids: Eerdmans, 1961), p. i.

"Methods" in Allen's thinking. Newbigin writes to the effect that Allen's use of the word *methods* in the title of his book is unfortunate for the simple reason that, though readers can be expected to look for certain methods that can be applied in their own missionary ministry or in the ministry of others, they will not find any. Or, if they do, they will do so because they misunderstand what Allen has in mind.[3] It seems strange that Newbigin would say that because before concluding his book, Allen includes an entire chapter on "application."[4] Nevertheless, Newbigin's point is well taken and for several reasons.

Since Allen does not stipulate a definition of "methods" he invites ambiguity. Allen seems to have much the same meaning in mind when he uses words such as *strategies* and *principles* as when he uses the word *methods*. But by neither adhering to the common definition of *method* nor supplying a clearly articulated stipulated definition, Allen invites confusion.

Under the rubric "methods," Allen discusses very diverse topics. Think, for example, of the differences between such topics as a typology of first century cities; basic principles of church finance; the importance of social class; the place of doctrinal content in missionary preaching; and the need for the empowerment and guidance of the Holy Spirit.[5] It is something of a stretch to think of all of this material as being missionary methods.

Allen's "methods" are inclusive of both theory and practice. The astute Hendrik Kraemer considered ministry/practice and theory/theology to be "indissoluble." Allen thinks similarly. "Paul's methods" are inclusive of the apostle's theology and ministry *taken together*. The word *baptism* as Allen understands it is a good example of "indissolubility." Allen says he uses the word *baptism* in its "full sense" and explains it this way, "I do not mean a mere form. I mean a composite whole. . . . I mean, not only washing, but repentance and faith and Grace of the Holy Ghost and Washing . . . all of these not merely together but in one unity."[6] In other words, something other than—and much more than—the act or practice of baptism is meant. Also involved is Anglo-Catholic sacramentarian theology. The indissolu-

---

[3]Ibid.
[4]Roland Allen, *Missionary Methods: St. Paul's or Ours?* (Grand Rapids: Eerdmans Publishers, 1961), pp. 51-163.
[5]Ibid., pp. 13, 49-61, 22-23, 68-69, 125.
[6]Ibid., p. 73 n. 1.

bility of his perspective is not always clear, inviting further confusion.

Once the definitional debris is cleared away it becomes apparent that Allen's methods are ultimately reducible to a single Method (capital *M*)—a process crucial to Paul and the apostles in the first century; crucial to Allen's generation at the beginning of the twentieth century; and crucial to our generation at the beginning of the twenty-first. The "Methods of Paul" enjoined by Roland Allen are really a process. It can be called "Generational Resubmission."[7]

Generational Resubmission in Allen's thinking. Quoting Allen, Newbigin says that it was never Allen's intention to convince missionaries of the rightness of this or that "method" but, rather, to urge *"the resubmission in each generation of the traditions of men to the Word and Spirit of God."*[8] Newbigin says, **"**There are no 'methods' here which will 'work' if they are 'applied.' There is a summons to everyone who will hear to submit inherited patterns of Church life to the searching scrutiny of the Spirit."[9]

Why this "summons"? Because Allen is thoroughly convinced that his generation of missionaries is going about the work of missions in ways that comport well with inherited colonial patterns and traditions but not at all well with the way of Paul. These patterns and traditions need to be *resubmitted* to the searching scrutiny of the Spirit. Certain aspects of this resubmission are especially important.

Resubmission is incumbent upon all Christians. Allen directs his summons to all Christians and all churches "who will hear." Christian missions move forward only to the degree that they are supported by knowledgeable and committed leaders and believers in the churches. In the final analysis, however, mission theorists and practitioners largely determine how the Christian mission will be understood and how it will be carried forward. So Allen speaks most directly to them.

Resubmission implies a prior submission of the patterns, proposals and practices of the present. Though Allen is especially concerned that inherited ideas and practices be resubmitted for examination, it is obvious that each

---

[7] I am indebted to Lesslie Newbigin for this insight. As they continue to read this chapter readers will become increasingly aware of how great that debt really is.

[8] Lesslie Newbigin, "Foreword," in Roland Allen, *Missionary Methods: St. Paul's or Ours?* (Grand Rapids: Eerdmans, 1961), p. ii (emphasis added).

[9] Ibid.

successive generation must submit its own ideas and practices to examination even as it resubmits to scrutiny those inherited from previous generations. Little if anything is absolutely new. Upon examination, many notions and approaches that appear to be new will have been tried and, in some cases, found wanting. Those that appear to be really new and novel will be in special need of testing. This is obvious, but more implicit than explicit in Allen's book.

Resubmission always and everywhere employs the Word of God and the Spirit of God as measures of legitimacy and effectiveness. Allen does not discuss his theology of inspiration and revelation, but neither does he speak of biblical revelation and Spirit guidance lightly or perfunctorily. Generational Resubmission is based upon a completely authoritative Bible and a genuine work of the Holy Spirit in true believers and churches of all generations and cultures. At the same time, however, it is to be acknowledged that, as an Anglican and High Churchman, Allen himself believes that the Holy Spirit works uniquely through the orders and sacraments of the church. That helps to explain his confidence in the ability of relatively new churches to govern their own affairs—they have both the bishops and the sacraments.

Resubmission is especially oriented to, and dependent upon, a biblical understanding of the mission and ministry of the apostle Paul. For Allen, *the way of Christ and the apostles* is *the way of Paul.* That is apparent not only from the book title but also from Allen's explicit statements, from his consistent use of Paul's mission as the measure of mission and from his preface to the second edition of *Missionary Methods* where he writes, "I myself am more convinced than ever that in the careful examination of his [Paul's] work, above all in the understanding and appreciation of his *principles,* we shall find the solution of most of our present difficulties."[10]

PRINCIPLES, PATTERNS AND PROPOSALS THAT NEEDED RESUBMISSION BY ROLAND ALLEN AND HIS GENERATION

Born in England in 1868, Allen was destined to be a member of the last generation of Kenneth Scott Latourette's "Great Century" of Christian missions

---

[10]Roland Allen, *Missionary Methods: St. Paul's or Ours?* 2nd ed. (Grand Rapids: Eerdmans, 1962), p. vii; emphasis his.

(dated by Latourette from 1800 to the beginning of the First World War in 1914).[11] When introducing it, Latourette takes note of three characteristics of the Great Century especially germane to Allen's summons to Generational Resubmission. First, the Great Century was characterized by almost unprecedented progress when viewed from a Western perspective. Western colonial powers considered it their duty to "civilize" and even "Christianize" the benighted peoples of the world. Christianity had been "taken to more peoples than ever before and entered as a transforming agency into more cultures than in all the preceding centuries," Latourette writes.[12]

Second, along with the acceptance of Christianity among non-Western peoples and cultures, "the rejection of Christianity among Western European peoples took place more openly than had been the case previously."[13] This means that though Allen's generation of Christians inherited a great advance abroad, they also inherited significant reversals at home. Philosophically and religiously, the skepticism and agnosticism associated with the Enlightenment flowered in the nineteenth century.

Third, Latourette says that it was more a "coming to fruition of previously existing movements rather than the injection of new ones which brought about the transition" to the twentieth century.[14] That being true, Allen's generation of missionaries must have had an ample supply of inherited ideas and practices to resubmit to Spirit-led scrutiny. History as well as Allen's book shows that to be the case.

For these reasons and more, Allen's generation was faced with a number of challenges to biblical mission that stood in need of both submission and resubmission. When studying and evaluating *Missionary Methods: St. Paul's or Ours?* then, it is important that readers have some of the most salient of these challenges in mind.

Rampant colonialism and the Westernization of mission principles and practice. As indicated above, a problem that Allen faces most directly and incisively in his book is colonialism, if not so much in mission theory at least in missionary mentality and practice. Rooted in revival, the nineteenth

---

[11]Kenneth Scott Latouette, *The Great Century in Europe and the United States of America: AD 1800–AD 1914*, vol. 4 of *A History of the Expansion of Christianity* (New York: Harper and Row, 1941).
[12]Ibid., p. 7.
[13]Ibid.
[14]Ibid., p. 6.

century Protestant missionary movement prioritized world evangelization. Millions heard and believed the gospel, thousands of churches were established and numerous cultures were transformed—all as parts of a missionary advance unprecedented in Christian history.

But that was not the whole story. Both the revivals and the larger missionary movement also focused on humanitarian and civilizing efforts to share the benefits of Western institutions with the wider world. These efforts reflected biblical principles, but they also mirrored Western colonialism. As a result, missions shared in the weaknesses as well as the strengths of the Great Century.

As much as anyone, Allen realized that the nineteenth and early twentieth century mission stations from which so much good emanated depended overly on a colonial mentality and methodology that stood in need of the kind of correctives modeled by the apostle Paul in the first century. Allen's book, therefore, is basically a response to a mission-station approach that more or less prevailed at his time and well into the twentieth century. In his final chapter he illustrates what he has in mind by describing the approach of two missionaries—one a sort of representative composite of many missionaries; the other extracted from the diary of an actual missionary. Allen's characterization of the practices of the former is particularly illuminating, but it is important to note that Allen is not impugning his motives. His "composite" missionary is, in fact, a "good man, devoted to his work" and "sincerely desirous of building up the native church."[15] The problem is not with the man nor with his motives, but solely with his methods—with his failure to submit his colonial and paternalistic patterns to careful examination in the light of the Word and the work of the Holy Spirit.

Encroaching liberalism/modernism and the Westernization of mission theology and doctrine. Though not always apparent, much of what Allen says in support of Paul's theology/missiology counters problems occasioned by the incursion of liberalism into churches and missions. In one sense, this incursion had a plus side in that it tended to refocus Christians on apologetics and doctrine in ways reminiscent of mission in the early centuries. Overall, however, the effect was deleterious because, in an effort to make

---

[15]Roland Allen, *Missionary Methods: St. Paul's or Ours?* (1961), p. 164.

Christian teachings acceptable to secular scholarship, some Christian scholars made concessions that were both unwarranted and hurtful to missions. These concessions were of various kinds.

Challenges to the authority of Scripture and the pivotal role of the apostle Paul. The nineteenth century witnessed the rise of two schools of thought especially inimical to evangelical theology in general and evangelical missiology in particular. One such was the Tübingen School under the leadership of F. C. Bauer (1826–1860). Bauer considered only four of Paul's principle letters to be authentic and called the historical reliability of Acts with its account of Paul's mission into question. The other was the Higher Critical school of thought initiated by Julius Wellhausen (1844–1918) and based on a critical process of ordering Bible documents in a way that undercut the authority of the Pentateuch and other portions of biblical text. The thinking of scholars such as Bauer and Wellhausen soon overtook many Western churches and seminaries. In fact, younger churches were affected as well, particularly in the East where Roland Allen himself had labored in the 1890s.

Challenges in the interest of Christian fellowship and unity. The last decades of the Great Century gave birth to the Student Volunteer Movement and an intensive effort to complete the task of world evangelization and "bring back the King." By the end of the nineteenth century, however, these efforts had already begun to fade, and they were in serious jeopardy at the beginning of the twentieth. In fact, at the very time Allen was preparing his manuscript for publication the famous ecumenical World Missionary Conference of 1910 was being planned to take place in Allen's own backyard of Edinburgh, Scotland. As the price of Anglican participation, the Archbishop of Canterbury, Randall Davidson, secured a pledge from John R. Mott and his fellow planners to exclude doctrinal discussion from the conference agenda. Concerning that decision, the late evangelical Anglican John R. W. Stott writes, "Theologically, the fatal flaw at Edinburgh was not so much doctrinal disagreement as apparent doctrinal indifference, since doctrine was not on the agenda. Vital themes like the content of the gospel, the theology of evangelism and the nature of the church were not discussed. . . . *In consequence, the theological challenges of the day were not faced.*"[16]

---

[16]John R. W. Stott, *Making Christ Known: Historic Mission—Documents from the Lausanne Movement 1974-1989* (London: Paternoster, 1996), p. xii; emphasis mine.

Challenges to the priority of evangelism and world evangelization. Founded in 1701, Allen's own missions agency, The Society for the Propagation of the Gospel, had featured both evangelistic and humanitarian endeavors. Over the years, however, the scales gradually tipped in favor of the latter, especially so when nineteenth century church leaders in both Europe and America wedded theology to social reform. Perhaps the best-known example of this was the leading theologian of the Social Gospel movement, Walter Rauschenbusch. He published his classic *Christianity and the Social Crisis* in 1907 just four years before the publication of Allen's *Missionary Methods.*[17] Rauschenbusch highlighted the social concerns of the Old Testament prophets, proposed that the kingdom of God was the central message of Christ, and advocated the transformation of the existing social order. After the passage of a few years Rauschenbusch died a despondent man upon witnessing the breakout of war between his native *Christian* Germany and adopted *Christian* America. But he and his work—and the Social Gospel itself—were riding the crest of a wave when Allen was readying his manuscript.

In view of the foregoing it is quite natural that we approach Allen's work with more than the ordinary questions having to do with the accuracy of his analysis and the viability of his suggestions. If Newbigin is correct—and I have no doubt that he is—we must also inquire as to how *Missionary Methods: St. Paul's or Ours?* measures up as an example of the kind of "Generational Resubmission" that Allen invokes upon his readers.

ALLEN'S BOOK AS GENERATIONAL RESUBMISSION:
STRENGTHS AND WEAKNESSES

As mentioned above, in anticipation of the publication of a second edition of *Missionary Methods* Allen writes that he is "more than ever convinced" of the validity of his argument.[18] Far from changing its substance, he carried his argument forward in a companion volume, *The Spontaneous Expansion of the Church and the Causes which Hinder It.*[19] That being the case, it would

[17]Walter Rauschenbusch, *Christianity and the Social Crisis* (New York: Macmillan, 1907).
[18]Allen, *Missionary Methods,* p. vii.
[19]Roland Allen, *The Spontaneous Expansion of the Church and the Causes which Hinder It* (London: World Dominion Press, 1927).

seem important, if not incumbent, upon us to attempt at least a very abbreviated evaluation of his work as a example of Generational Resubmission. I intend to undertake that evaluation now. At the outset, however, one caveat is in order. Namely, my comments and conclusions stem from a consideration of the text of the second edition of *Missionary Methods* only. They do not—nor are they intended to—apply to Allen's other writings.

The strengths of Missionary Methods: St. Paul's or Ours? *when viewed as an example of Generational Resubmission.* Mission books are notorious for having a short life. Yet fifty years after the publication of Allen's book, Lesslie Newbigin can write, "He [the reader] will find that this quiet voice has a strange relevance and immediacy to the problems of the Church in our day."[20] And Kenneth Grubb can write, "In recent years there has been a renewed interest in this book and in other writings of Allen. No doubt this is due to the fact that, in many parts of the world, churches and missions are being forced by circumstances to face the arguments which Allen so ably deployed nearly half-a-century ago."[21]

There are undoubtedly many reasons why this was the case, but I suggest three additional factors that probably contributed to a positive assessment back in 1960.[22]

Faithfulness to the Word of God and the Spirit of God. The decades that followed World War II were marked by serious controversies over the inspiration and authority of Scripture. Particularly pronounced within evangelicalism was the division between those who held to inerrancy of the autographs and those who settled for infallibility. Though, as I have said, Allen does not deal with inspiration and revelation much less inerrancy/infallibility, his case for the primacy of the methods of Paul exemplifies an unqualified dependence on the Bible. In 173 pages of text in *Missionary Methods* are to be found 153 specific references to the biblical text, many of them extensive. This undoubtedly resonated with multiplied thousands of evangelicals.

The passing of colonialism and the rise of an independent spirit among

---

[20]Lesslie Newbigin, foreword in Allen, *Missionary Methods,* 2nd ed., p. iii.

[21]Kenneth G. Grubb, Publisher's Foreword in Allen, *Missionary Methods,* 2nd ed., p. vi.

[22]I do not claim that Newbigin and Grubb would agree as to the importance of these three factors, only that they likely contributed to the generally positive reception with which the book was received at the time, especially by evangelicals.

younger churches. With the ending of World War II it was apparent to everyone that colonialism had had its day. Nation after nation in Africa and elsewhere in the Majority World achieved sovereignty and was received into the family of nations. Of equal missiological importance was the fact that the younger churches had come into their own. Henceforth they would not only make their own decisions but also their own distinctive contributions to Christian theology and the theory and practice of Christian mission. In a profound sense, Allen's book had proved to be prophetic.

Allen's methods were not only Pauline, they were also in accord with some of the best mission thinking of the day. In his book, Allen addressed five categories of proposals: (1) how Paul came to visit various central cities; (2) aspects of Paul's preaching, miracles and financial policies; (3) entrusting leadership to natural leaders and prophets; (4) issues of authority and discipline; and (5) basic principles and conclusions. These were and are critical areas for missions. To discuss Allen's recommendations would require considerably more space than is available here. But Newbigin's assessment is worth noting. He writes, "I shall be surprised if he [the reader] does not find before long that many of his accustomed ideas are being questioned by a voice more searching than the word of man."[23]

The weaknesses of Missionary Methods: St. Paul's or Ours? *when viewed as an example of Generational Resubmission.* One is indeed hesitant to speak in terms of the weaknesses of a missionary classic such as Roland Allen's *Missionary Methods,* but in a book of this size and scope we can be sure that there are such. Likely, some of them will surface elsewhere in this volume. For my part, while I was extremely appreciative of Allen's book early in my missionary career, I find myself even more appreciative today. Simply put, I think Allen is "on the side of the angels" when it comes to the main issues dividing evangelical missiologists today.

That said, I think it to be a sign of weakness that Allen is not more concerned to address challenges to biblical mission such as those mentioned above. Allen has his reasons for not dealing with them, and he expresses those, but I question whether his reasons are valid.

Allen believes that a true understanding of the "Apostle's Methods" depends

---

[23]Lesslie Newbigin, "Foreword" in Allen, *Missionary Methods,* 2nd ed., p. iii.

upon a true appreciation of facts, not upon a true interpretation of doctrine.
He writes,

> I am not writing a book on St Paul's doctrine. I do not feel it necessary to
> argue over again the foundations of the faith. I am a churchman and I
> write as a churchman. I naturally use terms which imply church doctrine.
> But the point to which I want to call attention is not the doctrine, which
> has been expounded and defended by many, but the Apostle's method. A
> true understanding of the method does not depend upon a true interpre-
> tation of the doctrine, but upon a true appreciation of the facts. About
> the facts there is very general agreement: about the doctrine there is very
> little agreement.[24]

I find Allen's reasoning at this point to be theologically and historically
problematic. Failure to deal with pertinent doctrinal issues has had a deleterious impact not only on how the church has *thought* about mission but
also how the church has set out to *do* mission. Over the years those proposals of the kind forwarded by Bauer, Wellhausen, Rauschenbusch and
numerous others have had a gravely adverse effect on Christian missions.
Not only that, but time and time again the willingness of men and women
like John Mott and his Edinburgh planners to overlook proposals such as
these has also proved hurtful to missions. Allen's fellow Anglican John Stott,
for example, considers their willingness to do so to have been Edinburgh's
"fatal flaw."[25] Stott diagnosed that "in the decades that followed, the poison
of theological liberalism seeped into the bloodstream of Western universities and seminaries, and largely immobilized the churches' mission."[26]

*Allen also believes that church unity is based as much or more on spiritual
ties as it is on doctrinal commitments.* With respect to first century churches
founded by the apostle Paul, Allen writes,

> [St Paul] was sent forth as the messenger of a Church, to bring men into
> fellowship with that body. His converts were not simply united one to
> another by bonds of convenience arising from the fact that they lived in
> the same place, believed the same doctrine and thought it would be a
> mutual assistance to form a society. They were members one of another

---

[24]Allen, *Missionary Methods,* 2nd ed., p. 7.
[25]Stott, *Making Christ Known*, p. xii.
[26]Ibid., emphasis mine.

in virtue of their baptism. Each was united to every other Christian everywhere, by the closest of spiritual ties, communion in one Spirit. Each
was united to all by common rites, participation in the same sacraments.
Each was united to all by common dangers and common hopes.[27]

Admittedly, this kind of thinking has some validity and is inherently ap-
pealing, especially from a sacramentarian perspective. But when tested by
Scripture and history, it will not stand. Returning again to Edinburgh 1910,
Ralph Winter once informed me that he believed Mott's decision to disallow
doctrinal discussion was based on Mott's experiences in the East just prior to
planning for Edinburgh. According to Winter, Mott had been so blessed in
missionary gatherings devoted solely to spiritual fellowship, mutual encouragement and corporate prayer that he deeply desired to replicate the spirit of
those gatherings at Edinburgh.

Perhaps so. But if so, Mott's decision to base unity on spiritual fellowship
rather than Christian doctrine at Edinburgh coupled with the World Council
of Churches' continuing failure to establish an adequate creedal basis for
itself and its subsidiaries produced a stultifying effect on twentieth century
mainline denominations and missions, including Allen's Church of England.
It is a matter of record that, though mainline churches contributed a lion's
share of both missionary personnel and finances at the beginning of the
twentieth century, this share was reduced to a trickle by the end of the
century. Similarly, indigenous churches in the places once reached with the
gospel through these mainline groups now denounce the founding church's
doctrine and practice as contrary to Scripture. For example, it is both ironic
and instructive to realize that, currently, Anglican bishops in England invoke
the blessing of the Church upon same sex marriages while Anglican bishops
in Africa refuse to do so!

GENERATIONAL RESUBMISSION AND EVANGELICAL MISSIONS TODAY AND TOMORROW

In spite of these weaknesses, Roland Allen's *Missionary Methods: St. Paul's
or Ours?* was of inestimable value in the twentieth century and remains an
invaluable resource for churches and missions today. We can forgive Allen

---

[27]Allen, *Missionary Methods*, 2nd ed., p. 126.

for not coming to grips with some of the most difficult and egregious theological/doctrinal issues facing missions in his day. In the past, Christians have behaved similarly. But they cannot afford to do so any longer. Too much is at stake. And so it is important to learn from what Allen does *not* write as well as from what he *does* write. Both are of tremendous importance. Avoiding the weakness of Allen's work, Christians should guard and guide Christian missions by submitting proposals of each generation to scrutiny in the light of Scripture and history, adopting those that pass the text and rejecting those that do not. At the same time, they should emulate the strengths of Allen's work by resubmitting his proposals (and those of other luminaries of the past) to the same kind process.

Recent proposals needful of submission by today's evangelicals. In almost every type of endeavor, but perhaps especially in thinking and doing mission, evangelicals especially have proved to be extremely resourceful, imaginative and creative. If, as we have interpreted it, Generational Resubmission implies the *submission* of contemporary proposals as well as the *resubmission* of inherited traditions and proposals to examination, this generation has its work cut out for it. Bible storying and the oral Bible, the 10-40 Window and the 4-14 Window, hidden peoples and Diaspora peoples, cyber Christians and cyber churches—the list is almost endless. All are more or less important and need vetting, but I will confine present consideration to theological/doctrinal issues of the kind that often fly under the radar of missions and that both Allen would and mission leaders today do tend to avoid. I do so because of their potential for good or—perhaps more likely—for ill.

Evangelicals and Catholics Together. As the price of togetherness and unity, proponents of this movement sometimes reinterpret Pauline doctrines such as *sola scriptura, sola fide,* and *sola gratia,* or equate the imputation of righteousness with the impartation of righteousness; or blend the "sacrifice of the Mass" with the "ordinance of the Lord's Supper."[28] Concessions such as these are often attributed to the unifying work of the Holy

---

[28]These illustrations are taken from Charles Colson and Harold Fickett, *The Faith: Given Once, For All* (Grand Rapids: Zondervan, 2008), p. 113, nn. 150-51. Compare their view with that of missionary James G. McCarthy, *The Gospel According to Rome: Comparing Catholic Tradition and the Word of God* (Eugene, Ore.: Harvest House, 1995), pp. 47, 166.

Spirit. However, the Holy Spirit does not work independently of the Spirit-inspired Word of God. Therefore, proposals such as these should be submitted and resubmitted to examination in the light of history and Scripture.

New Perspectives on Paul. Fundamental to much of the thinking of this particular movement is a recasting of Rabbinic Judaism as it existed from ca. 200 B.C. to ca. A.D. 200. Replacing the traditional view is a new understanding of post-Second Temple Judaism as being a religion of grateful response to God for Israel's covenant relationship with him. Sometimes called "covenantal nomism," this teaching is held to be the kind of religion known by Jesus and, most likely, by Paul as well. Its net effect can be rejection of the traditional Reformed understanding of Paul's teachings concerning the false gospel of Judaizers, justification by faith alone and the full authority of Scripture.[29] It deserves attention of the missions community lest the missionary message inherited from the apostle Paul and reclaimed by Protestant Reformers be modified or even lost.

The Emergent Church. A major leader of the Emergent Church defines "missional" as connoting that believers should first determine what the mission is and then construct a theology that supports it.[30] Some scholars consider the Emergent Church movement to be receding, at least in evangelical churches and missions. However, the idea that missionary vision precedes and even determines missionary theology is still very much with us. To the extent that it is, it threatens the very foundation of biblical mission by making the knowledge of God—which is what theology is and must be—subservient to a presumed knowledge of mission. That turns both theology and missiology on their head.

Supersessionism and "replacement theology." Supersessionism is a form of covenant theology holding that God's promises to Abraham in Genesis 12 are ultimately "spiritual promises" to be fulfilled in the Church of Christ as one body—multiethnic, multinational, multicultural and multigenerational. Personally, I think of extreme forms of supersessionism as being the

---

[29]See E. P. Sanders, *Paul and Palestinian Judaism: A Comparison of Patterns of Religion* (Minneapolis: Fortress, 1977), p. 422.

[30]See Brian D. McLaren, *A Generous Orthodoxy: Why I am a missional, evangelical, post-protestant, liberal/conservative, mystical/poetic, biblical, charismatic/contemplative, fundamentalist/calvinist, anabaptist/anglican, methodist, catholic, green, incarnational, depressed-yet-hopeful, emergent, unfinished Christian* (Grand Rapids: Zondervan, 2004), p. 105.

theological counterpart of the kind of ultradispensationalism that teaches that only the Pauline epistles (and not necessarily all of them) are directly applicable to the church in this dispensation of grace. "Ultrasupersessionism" (my word) holds to the position that ethnic Israel has no place in the economy of God today in spite of Paul's teaching to the effect that Israel's "partial hardening" is temporary until the "fullness of the Gentiles" is fulfilled, after which the "Deliverer" will come from Zion and fulfill God's covenant with Israel.[31] Perhaps due to a certain weariness that has overtaken evangelical discussions having to do with the Rapture, the Tribulation, the coming of Christ and the nature of the kingdom, various forms of supersessionalism are becoming increasingly pervasive.[32] Evangelicals are well advised to scrutinize them in the light not alone of Scripture, but also in light of the very positive impact premillennial eschatology, with its emphases on the Second Coming, Jewish evangelism and world evangelization, have had on modern missions.[33]

Revisionist holism. At one end of the missiological spectrum "holistic mission" holds that evangelism and sociopolitical action are more or less equal partners in mission.[34] At the other end of the spectrum, the "dichotomy between material and spiritual, between evangelism and social action, between loving God and loving neighbor" is rejected. Doing good deeds in Jesus' name *is* evangelism.[35] The "degree of partnership" involved here is important, but what is all-important is priority. The Christian mission is world evangelization. Doing good deeds is indeed Christian, but that does not make doing good deeds Christian mission. Making disciples is *prioritistic*—God decides exactly what is to be done and how to do it. That makes for clarity in mission. Doing good sociopolitical deeds is *holistic*—

---

[31]Rom 11:25-29.

[32]Kevin D. Zuber, "Supersessionism Rising. Dispensationalism. . . ?" *VOICE* (Sept./Oct. 2011): 19-21, 30-31.

[33]Craig A. Blaising, "The Future of Israel as a Theological Question," in *To the Jew First: The Case for Jewish Evangelism in Scripture and History,* ed. by Darrell L. Bock and Mitch Glaser (Grand Rapids: Kregel), p. 103.

[34]John R. W. Stott, *Christian Mission in the Modern World: What the Church Should Be Doing Now.* (Downers Grove, Ill.: InterVarsity Press, 1975), p. 27; see also David J. Hesselgrave, *Paradigms in Conflict: Ten Key Questions in Missions Today* (Grand Rapids: Kregel, 2005), pp. 120-22.

[35]Bryant L. Myers, "In Response . . . Another Look at Holistic Mission." *Evangelical Missions Quarterly* 35, no. 3 (1999): 287; see also James F. Engel and William A. Dyrness, *Changing the Mind of Missions: Where Have We Gone Wrong?* (Downers Grove, Ill.: InterVarsity Press, 2000), p. 93.

the people involved more or less decide all that is to be done and how to go about it. That makes for confusion.

In an attempt to get world evangelization on the agenda of the World Council of Churches' meeting in Uppsala in 1968, Donald McGavran repeatedly asked the question "What of the Two Billion [unevangelized]?" Preferring to deal with sociopolitical concerns and avoid the priority problem, planners adopted the slogan, "Let the world set the agenda." Evangelicals have never adopted that slogan, but missions observers will notice that the interests and involvements of evangelicals tend to follow the agendas of the world nevertheless. By way of examples, after World War II the evangelical missionary agenda highlighted apartheid and anticolonialism; later it centered on feminism and AIDS; most recently it prioritizes human trafficking—these along with periodic incursions of natural and national disasters. McGavran's observation, "These are good Christian things to do, but they are not Christian mission" merits consideration.[36]

Some century-old proposals by Roland Allen still worthy of resubmission by today's evangelicals. Before concluding it is incumbent upon us to consider at least a sampling of proposals Allen puts forward under the "methods" category and mentioned above.[37] Some if not all of these proposals will no doubt receive more thorough attention elsewhere in this volume, but I would be delinquent if I failed to at least illustrate their abiding relevance. By way of illustration, I will focus on just three aspects of apostolic preaching as practiced by Paul in the first century, enjoined by Allen in the twentieth and in need of resubmission now in the twenty-first.

The objectives *of apostolic preaching.* Allen maintains that some of the clear objectives of Paul's preaching that require emulation are (1) meaningful decisions on the part of hearers, (2) "total and entire conversion of the inner man" and the "absolute doing away of the old and acceptance of the new life," and (3) church incorporation or "gathering out of the world the elect of God into the fellowship of His Son."[38] Allen criticizes his contemporaries for being content with "scattering seeds" on the one hand,

---

[36]Personal correspondence from Donald McGavran to the author, April 7, 1988.
[37]Kenneth G. Grubb, "Publisher's Foreword" in Allen, *Missionary Methods,* p. vi.
[38]Allen, *Missionary Methods,* 2nd ed., pp. 74, 71 and 70, respectively.

while attempting to "Christianize the world" on the other.[39] Might not the same be true today?

The appeals *of apostolic preaching.* Allen says that Paul did not hesitate to appeal to "heathen" on the bases of both philosophy and morality. He made common cause with those confused by polytheism who nevertheless sought unity in a world of nature and an intelligent account of the world, its nature and end. Paul did not attack the religion of his hearers except in such respects as their own philosophers did, or would, denounce them. Moreover, there was in Paul's preaching a recognition of moral convictions and ethical sensibilities even in hearers who were downtrodden, hopeless and oppressed by a sense of sin.[40]

At the very least, Allen's analysis of Paul's preaching appeals should cause us to inquire into the ways we treat—or do not treat—the religious and ethical ideals of non-Christian peoples today.

The content *of apostolic preaching.* Simply stated and according to Allen, in mission preaching "the supreme subject is 'the Cross, Repentance, and Faith.'"[41] That seems simple and straightforward enough. Nevertheless, Allen finds the preaching of his missionary colleagues to be deficient with respect to content. First, he notes the "tendency today to avoid . . . stern doctrine."[42] "We have lost," he says, "two prominent elements of Paul's gospel: the doctrine of judgment at hand, and the doctrine of the wrath of God."[43] This, in turn, has made for an "easy doctrine of evangelization."[44]

Second, he says that it is often taken for granted that the gospel of Paul was purely individualistic. That is not true. Participation in the life of the church is more than an appeal in apostolic preaching; it is part and parcel of the apostolic gospel itself. Paul's gospel was calculated to gather believers into a society of which he himself was a member. Those who repented became one of the brethren, sharing in the sacraments but also in persecution.

Missionaries across the whole ecclesiastical/theological spectrum would do well to examine the content of their preaching with respect to biblical

---

[39]Ibid., pp. 75-76.
[40]Ibid., p. 77.
[41]Ibid., p. 67.
[42]Ibid., p. 70.
[43]Ibid., p. 72.
[44]Ibid.

doctrine, divine judgment and church incorporation. Is that preaching true to the whole counsel of God?

The importance of Allen's reliance on the apostle Paul in the practice of Generational Resubmission. Before concluding, I think it prudent to repeat and reinforce Allen's basic thesis yet once more. Paul is the divinely appointed model for missionaries of succeeding generations. This thesis was by no means original to Allen, of course. In effect, he himself had submitted a longstanding missiological tradition to scrutiny in the light of the Scripture and history and, finding it tenable and true, had resubmitted its implications to the consideration of his contemporaries. Then, when writing the preface to the second edition of *Missionary Methods,* Allen reviewed both what he had written in the first edition and how it had been received, concluding, "I myself am more convinced than ever that in the careful examination of his [Paul's] work, above all in the understanding and appreciation of his *principles,* we shall find the solution of most of our present difficulties."[45]

Though there are dissonant voices to be sure, were Allen alive and writing today he would still find corroborating voices as well. As for missions history, W. Paul Bowers says, "The mission of the apostle Paul in the first century has functioned as a principal inspiration and paradigm for Christian witness during the millennia since. The modern missionary movement in particular has routinely attempted to take bearings from the apostle's thinking and endeavors."[46]

And on the basis of a careful examination of both a large body of current missionary literature and the New Testament text, Kevin DeYoung and Gregory Gilbert conclude that Paul is indeed the model missionary and that "Paul's mission was threefold: (1) initial evangelism, (2) the nurture of existing churches by guarding against error and grounding them in the faith and (3) their firm establishment as healthy congregations through the full exposition of the gospel and the appointment of local leadership."[47]

---

[45]Ibid., "Author's Preface," p. vii; emphasis in original.

[46]W. Paul Bowers, "Paul and Mission," in *Evangelical Dictionary of World Missions,* ed. A. Scott Moreau (Grand Rapids: Baker Books, 2000), p. 731.

[47]Kevin DeYoung and Greg Gilbert, *What Is the Mission of the Church? Making Sense of Social Justice, Shalom, and the Great Commission* (Wheaton, Ill.: Crossway 2011), p. 62.

CONCLUSION

I close with two observations that appear to be especially relevant to Christian missions today.

First, I think that Allen's book "makes sense" of mission. Theologians and missiologists sometimes tend to so refashion mission as to make it inclusive of any and every good work and noble deed. Biblical mission is much more focused than that.

Second, lest we think the *latest* word on missions is also the *last* word, we do well to read and reread missionary classics like *Missionary Methods.* Allowing for the fact that every book is a product of its time, books such as this one nevertheless exhibit a timelessness born of a special blend of broad experience, encompassing intelligence and spiritual maturity. Books like *Missionary Methods: St. Paul's or Ours?* deter us from straying too far from the path of faith and fruitfulness.

9

PAUL'S STRATEGY:
DETERMINATIVE FOR TODAY?

♦ ♦ ♦

Michael Pocock

In the previous chapter David Hesselgrave pointed out, and others have agreed, that neither Paul nor Roland Allen seemed to have or advocate what we think of as a strategy or methods today. We can derive principles, emphases, values, and tendencies and observe oft-repeated practices, but not really methods, nor strategy. Some years ago Charles Bennett, writing on Paul's methods entitled his article, "Paul the Pragmatist."[1] His point was that whenever we treat a Pauline practice as a pattern, we immediately find examples where he did not follow that plan. Bennett's conclusion was that Paul "made hay while the sun shines."[2]

All who treat Scripture as normative for Christian faith and practice look with appreciation at the dynamic ministry of the apostle Paul. In varying degrees they attempt to implement or emulate his approaches. Paul's life and ministry were recorded in Scripture by an inspired writer, Luke, or by Paul himself in his Epistles, and this alone argues for serious consideration and acceptance by believers. But it is possible to drift from the practice and spirit of Scripture. Believers do this consciously or uncon-

---

[1]Charles T. Bennett, "Paul the Pragmatist," *Evangelical Missions Quarterly* 16, no. 3 (1980): 133-38.
[2]Ibid.

sciously by relegating historical narrative to a subservient place beneath direct scriptural instruction such as we find in the epistles. We will deal with this issue of interpretation and application later in this chapter. Roland Allen, in calling missionaries and his own Anglican mission society to examine their missionary practices a hundred years ago and resubmit them to the gaze of the Holy Spirit through Scripture, said in the early lines of his *Missionary Methods,*

> It is impossible but that the account so carefully given by St Luke of the planting of the church in the Four Provinces should have something more than a merely archeological and historical interest. Like the rest of the Holy Scriptures it was "written for our learning." It was certainly meant to be something more than the romantic history of an exceptional man doing exceptional things under exceptional circumstances—a story from which ordinary people of a later age can get no more instruction for practical missionary work than they receive from the history of the Cid, or the exploits of King Arthur.[3]

In this chapter, we want to show how and to what degree St. Paul's approaches, or "methods," are being implemented today and the degree to which this shows dependence on Roland Allen's work. We will then consider whether Pauline methodology should or should not be considered normative for today.

CONTEMPORARY PAULINE STRATEGY APPLICATION
AMONG MISSIOLOGISTS

Although it is commonplace to hear of Roland Allen's prediction that his emphasis on Pauline methodology would not be seriously considered until the 1960's, as a matter of fact, missiologists and missions conferences were busy digesting and using his work much earlier. In 1938, Hendrik Kraemer, in papers prepared for International Missionary Council conference in Tambaram, India, compared Allen's importance to that of John L. Nevius of China.[4] Importantly, Kraemer had grasped Allen's idea that each generation should carefully reexamine their doctrine, teaching and methodology in missions: "I have become convinced that, especially in our time . . . all the

---

[3]Roland Allen, *Missionary Methods: St. Paul's or Ours?* 2nd ed. (Grand Rapids: Eerdmans, 1962), p. 4.
[4]Hendrik Kraemer, *Christian Message in a Non-Christian World* (Grand Rapids: Kregel, 1956), p. 413.

fundamentals and principles have to be re-examined. . . . The highest ambition I foster [in regard to the publication of his book *The Christian Message in a Non-Christian World*] is that it may contribute to the Church's rediscovery of its apostolic nature."[5]

The significance of Allen's call to missional reexamination in the light of Pauline methodology could clearly be seen by Alexander McLeish in 1958 when he said of Allen, "His exposition of missionary methods and principles is far more revolutionary than is usually thought."[6] This is likely the reason InterVarsity Christian Fellowship distributed *Missionary Methods* to every attendee at the Urbana Student Missionary Convention of 1962, almost the exact time Allen had said it would be more widely read.

Harry R. Boer detailed Allen's emphasis on Pauline work as Spirit-dependent work.[7] The German Peter Beyerhaus was impressed with Allen's penetrating emphasis on what was already known as the "Three Self Principle."[8] And South African David Bosch followed Allen in his assertion that "Intimately related to the resurrection, almost part of the Easter event itself, is the gift of the Spirit, which is equally integrally linked to mission."[9]

David Hesselgrave cites Allen for five of the ten steps in his Pauline cycle of church planting, and Latin American Samuel Escobar, in two excellent chapters of *Global Missiology for the Twenty-first Century,* shows how Allen, following Paul's belief in the power and ability of the Spirit to guide new Christian churches toward spontaneous expansion, practically prophesied today's rapid Christian expansion in what Philip Jenkins called "Southern Christianity" (in his book *The Next Christendom*) and later, "The Global South."[10]

---

[5]Ibid., p. v.

[6]Alexander McLeish, *The Priority of the Holy Spirit in Christian Witness. Being an Examination of the Objective Aimed at in the Writings of the Rev. Roland Allen* (London: World Dominion Press, 1961), p. 2.

[7]Harry R. Boer, *Pentecost and Missions* (Grand Rapids: Eerdmans, 1961), p. 63.

[8]Peter Beyerhaus and Henry Charles Lefever, *The Responsible Church and the Foreign Mission* (Grand Rapids: Eerdmans, 1964), pp. 33-39.

[9]David Jacobus Bosch, *Transforming Mission: Paradigm Shifts in Theology of Mission* (Maryknoll, N.Y.: Orbis Books, 1991), p. 40.

[10]David J. Hesselgrave, *Planting Churches Cross-Culturally: North America and Beyond*, 2nd ed. (Grand Rapids: Baker Books, 2000), pp. 76, 114-15, 124, 225, 275, 284-85; William David Taylor, ed. *Global Missiology for the 21st Century: The Iguassu Dialogue* (Grand Rapids: Baker Academic, 2000), p. 28; Philip Jenkins, *The Next Christendom: The Coming of Global Christianity* (Oxford; New York: Oxford University Press, 2002), p. 7; Philip Jenkins, *The New Faces of Christianity: Believing the Bible in the Global South* (New York: Oxford University Press, 2006).

Hardly any evangelical missiologist fails to acknowledge the seminal contribution of Roland Allen in driving mission thinking, planning and praxis on the basis of biblical—and specifically Pauline—principles. Yet there are probably a myriad of evangelicals who hope that their *theology* is both biblical and Pauline but who fail to understand the *missiological* significance of how Paul did his work. This is especially true for the many churches that attempt to do mission work directly without reference to a mission agency. It is possible to boast of Pauline *doctrine* without fully recognizing the intention of Paul, that his *example* be far more than suggestive for those who followed him. These churches are frequently unaware of historical issues in missions. As a result, they move straight into the errors Roland Allen urged his readers to avoid.

Let us turn from recognizing the extent to which missiologists have engaged with both Roland Allen and Paul to observe how both Paul and Allen's thinking and practice actually affect or can be observed in mission today. In each case we will show Allen's emphasis followed by contemporary phenomena or practice in Christian work and missions.

Implementation of Roland Allen's principles of submission and dependence on the Holy Spirit and the Word of God. Luke gives us the picture of Jesus in his Gospel and a selective account of the Holy Spirit's work through the apostles in Acts. He shows the centrality and indispensability of the Spirit in the amazing spread of the gospel and establishment of churches in the Northern Mediterranean region during the first century.

Paul was clearly cognizant of the Spirit's work. Following his conversion on the Damascus road, he went north to Tarsus, from which Barnabas retrieved him to help teach the rapidly growing church in Antioch. The first mission from Antioch was instigated by the Spirit of God prophesying through Agabus (Acts 11:28). This had to do with relieving the saints in Jerusalem in the long drawn out famine they were about to experience. This was really the first installment of a relief program that occupies Paul's concern throughout his ministry and to which he gives witness in Romans 15 and 2 Corinthians 8–9.

After worshipping and fasting, the leaders of the church in Antioch commissioned Paul and Barnabas as missionaries (Acts 13:1-3). The Holy Spirit clearly chose them for service, and the Spirit sent them out (Acts 13:4). Thus the Holy Spirit selected them for service, and the church leaders affirmed their mission. Luke records that as Paul ministered to the Proconsul in Cyprus and reprimanded the sorcerer Elymas, he was filled with the Holy Spirit (Acts 13:9). As disciples grew, Luke records, "The disciples were filled with joy and with the Holy Spirit" (Acts 13:52).

The Acts 15 letter to the Gentile believers communicating the decision of the elders in Jerusalem acknowledged that it was the Holy Spirit who had encouraged them in the decision they made (Acts 15:28). As Paul and Barnabas continued on their second missionary journey, the Spirit stopped them from entering one area and instead they were guided to Macedonia in a vision (Acts 16:7-10). The believers at Ephesus had to be oriented to the reality, presence and power of the Holy Spirit (Acts 19:1-7).

Paul was clearly and strongly christocentric in his teaching, but he usually explained his movements as instigated by the Holy Spirit. For this reason, he told the Ephesians that he was "constrained by the Spirit" to go to Jerusalem, and that as in every city, the Holy Spirit had warned him of prisons and hardships that awaited him (Acts 20:22-23). The same Ephesian elders are told in Paul's farewell address that they should keep watch over themselves and "all the flock, in which the Holy Spirit has made you overseers" (Acts 20:28). This last point becomes very significant in Roland Allen's argument that local leadership can be trusted to lead because of the Holy Spirit in and among them.[11]

We could go on to show that what the book of Acts gives examples of is also taught in Paul's epistles. At the beginning of his letter to the Romans, Paul declared that the gospel of Christ had been preached through the power of the Spirit (Rom 1:4). True circumcision was that of the Spirit (Rom 2:29). The secret to overcoming the flesh was dependence on the Holy Spirit (Rom 8:1-15; Gal 5:16). The fullness of the kingdom was a matter of righteousness, peace and joy in the Holy Spirit (Rom 14:17), and the Holy Spirit produces fruits of morality, ethics and joy (Gal 5:22-26).

The demonstration of the Spirit's power is the basis of real impact in gospel proclamation, and the ability to understand deep spiritual truths is a capacity given by the Spirit (1 Cor 2:4, 6-16). To be the body of Christ is to

---

[11]Allen, *Missionary Methods*, p. 114; Roland Allen, *The Spontaneous Expansion of the Church and the Causes which Hinder It,* American ed. (Grand Rapids: Eerdmans, 1962), p. 59.

be individually and collectively the temple of the Holy Spirit (1 Cor 3:16-17; 6:19). Gifts for edifying the body are given by the Spirit (1 Cor 11–14). Believers are delivered from fear and timidity, and given love, power, and self control by the Spirit (2 Tim 1:7). Believers are to defend themselves by the sword of the Spirit (Eph 6:17). The Spirit works continually to sanctify believers (2 Thess 2:13). The Spirit helps young leaders like Timothy to guard the truth, whether Paul is present with him or not (2 Tim 1:14).

This all seems a lot to say about the work of the Holy Spirit, most of which was also predicted by Jesus in the Gospel of John (Jn 3:5-6; 7:37-39; 14:15-26; 15:26; 16:5-15). But this is what struck Roland Allen as he surveyed missionary endeavor at the opening of the twentieth century: There was an insufficient emphasis and dependence on the reality, presence and power of the Holy Spirit to produce the maturity and capability of new believers to spontaneously care for themselves and extend their witness. What Allen begins to say about the Spirit in *Methods,* he develops much further in subsequent works, like *The Spontaneous Expansion of the Church,* and *The Ministry of the Spirit.* As Harry Boer, citing Allen, notes, "So bright a light (as the Holy Spirit) could not be wholly hid . . . but the light of understanding as to the nature and practical missionary significance of this power has been dim. . . . How then has this revelation been treated by the great teachers of our day? . . . I venture to say it has been practically ignored."[12] This, to me, is the most significant part of Allen's criticism of mission work in his day. It is the emphasis that has been rescued in large measure since his time.

What amazes me about the ministry of Roland Allen is that his concerns about the place of the Spirit in the work of missions in 1912 when *Methods* first appeared was the same as the Pentecostalism that burst forth in Kansas City and in Azusa Street, California in 1900 and 1906, but Allen does not seem to be aware of it.[13] Neither does he acknowledge the awakening closer to his home, in Wales, in 1904-1905 during which over 200,000 came to Christ. Communication would have been slower in their day, and we may have to conclude that God himself was doing something spontaneously and simultaneously in various parts of the world exactly as Allen said he would.

---

[12]Boer, *Pentecost and Missions*, p. 48.

[13]Gary B. McGee, "William Seymour and the Azusa Street Revival," *EJ* (Fall 1999), http://enrichment journal.ag.org/199904/026_azusa.cfm.

Where there had been spiritual deadness, even alongside biblical orthodoxy, God was impressing on Congregationalists, Anglicans, Presbyterians and Independents, all without reference to one another, the need to reemphasize the person and work of the Holy Spirit.[14]

Allen did not become a Pentecostal in the same way as the followers of Seymour and Parham, nor did his Anglican contemporaries pay much attention to Allen himself, but the spark had been lit in such a way that others in mainline denominations began to pay attention. Harry Boer, a Christian Reformed missionary and professor, was so exercised about the need to consider afresh the role of the Spirit that he wrote the influential book *Pentecost and Missions*.

Although Dallas Theological Seminary cannot be viewed as either Pentecostal or Charismatic in its emphasis, its founder, Louis Sperry Chafer, a Congregationalist, wrote what for many evangelicals became the handbook for a walk in the Spirit, *He That Is Spiritual*.[15] There is no mistaking Chafer's conviction that the Holy Spirit is the indispensable agent in producing a truly Christ honoring life or ministry. What Chafer could see in 1918 reflected what many were realizing regardless of their denominational background.

We cannot conclude that Roland Allen's emphasis on the role of the Spirit was the sole impetus behind movements focused on the recognition and acceptance of the Holy Spirit's role in missions, but we certainly can see the change in both Pentecostal and Charismatic growth, among Protestants and Roman Catholics during the Catholic Renewal movement of the 1960s and 70s, and in neo-Pentecostal movements worldwide. These constitute some 70 percent of the global evangelical movement today. From the West, a single Charismatic mission agency, Youth with a Mission (YWAM), founded in 1960, grew globally to 18,000 workers by 2012.[16]

The growth of a church movement in proportion to diminished foreign control. Roland Allen, following Rufus Anderson, Henry Venn and John Nevius, was an advocate of the "three-self principle" and all it implied— churches that are self-supporting, self-governing and self-propagating. Allen

[14]Michael Pocock, Gailyn Van Rheenen and Douglas McConnell, *The Changing Face of World Missions: Engaging Contemporary Issues and Trends* (Grand Rapids: Baker Academic, 2005), p. 186.
[15]Lewis Sperry Chafer, *He that is Spiritual* (Chicago: Moody Press, 1918).
[16]About YWAM Page, Youth with a Mission (YWAM, 2010) www.ywam.org/About-ywam.

believed that missions in his day stultified the growth of indigenous churches by maintaining too much control in leadership, administration, education, finance and propagation of the gospel. In short, he charged the missions with paternalism. Mission agencies, he said, exercised ongoing control because they did not trust the Holy Spirit in new believers to guard the integrity of sound doctrine and practice. When he reached the point of application in his *Missionary Methods,* he wrote,

> Now if we are to practice any methods approaching the Pauline methods in power and directness, it is absolutely necessary that we should first have this faith, the Spirit. Without faith—faith in the Holy Ghost, faith in the Holy Ghost in our converts—we can do nothing. . . . If we have no faith in the power of the Holy Spirit in them, they will not learn to have faith in the power of Holy Spirit in themselves. We cannot trust them, and they cannot be worthy of trust; the trust which begets trustworthiness, is the one essential for any success in the Pauline method.[17]

This failure to trust the work of the Spirit in and among new believers was at the heart of missionaries' failure to allow indigenous leadership, teaching, financial responsibility and expansion to move forward spontaneously. In the years since Allen lodged these allegations against the Church Mission Society and missions in general, we have seen a marked increase among missionaries and agencies to trust in the capacity of new believers to conduct their own affairs effectively. The end of colonialism had a lot to do with this, but so has the maturation of churches in formerly receiving countries. There has also been a vast explosion of movements having no reference at all to foreign agency involvement, much less control. An example would be the spontaneous explosion of movements like the African Initiated Churches (AIC). AICs include the Zionist movement of southern Africa, the Vapastori movement of Zimbabwe, the Aladura, Kimbanguist and about six thousand other AICs first catalogued by David Barrett and more recently by Barrett and Johnson.[18]

---

[17]Allen, *Missionary Methods,* p. 152.
[18]David B. Barrett, *Schism and Renewal in Africa: An Analysis of Six Thousand Contemporary Religious Movements* (Nairobi, Kenya: Oxford University Press, 1968); David B. Barrett, George Thomas Kurian and Todd M. Johnson, *World Christian Encyclopedia: A Comparative Survey of Churches and Religions in the Modern World,* 2nd ed. (New York: Oxford University Press, 2001), p. 4.

Sometimes events like the Marxist revolution in China forced the hand of foreign missions in regard to control of churches. Believing as Marx did that "religion is the opiate of the masses," the Maoists were convinced that religion would eventually die out as humanity progressed. They decided to simply oversee the Christian movement while it died out. Churches in China were required to belong to the Three Self Patriotic Movement (TSPM). In a sense, this was taking Western missions at their own word that such "three-self churches" were the ideal, and if so, foreigners were no longer necessary.

The Chinese central government maintained a pivotal role in the TSPM. This resulted in many house churches deciding that they could not collaborate with the TSPM because Christ alone is the true authority in His church. Ironically, the house church movement now numbers between 60 and 70 million members. These house churches are truly "three-self" churches, free from foreign control, fulfilling Roland Allen's prediction.[19] TSPM churches themselves count approximately 16 million adherents.

Is Pauline Methodology Normative for the Church and Missions Today?

The question this chapter has sought to answer is whether Paul's missionary methods are applicable to modern missions. Or, to put it another way, should modern missionaries seek to imitate Paul? The answer from Roland Allen is "yes," at least in the sense of taking very seriously the approaches of Paul in Acts and his Epistles. Allen believed Scripture gives the churches their marching orders today. We have already noted Allen's statement in his introduction to *Missionary Methods* to this effect. But is this in accord with generally accepted principles of hermeneutics? Frequently, the teaching we encounter in the epistles is taken to be more binding than examples in historical or narrative portions of the scripture like the Acts of the Apostles, as mentioned earlier in the chapter. Both example and narrative passages provide principles that missionaries should take seriously, but missionaries need not imitate the apostles slavishly in every regard.

---

[19]"Christian Population in China," *Christians in China: First-hand Reports on the Current State of Christianity in China* (December 26, 2009), www.christiansinchina.com/2009/12/26/christian-population-in-china.

Bernard Ramm makes this observation: "Holy Scripture is not a book of theoretical abstractions, but a book that intends to have a mighty influence on the lives of its readers."[20] Walter Kaiser and Moisés Silva more recently have pointed out that two-thirds of the Bible is narrative in nature, and this argues for the importance of such material for the Body of Christ. "Narrative is clearly the main supporting framework of the Bible."[21]

St. Paul himself gives a "minitheology" of the significance of historical portions of the Bible when he reminds the Corinthians that the events of the Exodus and wilderness experience happened and were recorded for the admonition of those who would come much later, even to the present generation of his readers (1 Cor 10:6, 11). This clearly implies that historical narrative in Scripture has a pedagogical intent and value.

Add to this Paul's own teaching to Timothy that "all scripture is God-breathed and is useful for teaching, rebuking, correcting and training in righteousness, so that the servant of God may be thoroughly equipped for every good work" (2 Tim 3:16-17 NIV). This does not imply slavish repetition of Scriptural patterns; that would result in a new legalism running counter to grace. But it certainly does mean that patterns of ministry like that of Paul are applicable and recorded precisely because they are of value in formulating ministry approaches. They constitute benchmarks against which we can and should evaluate contemporary missionary practice.

Roland Allen was also positive about the ability of indigenous believers to understand and interpret Scripture. He discouraged foreigners from handing down directives about the meaning of scriptural passages and their application to newly planted churches. The ability of believers, imbued with the Spirit, to make sound joint decisions was clearly recognized by Paul when he admonished the Corinthians to trust their own common members to make right decisions in momentous matters (1 Cor 6:1-6). Peter advocated the priesthood of all believers in 1 Peter 2:4-10. This had the effect of establishing believers as reliable arbiters of their own affairs.

The late Christian missiologist and anthropologist Paul Hiebert laid out

---

[20]Bernard L. Ramm, *Protestant Biblical Interpretation: A Textbook of Hermeneutics*, 3rd ed. (Grand Rapids: Baker, 1970), p. 113.

[21]Walter C. Kaiser and Moisés Silva, *An Introduction to Biblical Hermeneutics: The Search for Meaning* (Grand Rapids: Zondervan, 1994), p. 123.

an argument for what he termed "the hermeneutical community" when he discussed "critical contextualization."[22] Hiebert maintained that decisions about the meaning and application of Scripture in resolving indigenous issues should always be done by a plurality of indigenous believers. In the process of critical contextualization, local people describe what would usually be done in a particular situation. Next, possibly with expatriate missionary help, they discover what Scripture says on the topic. Finally, local Christians, "the hermeneutical community," decide how the Scripture relates to the issue at hand and what to do about it. Roland Allen would have loved this! In all events, Hiebert would have anchored Christian indigenous decision-making in the Word of God.

The application of the principle of the hermeneutical community in missions today is evidenced in Wycliffe Bible Translators' approach to their "Vision 2025." This strategy intends to arrive at the point where all the languages of the world needing a separate translation of the Bible actually have it available or under way by 2025. Wycliffe does not intend to do this alone, but seeks to partner with other agencies and church fellowships to reach the goal. A key ingredient is the training of many indigenous and vernacular translators who work as teams to produce reliable translations. This is an example not only of Hiebert's "hermeneutical community," but also of Roland Allen and St. Paul's emphasis on indigenous believers reading, reflecting and deciding what they should believe and how they should act. In the New Testament, the Berean Christians were examples of this approach, as Luke notes: "Now these Jews were more noble than those in Thessalonica; they received the word with all eagerness, *examining the Scriptures daily to see if these things were so*" (Acts 17:11, emphasis mine).

Roland Allen believed that "fear for the doctrine," fear that indigenous believers could not be trusted to stay orthodox, had had a limiting affect on the growth of indigenous churches.[23] "We dread the possible mistakes of individual zeal," he wrote.[24] Indeed it has happened that churches left to themselves have developed heresies or grave misapplications of the Word. Not all house churches in China, for example, are orthodox, and

[22]Paul Hiebert, *Anthropological Issues for Missionaries* (Grand Rapids: Baker Books, 1985), pp. 186-90.
[23]Allen, *The Spontaneous Expansion of the Church*, p. 43-47.
[24]Allen, *Missionary Methods*, p. 94.

the African Initiated Churches are sometimes termed "marginally Christian."[25] But this does not mean they are inauthentic or will be permanently heretical.

The kind of spontaneously growing churches Roland Allen envisioned may have been similar to what have been termed "insider movements" today. These are usually house church movements that in several respects remain inside their cultural context. They may continue to practice some elements of the religion from which they are emerging and would be judged as odd or even heterodox by many outside, or even close Christian observers.[26] Nevertheless, they are Jesus-oriented movements, regarding the Bible as their authority, but still respecting or reading the sacred writings of their old religious commitments. What should we think about these movements?

We know that such movements grow rapidly, as David Garrison documented in *Church Planting Movements*.[27] Spontaneously growing house church movements have multiplied in Asia, Africa and Latin America. If Roland Allen were present today, he would welcome such growth and declare it to be what he predicted could happen if missionaries would only allow the new churches to develop spontaneously, without excessive missionary control.

Timely correction or instruction of new believers helps correct the excesses and misunderstandings of new believers. This could have been why Barnabas invited Paul to teach new believers at Antioch in Acts 11 and why Priscilla and Aquila had to "explain the way of God more adequately" to the zealous and authentic preacher Apollos, in Acts 18:18-26. We are not told what constituted his errors or mistaken teaching, but apparently he was trusted with evangelistic and pastoral responsibility immediately after his time with Aquila and Priscilla (Acts 18:27-28).

Ralph Winter has asked: "Do we need more heresies on the mission

---

[25]Barrett, Kurian, and Johnson, *World Christian Encyclopedia*, p. 4.

[26]Joshua Lingel, Jeffery J. Morton, and Bill Nikides, eds. *Chrislam: How Missionaries are Promoting an Islamized Gospel* (Garden Grove, Calif.: i2 Ministries, 2011). This work contains strong condemnation of Insider Movements and Bible translations for Muslims, by a variety of authors, many indigenous believers in Muslim contexts.

[27]V. David Garrison, *Church Planting Movements: How God is Redeeming a Lost World* (Midlothian, Va.: WIGTake Resources, 2004), www.churchplantingmovements.com.

field? Can heresies be clouds with a silver lining?"[28] His point, developed in many more articles in *Mission Frontiers* and *The International Journal of Frontier Missiology* in the intervening years, is that new movements to Christ have been historically regarded as heretical, but many of these have moved back to a more biblical orthodoxy with the passage of time. This is evident in South Africa where the African Initiated Church called "Amaziones" (Zionist Churches of Southern Africa) now welcome traditional evangelical teachers among them in an attempt to lay more biblical foundations under their massive movement. Similar phenomena can be found in China today.

Some who have read Roland Allen's work have concluded that they could work as rapidly as Paul, establishing churches in a few weeks or months and move on to other regions. Roland Allen would never have advocated the precipitous abandonment of newly established churches. His overarching conviction that the Holy Spirit is capable of instructing new believers would not have led him to leave new believers and churches without guidance.[29] What he did advocate was the willing transfer of authority, responsibility, and self-support to young churches before the missionary was obligated unwillingly by circumstances to do so.[30]

CONCLUSION

As several have shown in this book, Roland Allen hoped that missionaries and missions agencies would examine and resubmit their theories and practices to the judgment of the Bible and the Holy Spirit. We have shown that missiologists and large missionary consultations have done just that. There are probably many groups and individuals who need to go through a fresh process of reexamination, but many have already done so. The challenge for our age is that emerging mission agencies from the Global South and mission-sending churches may ignore the history of missions and the exemplary practice of St. Paul.

We have shown that narrative or historically descriptive portions of

---

[28]Ralph D. Winter, "Do We Need More Heresies on the Mission Field? Can Heresies be Clouds with a Silver Lining?" *Mission Frontiers* (September 1, 1996).

[29]Allen, *Missionary Methods*, pp. 153-54.

[30]Ibid., pp. 158-59.

scripture are always to be taken seriously. They may not be normative in the sense that they should be slavishly replicated, but the patterns and principles derived from scriptural example are definitely meant to guide our practice in contemporary ministry. Moreover, the general principles and patterns of Paul's work pragmatically and spiritually apply to our times.

The only way to maintain a scripturally authentic approach to our work while avoiding the repetition of methods that stifled qualitative and quantitative growth in the past is fresh dependence on the Holy Spirit, modeling and teaching dependence on Him. It is not enough to have Christian *orthodoxy* in missionary work. We must also have *orthopraxis* that acts in accord with our beliefs regarding the preeminence of Jesus Christ, the indispensable power of the Holy Spirit and the guidance of the Word of God.

10

Paul and Indigenous Missions

♦ ♦ ♦

John Mark Terry

The term "indigenous" comes from biology and indicates a plant or animal native to an area. For example, oak trees are indigenous to North America like mango trees are indigenous to the Philippines. In the nineteenth century, missiologists adopted the word and used it to refer to churches that are able to reproduce themselves in a particular culture and reflect the cultural distinctives of their ethnolinguistic group. The missionary effort to establish indigenous churches is an effort to plant reproducing churches that fit naturally into their environment and to avoid planting churches that replicate Western patterns.[1]

The Apostle Paul's Indigenous Strategy

Missionary efforts to establish indigenous churches are attempts to do missions as the apostle Paul did. In fact, all advocates of indigenous missions base their writings on Paul's missionary strategy. Even a cursory review of the literature on indigenous missions reveals this fact. Advocates of indigenous missions seek to emulate the apostle Paul's strategy.

---

[1]Much of this chapter appeared in an abbreviated form in my article, "Indigenous Churches," in *The Evangelical Dictionary of World Missions*, ed. A. Scott Moreau (Grand Rapids: Baker Books, 2000), pp. 483-85.

What was the apostle Paul's missionary strategy? Missiologists have debated whether Paul had an overarching strategy. J. Herbert Kane, long-time professor of missions at Trinity Evangelical Divinity School, addressed this question: "If by strategy is meant a deliberate, well-formulated, duly executed plan of action based on human observation and experience, then Paul had little or no strategy; but if we take the word to mean a flexible *modus operandi* developed under the guidance of the Holy Spirit and subject to His direction and control, then Paul did have a missionary strategy."[2]

Almost certainly, Paul and Barnabas did not formulate a strategy before departing on their first missionary journey, but it seems clear that over time Paul did develop a pattern of ministry that could be described as a strategy. What, then, was Paul's strategy or *modus operandi*?[3]

Paul served as an itinerant church planter. He traveled from city to city, planting churches. In some cities he only stayed a few weeks or months, but he clearly functioned as an itinerant church planter. In fact, he never stayed more than three years in any city during his missionary journeys. Paul often described himself as an *apostle*. John Polhill defines an apostle as "a sort of pioneer missionary who had received a direct calling from the risen Christ to establish work on a new field. An apostle was a groundbreaker."[4] This description fits Paul very well. He explained his aim in Romans 15:20—"I make it my ambition to preach the gospel, not where Christ has already been named, lest I build on someone else's foundation." The theory and practice of indigenous missions emphasize the responsibility of missionaries as pioneer church planters who do not remain to pastor the churches they plant.

Paul's approach to evangelizing regions was to plant churches in cities from which the gospel would permeate the surrounding areas. Luke mentioned this in Acts 19:10—"all the residents of Asia heard the word of the Lord, both Jews and Greeks." Roland Allen notes this, also: "St Paul's theory of evangelizing a province was not to preach in every place in it himself, but to establish centres of Christian life in two or three important places from which the knowledge might spread into the country round. . . . He intended

---

[2] J. Herbert Kane, *Christian Missions in Biblical Perspective* (Grand Rapids: Baker Book House, 1976), p. 73.
[3] Ibid., pp. 75-85. This material by Herbert Kane is the basis for this section of the chapter.
[4] John B. Polhill, *Paul & His Letters* (Nashville: Broadman & Holman, 1999), p. 441.

his congregation to become at once a centre of light."[5]

It is not clear why Paul chose to work in some cities but not in others. At least at some times the Holy Spirit guided Paul to a particular place. Acts 16:6-10 reveals how God guided Paul to Macedonia by means of a vision. Perhaps Paul ministered in other cities because he had contacts there or because of a city's importance. Ephesus' importance surely influenced Paul to work there. Roland Allen summarizes:

> At first sight it seems to be a rule which may be unhesitatingly accepted that St Paul struck at the centres of Roman administration, the centres of Hellenic civilization, the centres of Jewish influence, the keys of the great trade routes. We must not, however, allow ourselves to lay over-much stress on these characteristics of the places at which St Paul established his churches. . . . St Paul, plainly did not select where he would preach simply on grounds like these: he was led of the Spirit, and when we speak of his strategic centres, we must recognize that they were natural centres; but we must also recognize that for missionary work they were strategic centres because he made them such.[6]

Paul primarily concentrated his work in four Roman provinces: Galatia, Asia, Macedonia and Achaia. In doing this, the Apostle demonstrated a "concentration strategy" rather than a "diffusion strategy." In a diffusion strategy missionaries present the gospel to as many people as they can as quickly as they can. Using a concentration strategy, missionaries concentrate on a limited area (like Paul) or a particular people group or city. The idea is to establish churches that will be able to reach out to other places and peoples. Herbert Kane described Paul's concentration strategy: "His aim was not simply to cover territory but to plant churches. To accomplish this it was necessary not only to sow the seed but also to reap a harvest. This could best be done by confining his efforts to a fairly restricted area."[7]

Paul normally began his gospel ministry in the local synagogue if there was one (Acts 13:10-15). There were several reasons for this. First, it was Paul's custom to go to the synagogue on the Sabbath. Second, Paul and

---

[5]Roland Allen, *Missionary Methods: St. Paul's or Ours?* 2nd ed. (Grand Rapids: Eerdmans, 1962), p. 12. Michael Green affirms Allen's position in his helpful book, *Evangelism in the Early Church* (Grand Rapids: Eerdmans, 2003), p. 362.

[6]Allen, *Missionary Methods*, p.16.

[7]Kane, *Christian Missions in Biblical Perspective*, p. 75.

Barnabas knew that in the synagogues of the Diaspora they would be invited to read from the Old Testament and make comments on the passage. This would give them at least one opportunity to speak to the synagogue worshipers. Third, Paul believed the gospel was "to the Jew first" (Rom 1:16). Fourth, Paul knew that in the synagogues he would encounter three types of worshipers: Jews, Gentile proselytes to Judaism and God-fearers. The God-fearers were Gentiles who had expressed an interest in the Jewish religion but had not yet formally converted, as had the proselytes. The God-fearers proved to be Paul's most receptive audience. Fifth, the worshipers in the synagogues already knew the Old Testament, and they were already expecting the Messiah. Thus, Paul did not have to explain as much to them as he did to Gentile audiences who had no prior knowledge. Usually, Paul's teaching ministry in the synagogues was short-lived; but when he was expelled, he carried on his teaching and preaching in another place (Acts 18:6-7; 19:9).

Paul never appealed to the churches in Antioch or Jerusalem for funds with which to support the new churches. Rather, he expected the churches to support themselves from the beginning.

Paul appointed elders to lead all the churches he planted. Acts 14:23 (NIV) states: "Paul and Barnabas appointed elders for them in each church and, with prayer and fasting, committed them to the Lord." The process by which the elders were chosen is not clear. John Polhill explains, "The final ministry of the apostles was to establish leadership in the new congregations. For these early churches there was no professional clergy to assume their leadership. Consequently, the pattern of the Jewish synagogues seems to have been followed by appointing a group of lay elders to shepherd the flock. There is some question in this particular instance about who appointed the elders—the apostles or the congregation. The NIV follows the most natural rendering of the Greek construction: Paul and Barnabas appointed the elders" (v. 23).[8]

Paul gave the churches over to the care of the Holy Spirit, but he also visited them and wrote to them periodically. For example, on his second and third missionary journeys, Paul returned to visit the churches in Asia

---

[8]John B. Polhill, *Acts*, NAC (Nashville: Broadman Press, 1992), p. 319.

Minor and Greece. Paul wrote the letters we call the Pauline Epistles in the New Testament to encourage the young churches and address issues that arose in them.

Paul employed a team ministry. We never see Paul working alone; rather, he always worked with a team of missionaries. On his first missionary journey he worked with Barnabas and John Mark. On his second missionary journey Silas, Luke and Timothy accompanied him—Silas from the beginning, with Timothy and Luke joining the team in Asia Minor. This teaming provided Paul with the opportunity to train apprentice missionaries who could undertake important tasks in the future (2 Tim 2:2). Using a team approach also provided Paul with enhanced security and extra workers to assist in his gospel ministry.

Paul preferred to preach to responsive people. The apostle Paul was determined to be both faithful and fruitful. Therefore, he preached where he could achieve good results. Not all people or people groups are equally responsive. Jesus alluded to this in the parable of the sower (Mt 13:1-23). In both Antioch of Pisidia and in Corinth, Paul began his gospel ministry among the Jews; but when they rejected Christ, he turned to the Gentiles (Acts 13:46; 18:6).

Paul maintained close contact with his home church, Antioch of Syria. After his missionary journeys Paul returned to Antioch to report to the church what God had accomplished among the Gentiles (Acts 14:26-28).

Paul became all things to all men. Paul never changed or compromised his message or the doctrines he taught, but he demonstrated flexibility in other ways. When he lived and worked among the Jews, he lived like a Jew. When he lived among the Gentiles, he lived like a Gentile. This must have been difficult for Paul, the former Pharisee, but the love of Christ compelled him to make cultural adaptations for the sake of the gospel (1 Cor 9:19-23).

EARLY INDIGENOUS MISSIONS ADVOCATES

Henry Venn (1796–1873) of the Church Missionary Society (Anglican Church) and Rufus Anderson (1796–1880) of the American Board of Commissioners for Foreign Missions (Congregational Church) first used the term "indigenous church" in the mid-nineteenth century. They developed their theories separately, but they later harmonized their positions through correspondence. Based on their study of the apostle Paul's approach, they wrote about the necessity of planting "three-self" churches—churches that would be self-supporting, self-governing and self-propagating. (Venn originally used the term "self-extending.") They exhorted missionaries to establish churches that could support themselves financially, govern their own affairs and carry out a program of evangelism and missions. They cautioned missionaries about becoming absorbed in pastoring and maintaining churches, insisting that the missionary's primary task must be planting new churches that would be "self-reliant" and "purely native." They instructed their missionaries to train national pastors and hand the care of the churches over to them at the earliest opportunity. Venn coupled the concept of indigenous churches with "euthanasia" in missions. By euthanasia he meant that missionaries should plant churches, train leaders and then move on to new, unevangelized regions. That is, as the national church develops, the mission should decline and eventually disappear in that place. The missionaries would then be assigned to another area. Henry Venn believed that missionaries should always be temporary workers, not permanent fixtures.[9]

John L. Nevius (1829–93), a Presbyterian missionary to China, built on Venn and Anderson's indigenous principles in his classic work *Planting and Development of Missionary Churches*. Nevius developed a set of principles that came to be called "The Nevius Plan":

1. Christians should continue to live in their neighborhoods and pursue their occupations, being self-supporting and witnessing to their co-workers and neighbors.

2. Missions should only develop programs and institutions that the national church desired and could support.

3. The national churches should call out and support their own pastors.

4. Churches should be built in the native style with money and materials given by the church members.

---

[9]To learn more about Henry Venn, see Max Warren, ed., *To Apply the Gospel: Selections from the Writings of Henry Venn* (Grand Rapids: Eerdmans, 1971). To learn more about Rufus Anderson, see R. Pierce Beaver, ed., *To Advance the Gospel: Selections from the Writings of Rufus Anderson* (Grand Rapids: Eerdmans, 1967).

5. Intensive biblical and doctrinal instruction should be provided for church leaders every year.

In his writings, Nevius criticized the heavily subsidized work that most missions carried on in China. Nevius's principles had little impact in China, because most of the missionaries there rejected his method. They preferred to maintain their mission stations, control the Chinese, and financially subsidize churches, pastors, and institutions. However, when the American Presbyterians and Methodists began their work in Korea in the 1880s, the new missionaries realized their inexperience. One of them had read some articles by Nevius, so he suggested they invite John Nevius to teach them. He and his wife traveled to Korea in 1890 and spent several weeks coaching the novice missionaries. They adopted his plan and enjoyed great success.[10]

ROLAND ALLEN

Roland Allen (1868–1947), an Anglican priest, served as a missionary in China with the Society for the Propagation of the Gospel in Foreign Parts from 1892 until 1904. Like Nevius, he criticized the methods employed by most missionaries in China. He wrote several books and many articles, but he expressed his philosophy of indigenous missions most clearly in two books: *Missionary Methods: St. Paul's or Ours?* (1912) and *The Spontaneous Expansion of the Church* (1927).

Allen devoted much of his writing to exhorting missionaries to follow the pattern set by the apostle Paul. For example, in *Missionary Methods: St. Paul's or Ours?* he stated, "We must allow to his methods a certain character of universality, and now I venture to urge that since the Apostle, no other has discovered or practiced methods for the propagation of the Gospel better than his or more suitable to the circumstances of our day. It would be difficult to find any better model than the Apostle in the work of establishing new churches. At any rate this much is certain, that the Apostle's methods succeeded exactly where ours have failed."[11]

Allen emphasized the role of the Holy Spirit in missions and encouraged missionaries to work in itinerant church planting, trusting the Holy Spirit

---

[10]John L. Nevius, *The Planting and Development of Missionary Churches* (Hancock, N.H.: Monadnock Press, 2003).

[11]Allen, *Missionary Methods*, p. 147.

to develop the churches. He certainly affirmed the three "selfs," but he emphasized "self-propagating" most of all. He believed a church could not be indigenous if it was not reproducing itself. Allen's main principles are these:

All permanent teaching must be intelligible and so easily understood that those who receive it can retain it, use it and pass it on. Allen insisted that the teaching provided by missionaries must be easily understood so that the learners could teach it to others.

All organizations should be set up in a way that national Christians can maintain them. By Allen's time, the work in China had become highly institutionalized. There were missionary stations (compounds), schools, Christian colleges and universities, orphanages, seminaries, publication centers, agricultural centers, hospitals, dispensaries and vocational training centers. Allen doubted that the Chinese churches desired all these institutions, and he was certain they could not support them all.

Church finances should be provided and controlled by the local church members. Roland Allen fervently believed that the local churches should be supported financially through the tithes and offerings given by the members. He disagreed with the common practice of remitting all the contributions to the diocese or missions headquarters.

Christians should be taught to provide pastoral care for each other. The people of China often suffered famine due to drought, floods and pestilence. During the periodic famines, the missionaries provided rice for the members of the churches. This is understandable, even commendable, because the missionaries could not bear to see their converts starve. On the other hand, during the famines many Chinese would join the local church to receive the rice. This practice gave birth to the phrase—"rice Christian." Roland Allen did not oppose feeding the hungry, but he believed the local Christians should be taught to care for each other, rather than relying on foreign missionaries.

Missionaries should give national believers the authority to exercise spiritual gifts freely and at once. Consistent with his emphasis on the Holy Spirit, Allen believed strongly that the Holy Spirit had given the local Christians all the spiritual gifts necessary to lead the churches. He believed one of the main hindrances to the growth of the churches overseas was that the missionaries refused to relinquish control to local Christian leaders.

Allen's principles have influenced many twentieth-century missiologists, most prominently Donald McGavran, the founder of the Church Growth Movement.

TWENTIETH-CENTURY ADVOCATES

Melvin Hodges (1909–1986), a missionary to Latin America and mission administrator with the Assemblies of God, wrote *The Indigenous Church* (1953). Widely used in Bible college and seminary missions courses, this book expressed the ideas of Venn, Anderson, Nevius and Allen in an updated, popular format. Hodges acknowledged the difficulty missionaries experience in changing a mission field from a subsidized approach to an indigenous approach. He also emphasized training national workers and giving them responsibility for the care of the churches, freeing the missionaries to concentrate on starting new churches. Another prominent advocate of indigenous missions has been Charles Brock. After a long and successful career as a church planter in the Philippines, Brock has circled the globe teaching indigenous church planting.[12]

CHURCH GROWTH MOVEMENT

In the 1950s Donald McGavran founded what came to be called the Church Growth Movement. We can mark the beginning of the movement with the publication of McGavran's book *The Bridges of God* in 1955. After McGavran retired from missionary service he became the founding dean of the School of World Mission at Fuller Theological Seminary in 1965. One of the first professors he hired was Alan Tippett, an Australian Methodist who had served as a missionary in the South Pacific. In his book *Verdict Theology in Missionary Theory*, Alan Tippett (1911–88) updated the three-self formula of Henry Venn. The writings of Tippett, McGavran and others show that the Church Growth Movement accepted and built on the work of the earlier proponents of indigenous missions.

In *Verdict Theology* Tippett proposed a six-fold description of an indigenous church:

1. Self-image. The church sees itself as being independent from the mission;

---

[12]See Charles Brock, *Indigenous Church Planting* (Neosho, Mo.: Church Growth International, 1994).

that is, the church has self-identity. It is serving as Christ's church in its locality.

2. Self-functioning. The church is capable of carrying on all the normal functions of a church—evangelism and missions, worship, discipling, fellowship and ministry—without the assistance of expatriate missionaries.

3. Self-determining. This means the church can and does make its own decisions (self-governing in earlier writings). The local churches do not depend on the missionary to make their decisions for them; rather, they rely upon the guidance of the Holy Spirit and the Holy Bible. Tippett echoes Venn in saying that the mission has to die for the church to be born.

4. Self-supporting. The church carries its own financial burdens and finances its own service projects. This means the national church supports itself with the tithes and offerings given by its own members rather than with financial assistance from abroad.

5. Self-propagation. The national church sees itself as responsible for carrying out the Great Commission. The church gives itself wholeheartedly to evangelism and missions—locally, nationally and internationally.

6. Self-giving. An indigenous church knows the social needs of its community and endeavors to minister to those needs.

Tippett summarizes his understanding of the indigenous church with this definition: "When the indigenous people of a community think of the Lord as their own, not a foreign Christ; when they do things as unto the Lord, meeting the cultural needs around them, worshipping in patterns they understand; when their congregations function in participation in a body which is structurally indigenous; then you have an indigenous church."[13]

In recent years some missiologists have suggested adding a seventh mark to Tippett's list: self-theologizing. They believe a truly indigenous church will develop its own theology, true to the Bible but expressed in culturally appropriate ways. These theologies would affirm the central doctrines of

---

[13]Alan R. Tippett, *Verdict Theology in Missionary Theory* (Lincoln, Ill.: Lincoln Christian College Press, 1969), p. 136.

the Christian faith, but they would express them using metaphors and concepts that reflect their own unique cultures. Historically, this has been the last mark to manifest itself.

CONTEMPORARY APPLICATION

Today, missiologists talk and write more about "contextualization" than they do about indigenous missions. Students find it difficult to differentiate the two concepts. Actually, contextualization emphasizes the clear and accurate communication of the biblical message of salvation. That is, contextualization focuses on effective crosscultural communication. Indigenization focuses on the churches that result from good missionary work. It has been said that good contextualization will result in indigenization, and that is true.

Missionaries who seek to establish indigenous churches should keep these principles in mind as they begin their work:

Missionaries should plant churches with their desired goal in mind. Sometimes missionary trainers call this "the End Vision." This means that the desired outcome—indigenous churches—should influence the methods employed. The Bible teaches us that we shall reap what we sow (2 Cor 9:6). That is certainly true in church planting. If you employ a highly subsidized approach to church planting, then it will prove quite difficult to transition to a self-supporting national church.

There will always be a dynamic tension between supracultural doctrines and variable cultural traits. Basic Christian doctrines like the virgin birth of Jesus Christ and the inspiration of the Scriptures are true in every culture and at every time. However, the church must adapt itself to the cultures it enters. For example, many churches in Indonesia worship on Fridays because that is the day off for their members. Sunday is certainly the preferred day for worship, but in light of the situation in Indonesia, worshiping on Friday is permissible. Or, Christians in North America typically sit on pews or chairs during the worship services; however, worshipers in Indonesia often sit on mats on the floor. Many other examples could be mentioned.

Church planters should expect the churches to support themselves from the beginning. We do not find any mention in the New Testament of the apostle Paul soliciting the church in Antioch of Syria or in Jerusalem for money for the new churches in Asia Minor. On the contrary, Paul solicited donations from the new churches in Greece and Asia Minor to relieve the suffering of the saints in Jerusalem, who were suffering because of a famine in Judea (1 Cor 16:1-3). This approach could be compared to "tough love." An indigenous approach to church planting teaches the new congregations to be self-supporting from the beginning. Sometimes this results in slower growth in the beginning, but it produces greater results later. If the church planter uses lots of money in church planting, then the availability of funds will determine the number of churches that can be planted. However, if the church planter employs an indigenous approach, then there is no limit on the number of churches that can be planted.

Bible study groups should be encouraged to make basic decisions even before they organize as churches. Often, the church planter will invite people to gather for Bible study on a regular basis. These Bible study groups develop naturally into house churches. The church planter can encourage indigenous decision-making by encouraging the members of the Bible study group to make their own decisions—like when and where to meet—long before the Bible study group becomes a church.

Missionaries should encourage new congregations to evangelize their communities and seek opportunities to begin new churches. The church planter should inculcate evangelism and church planting and missions into the DNA of the new congregations. The church planter should encourage new believers to share their testimony with their family, friends, neighbors and coworkers. The church planter also should assist the new congregations to identify opportunities for church planting. Church planters should teach the missionary mandate of the Bible. In this way even new Christians and congregations will understand their part in the expansion of Christ's Kingdom.

Missionaries should always use reproducible methods of evangelism, teaching, preaching and leadership. This means the church planter should evangelize, pray, lead worship, preach and lead in ways the local believers can copy. In other words, the church planter should intentionally model methods the new believers and novice pastors can imitate. For example, in the 1950s, a missionary church planter worked hard at planting churches in the southern Philippines. He purchased a truck, tent, lights, benches, electrical generator, movie projector and films. He would go to a village or town and set up his tent, lights, projector, etc. Then he would publicize free movies. This was quite an attraction in the rural Philippines in that era. He would show half of a movie, preach a gospel message and show the second half of the movie. He would remain in the town or village until he had won some people to Christ, baptized them, discipled them and organized them into a church. Then, he would go on to the next village. Using this method, the faithful missionary planted more than forty churches. Sadly, few of these churches ever reproduced. The church planting method demonstrated for them required a truck, tent, generator, projector and films. They could not afford that equipment, so they did not plant daughter churches.

Missionaries should give priority to developing nationals to serve as church leaders. There will never be enough foreign missionaries to evangelize the world. The only hope for world evangelization is to multiply pastors, evangelists, church planters and missionaries. Jesus spent a lot of time training his twelve disciples so they could continue his mission (Jn 20:21) Paul understood this principle also, and he trained a number of workers to assist him in his missionary endeavors. From the beginning, missionary church planters should pray that God will raise up workers from among the new disciples (Mt 9:35-38). They should be sensitive to the leading of the Holy Spirit in this regard and then mentor those who demonstrate spiritual gifts.

Missionaries should view themselves as temporary church planters rather than permanent pastors. Henry Venn and Rufus Anderson stressed the temporary nature of missionary work. They taught that church planters should seek to work themselves out of a job. If they do their work well, the time will come when they are no longer needed in that place or among that people group. This is a difficult thing for some missionaries. Many missionaries were trained in seminary to serve as pastors, and they may have had experience in pastoring a church. Thus, when they have established a church, there is a natural desire to stay and develop that congregation. This approach could be called *entrepreneurial church planting*. That is not a bad thing in some contexts, but generally in international missions, church planters are expected to be *apostolic* church planters. This means they are expected to plant a cluster of reproducing churches and then move on to another area—just as the apostle Paul did. Another difficulty for missionary church planters is psychological bonding. It is difficult to pour oneself into a group of people and then leave them. Acts 20 shows how Paul had bonded with the believers in Ephesus. Separation was hard for the Ephesians, and we can assume it was difficult for Paul, also. Tom Steffen's helpful book *Passing the Baton* explains how church planters can develop and implement an effective exit strategy.[14]

Missionaries should resist the temptation to establish institutions and wait for the national church to take the initiative. It is a temptation for missionaries to insist that the new national churches need all the institutions and programs the missionaries knew "back home." These include: Christian camps or retreat centers, Christian bookstores, Bible colleges, etc. These are certainly not bad things, but their development should arise from felt needs expressed by local believers. One missionary sought to raise money for choir robes for the choir at the church he planted in Central Asia. When asked why his choir needed robes, he replied, "My church back home uses choir robes, and we need them here, also."

Missionaries must allow the national churches to develop theologies and practices that are biblical yet appropriate in their cultural settings. One telling criticism of Christianity around the world is that it is a "foreign religion." Truly indigenous churches should manifest worship and practices that are consistent with the Bible but also reflect the local culture. In this way the national church will not seem "imported."

SUMMARY

As you have read, the key descriptors of an indigenous church are self-supporting, self-governing and self-propagating. Were Henry Venn and Rufus Anderson correct? Do these three "selfs" accurately reflect the apostle Paul's missionary practice? It is clear that Paul expected the churches he planted to support themselves financially from the first. This was not difficult for them because they were house churches led by elders who served voluntarily, at least in the early years of the church. It is also clear that Paul en-

---

[14]Tom Steffen, *Passing the Baton* (La Habra, Calif.: Center for Organizational & Ministry Development, 1993).

couraged his churches to govern themselves under the guidance of the Holy Spirit. Paul did not hesitate to correct doctrinal or ethical errors, but neither did he try to micromanage the churches. Rather, he allowed them to govern their own affairs and only counseled them when asked for advice or when a crisis arose. Last, Paul praised the churches for their efforts in evangelism. For example, Paul applauded the church in Thessalonica for its evangelism: "The Lord's message rang out from you not only in Macedonia and Achaia— your faith in God has become known everywhere. Therefore, we do not need to say anything about it" (1 Thess 1:8 NIV).[15] So, yes, the apostle Paul did establish the approach to missionary work that we call indigenous missions. Therefore, missionaries in this generation should seek to follow his example and plant reproducing churches.

---

[15]For more on Paul's understanding of the church's responsibility in regard to evangelism and missions see Robert. L. Plummer, *Paul's Understanding of the Church's Mission* (Waynesboro, Ga.: Paternoster, 2006).

11

Paul and Church Planting

♦ ♦ ♦

Ed Stetzer with Lizette Beard

The one-hundredth anniversary of Roland Allen's *Missionary Methods: St. Paul's or Ours?* raises the issue of whether Allen's work is relevant to missions study today. To reevaluate a previous analysis of Paul's method is not to dismiss its value but to seek a better understanding of how its insights speak in today's contexts. A study of this nature can help guide missiological thought—specifically that of church planters—on how one begins to study Paul and his methods with a holistic theological, practical and contextual approach.

In our time, church planters can quickly jump to a model to replicate—and there are so many—or a method to use, rather than seek transformative change in how they think about or do missionary work.[1] To learn from Paul is not to glean merely one new good idea but to see the whole of his efforts and strategy and understand how they worked in his time. As W. M. Ramsay concluded, "The life and the nature of one who has influenced human history so profoundly as St Paul must be studied afresh by every successive age," recognizing that these attempts will not be perfect but rather will

---

[1] Roland Allen, *Missionary Methods: St. Paul's or Ours?* (London: Robert Scott, 1912; repr. Mansfield Centre, Conn.: Martino Publishing, 2011), p. 6.

guide believers today to study Paul's ministry and writings for themselves.[2]

Christians must look at their time, culture, and situation; seek the Spirit for guidance in their work; and do missions in their own day and time. Beginning with a holistic view of how Paul did these very things will move believers to a similar process for today. In this section, we will look at how Roland Allen and other Pauline scholars outline the success of Paul's methodologies.

In *Missionary Methods*, Allen contends that Paul's effectiveness did not rest in his lineage, his education, or the culture or time in which he lived and ministered.[3] It had become common, according to Allen, for missionaries to dismiss Paul as a model due to his unique apostolic authority and blessing. However, Allen argues that simple and practical examples from Paul's ministry are still applicable to missionaries. The problem many people have with the effectiveness of Paul's church planting methodology, Allen says, has less to do with an understanding and practice of them and more that so many ineffective methodologies have claimed to be based on Paul's methodology when they actually showed no resemblance at all.[4] While these missionaries may have traveled widely and preached the gospel, all the while claiming they followed Paul's example, Allen believes that often they fail to establish the foundational elements of the local church that are necessary to foster and sustain growth. This firm establishment of a church body, he says, was integral to Paul's church planting success.[5]

Eckhard Schnabel, in his book *Paul the Missionary*, affirms the need for Allen to be read today, summarizing Allen's view that the "political, geographical, moral and social conditions" of Paul's time afforded the apostle no advantage in proclaiming the gospel over those available to the missionaries of Allen's day.[6] Allen identifies another reason why Paul's methods are often disregarded in the Western context: Western pride. In general, he says, Western missionaries tend to be impatient, self-assertive, self-reliant and

---

[2]Sir W. M. Ramsay, *Pauline and Other Studies in Early Christian History*, rev. ed. (New York: Church Growth International, 1908).

[3]Allen, *Missionary Methods*, p. 4.

[4]Ibid., p. 5.

[5]Ibid.

[6]Eckhard J. Schnabel, *Paul the Missionary: Realities, Strategies and Methods* (Downers Grove, Ill.: IVP Academic, 2008), p. 11-12.

have an attitude of superiority—believing that the expansion of Christianity is entirely dependent on their endeavors. Western missionaries also hold tightly to their own methods and models through their own law and customs, and Allen is adamant that this obstinacy does not follow the example of Paul who emphasized first a reliance on the Holy Spirit. Paul cultivated a spirit of humility and emphasized the need to die to self and live for Christ. According to Allen, Paul so distrusted established and organized structures that he seemed nothing less than "dangerous" to the Jewish Christians of his day.[7]

In his book *Paul: Apostle of God's Glory in Christ: A Pauline Theology*, Tom Schreiner describes Paul as an "apostolic missionary" who was called and commissioned to start churches.[8] Understanding Paul as a missionary helps one to understand the nature of his letters, written to help the new converts remain and be fruitful in their new faith in Christ.[9]

Schreiner describes Paul's posture as a missionary, emphasizing his task of communicating God's grace, yet always reminding his readers that in that grace also came a great deal of work.[10] Paul compares the missionary task to the work of a wrestler, a runner and a boxer—reminding his readers that church planting is not a passive effort.

PAUL'S PREPARATION AS CHURCH PLANTER

In *The Apostle Paul and the Missionary Task*, Arthur Glasser notes that during his renowned conversion, Paul received his call to go out as a missionary and share the gospel.[11] After Paul arrived in Damascus, having been blinded by his encounter, he was instructed in more detail by Ananias, a local Christian, on his assignment to tell about Jesus throughout the world.[12] Because other contributors to this volume have already covered much of this topic, I will just touch on it briefly here.

---

[7]Allen, *Missionary Methods*, pp. 6-7.

[8]Thomas R. Schreiner, *Paul: Apostle of God's Glory in Christ* (Downers Grove, Ill.: InterVarsity Press, 2001), pp. 38-39.

[9]Ibid., pp. 40-41.

[10]Ibid., p. 41.

[11]Arthur F. Glasser, "The Apostle Paul and the Missionary Task," in *Perspectives on the World Christian Movement: A Reader*, ed. Ralph D. Winter and Steven C. Hawthorne (Pasadena, Calif.: William Carey Library, 1999), p. 128.

[12]Schnabel, *Paul the Missionary*, pp. 45-46.

Little is known about Paul's ministry and travels between the time of his conversion and his first missionary journey with Barnabas; however, enough information exists to bring clarity to areas of confusion. Many people assume that it was a relatively short period (a few months to two years) between the two milestone events, which suggests that Paul had little opportunity to observe and experience missions work before his recorded ministry endeavors. These conclusions lead to grossly diminishing the value of Paul's experience and training and assume an almost instantaneous acquisition of expertise as a missionary and church planter.

Glasser offers a rather bold and romantic description of Paul's movements during what he describes as these "hidden years" of Paul where little is recorded and known about the apostle's movements. He notes that in Damascus, Paul fellowshipped with other Jewish believers and witnessed with them in Jewish synagogues.[13] He then describes a persecuted Paul who retreated for three years for "personal withdrawal, spiritual communion, and divine instruction" where Paul discovered God as his strength.[14] From here, it appears that Paul returned to Jerusalem to visit with believers and confirm his understanding of the gospel was correct, and then returned home to Tarsus in Cilicia where he was to serve. Glasser's description and accounts of Paul's ministry preparation invite appreciation but also caution; he takes too many liberties and backs up his ideas with little Scripture. While an abundance of diverse ideas on Paul's movements after his conversion exist, one general outline, compliments of Eckhard Schnabel's *Paul the Missionary,* is as follows: Just a few days after his conversion, Paul was spending time with disciples and was preaching the gospel in Damascus (A.D. 31-32).[15] Paul preached the gospel in Arabia (A.D. 32-33) and Damascus.[16] Paul traveled to Jerusalem to preach in synagogues (A.D. 33-34). He then preached the gospel in Syria and Cilicia where he was proclaiming the faith "he once tried to destroy" and planted churches (A.D. 33-42).[17]

Schnabel disagrees with those who claim Paul's time in Arabia was spent working through theological issues of the Gentile mission; he insists Paul

---

[13]Glasser, "The Apostle Paul and the Missionary Task," p. 128.
[14]Ibid., p. 128.
[15]Schnabel, *Paul the Missionary*, pp. 58-59.
[16]Ibid., p. 58.
[17]Ibid., pp. 40, 58.

saw that Arabia—a "flourishing civilization"—was close enough to Damascus, far enough away from Jerusalem to avoid problems, and a prime
place to go for mission work. Schnabel notes that while Paul does not report
on the degree of success he experienced in Arabia, the aggressive reaction
by officials in the area indicate there were significant numbers of converts,
which was beginning to cause tensions in the cities.[18] The accounts of Paul's
visit to Jerusalem include reports of him preaching the gospel in synagogues,
which would mean he preached to Hellenistic (Greek-speaking) Jews.

From there, Paul went to Cilicia and Syria where he preached the gospel.
Very few details about his activities are available for this period, but it appears that he planted churches he would visit later during his ministry.[19] In
this area, specifically his hometown of Tarsus, Barnabas recruited him in
A.D. 42.[20] It appears the apostle had already established a reputation as an
experienced and capable missionary who would be able to instruct the
large number of Gentile converts in Antioch.[21] In their book *Paul Between
Damascus and Antioch,* Martin Hengel and Anna Maria Schwemer observe
that it is reasonable to conclude that for Barnabas to find Paul, he had established a reputation in Tarsus and had maintained connections with the
"Gentile Christians" in Antioch.[22]

Even without fulsome information, it is reasonable to believe that Paul
was regularly preaching the gospel, engaging in mission, moving throughout
the area, building relationships, and learning and honing the skills of how
to establish churches before he arrived in Antioch with Barnabas. Schnabel
notes that we do not know what Paul was doing as far as his missionary
preaching in the early years, but by the time we have significant information
on him, Paul had twelve years of ministry and missionary experience.[23]

Paul serves as an excellent model for church planters today because he
obeyed Jesus as Lord, fulfilled his calling to share the gospel, and teamed
with other believers in proclaiming this gospel and establishing churches.

---

[18] Ibid., p. 65.
[19] Ibid., p. 67.
[20] Ibid., pp. 69-71.
[21] Ibid., p. 72.
[22] Martin Hengel and Anna Maria Schwemer, *Paul Between Damascus and Antioch: The Unknown Years,* trans. John Bowden (Louisville: Westminster John Knox, 1997), p. 178.
[23] Schnabel, *Paul the Missionary,* p. 31.

We may not know everything Paul did between his conversion and his first missionary journey, but clearly he had become a man of reputation and was known for his work. Paul's experience provides a strong argument for the need for church planters to gain active experience and exposure to churches and ministry opportunities as they prepare to plant churches.

PAUL'S CHURCH PLANTING STRATEGY

According to Allen, Paul's church planting activity followed a pattern of preaching and starting churches in places that were central and influential. From there, the message of the gospel could spread throughout the province. Paul focused on provinces as a whole rather than on specific cities, villages or towns.[24] Allen also notes that Paul limited himself to working within the Roman Empire.[25] His goal did not seem to be planting a church that would become big and important in and of itself, but planting a church that would start new churches in the areas around it.[26]

Allen notes that Paul preached in South Galatia, next to his home region of Cilicia. He was familiar with this area, but he chose to preach in some cities and not in others. Why would Paul intentionally pass through these areas and miss an opportunity to share the gospel and invest in these people? Paul chose to minister and plant churches in areas of higher influence, Allen says, and these churches had strong potential for long-term influence in particular provinces.[27] While current church planting efforts need not deem such a strategy the only model worthy of emulation, there is value in noting this as Paul's preferred option.

Allen points out that Paul was savvy in his selection of significant centers in the Roman civilization for several reasons. First, as a Roman citizen, Paul was able to rely on the protection of Roman officials against the anger of the most radical Jews. Second, he enjoyed the ability to travel peacefully and broadly. And third, despite being expelled from the synagogues, Paul found a relatively tolerant and open field for sharing the gospel message among the Jews of the Diaspora. Allen points out that the idea of the worldwide

---

[24]Allen, *Missionary Methods*, pp. 11-12.
[25]Ibid., p. 12.
[26]Ibid., p. 12-13.
[27]Ibid., p. 12.

Empire, common citizenship, the Empire's multiple ethnicities and the *pax Romana* (peace of Rome) prepared people to grasp Paul's teaching on the Kingdom of Christ. [28] Along the same lines, Rodney Stark, in his book *The Rise of Christianity*, observes that the more urban an area is, the more unconventional it tends to be; and the larger the population of an area, the easier it is to gather and start a group that differs from the accepted norms.[29]

Schnabel does not agree completely with Allen's argument that Paul was attempting to establish "centers of Christian life." Schnabel says Paul intended to spread the gospel throughout a province.[30] He argues that the cities Paul preached in were locally governed and their "radiation" impact would likely have only reached the border of the cities themselves.[31] Social identity was tied to a person's city of origin rather than his province of origin; it seems unlikely to anticipate automatic and significant social influence would spread throughout an entire province.

Schnabel offers a few possible reasons why Paul selected the particular areas in which he planted churches. Paul was called to preach to Gentiles, so he went where he would find them, even when he preached to the Jews first. Proximity also was likely a factor since Paul often went to places near to where he had already preached and planted churches. Established relationships—to him or someone in his traveling party—were likely another reason why Paul chose to travel to Cyprus (Barnabas' home place) and return to Cilicia. Finally, the existence of a Jewish community was a consistent factor due to Paul's practice of beginning in the synagogue and preaching to the Jews before eventually going out to preach to the Gentiles.[32]

Although I tend to agree more with Allen (that Paul did have provinces in mind) than Schnabel, Allen's premise is not without flaws.[33] While it does seem unlikely that Paul saw the evangelization of a province as a foregone conclusion once a church was established in a city, it does not follow that Paul was not intentional in planting churches in cities with the goal of

---

[28]Ibid., p. 14.
[29]Rodney Stark, *The Rise of Christianity: How the Obscure, Marginal, Jesus Movement Became the Dominant Religious Force in the Western World in a Few Centuries* (San Francisco: HarperCollins, 1996), pp. 134, 149.
[30]Schnabel, *Paul the Missionary*, pp. 260-82.
[31]Ibid., p. 283.
[32]Ibid., pp. 260, 282.
[33]Ibid., p. 286.

reaching the provinces. Just as organizations today often place key leaders and offices in centrally located cities to ease travel, Paul equipped churches that could reach out into the provinces and plant churches. Still, planting churches in central cities does not guarantee effective outreach into the surrounding area. Allen wisely cautions that often the best leaders get stuck in these strategic city centers—they get into the cities, but they never mobilize the church to go out into the surrounding area.[34] He says it is important to recognize particular signs in a strategic city center he calls "signs of life": influence, change and significance. "We are sometimes so enamored with the strategic beauty of a place that we spend our time in fortifying it whilst the opportunity for a great campaign passes by unheeded and neglected."[35] In a popular sense, I have called this planting a church in one's head rather than in one's actual location.[36]

The way Paul equipped the new churches in these centers enabled them, while depending on the Holy Spirit, to spread the gospel rather than contain it. Although Allen is adamant that city centers were a part of Paul's strategy, he is quick to point out that Paul's sensitive dependence on the Holy Spirit combined with his understanding of the culture and people, rather than a finely drafted plan or model, led him to these locations and opened the opportunity for him to plant churches of tremendous influence.[37]

PAUL'S INTENTIONAL AND INCLUSIVE STRATEGY

While Paul traveled great distances throughout his missionary career and preached in a variety of settings, his travel strategy appears to have focused on staying in cultural contexts he understood and could build upon, according to Stark.[38] Paul developed a strategy and basic plan as he moved about on his journeys. Allen says that Paul would preach in some cities and skip others; he would start out preaching in a synagogue but be sent away.[39] Glasser notes that in Romans 1:16, Paul writes that the gospel was

---

[34]Allen, *Missionary Methods*, p. 17.
[35]Ibid.
[36]Ed Stetzer, "Planting / Pastoring in Your Head or Your Community?" www.edstetzer.com/2009/11/planting-in-your-head-or-your.html (accessed August 9, 2012).
[37]Allen, *Missionary Methods*, p. 17.
[38]Stark, *The Rise of Christianity*, p. 135.
[39]Allen, *Missionary Methods*, p. 18-19.

"to the Jew first": although known as an apostle to the Gentiles, his actions reveal a commitment to the Jewish community first even in the exercise of that mission.[40]

Allen writes that some of Paul's converts came from the synagogue—Jewish Christians and God-fearing Greeks who brought with them foundational beliefs, familiarity with the Old Testament and experience with public worship. The believers' background was helpful to Paul as he began to instruct young churches.[41] Though they were not the largest group of converts, Allen observes, they were an essential key to the sustained and ongoing teaching of the Old Testament after Paul moved on to his next location.

It appears the majority of Paul's converts came from the "lower commercial and working classes, laborers, freed men, and slaves," Allen writes; yet, Paul did not target them exclusively.[42] It is likely that Paul attracted people who were easily drawn into what is new and different. According to Allen, there is no indication that he tried to keep these people away, but he did not make these his first converts. Instead, he ensured that the churches he planted began with a strong foundation of respectable leaders.[43] While Paul understood cultural differences, he did not foster them. In his book *The Spirit, the Church, and the World*, John Stott argues that when Paul insisted these young churches have pastoral oversight in place and not remain dependent upon the missionaries, he was ensuring their continuation.[44]

PAUL'S CONTEXTUALIZATION IN CHURCH PLANTING

Paul appeared to have strong sociological instincts regardless of whether they were intuitive or intentional. Stark provides several key principles for understanding how and why people adopt a new religion or system of beliefs. One of his first principles is that the willingness of a person or group of people to change beliefs is related to the degree of "cultural continuity" with their current religious beliefs and practices.[45] Stark describes this as a

---

[40]Glasser, "The Apostle Paul and the Missionary Task," p. 130.

[41]Allen, *Missionary Methods*, p. 21-22.

[42]Ibid., p. 24.

[43]Ibid.

[44]John Stott, *The Spirit, The Church, and the World: The Message of Acts* (Downers Grove, Ill.: Inter-Varsity Press, 1990), p. 236.

[45]Stark, *The Rise of Christianity*, p. 137.

natural human tendency to "maximize" a situation or to get the largest benefit with the least amount of sacrifice. This is measured by how much of the old people have to discard (beliefs, actions and relationships) to make room for the new. When a religious convert can hold to parts of their original cultural heritage, Stark says, the sense of cost or sacrifice is lessoned during the transition.[46]

In Paul's ministry, the Gentiles knew something about Jewish culture—especially the "God-Fearers" who were familiar with Jewish theology and monotheism but unwilling to fully convert to the Jewish religion.[47] Glasser believes that God-fearers had already been willing to break with their pagan idolatry but were unwilling to make the full transition to Judaism. They were not well integrated into the Jewish religious community, and they were open to this new one.[48] Stark contends that the mission to the Jews was successful in terms of the steady number of Hellenized Jewish converts to Christianity through the first four or five centuries.[49] He believes this success in reaching the Hellenized Jews related to the cultural continuity of their Jewish heritage and Hellenic cultural elements with Christianity. Stark believes further that the existing social networks facilitated rapid growth.[50] For Michael Pocock, the goal was not simply sharing a message of the faith but equipping the new adherents to live out the faith in their cultural setting.[51] Whole books have been written on Paul's approach to contextualization, and the topic is addressed elsewhere in this volume. While this is not our main focus here, contextualization is an important consideration in church planting.

PAUL'S PREACHING

In his letters to the churches he established, Paul continually requested prayers for the ongoing mission work that was advanced through the "word of the gospel."[52] According to Schreiner, "Paul has no conception of his

---

[46]Ibid., p. 55.
[47]Ibid., p. 137.
[48]Glasser, "The Apostle Paul and the Missionary Task," p. 130.
[49]Stark, *The Rise of Christianity*, p. 138.
[50]Ibid., p. 55.
[51]Michael Pocock, Gailyn Van Rheenen and Douglas McConnell, *The Changing Face of World Missions: Engaging Contemporary Issues and Trends* (Grand Rapids: Baker Academic, 2005), p. 323.
[52]Schreiner, *Paul*, p. 64.

mission advancing apart from the proclamation of the gospel" and that fundamentally the "Pauline mission advances in and through the preached word."[53] Paul planted churches through preaching.

William Baird, in *Paul's Message and Mission*, contends that Paul's conviction about the lost condition of both Jews and Gentiles motivated him to preach the gospel.[54] Paul saw the Gentiles as under the condemnation of God (1 Cor 11:32) and referred to the time as "the present evil age" (Gal 1:4).[55] "After his conversion, the apostle saw all men as standing under the shadow of the cross of Christ which stood in stark judgment on all the pride and pretentions of men," according to Baird.[56] Paul clearly understood that neither legalistic religion nor the Jewish law could justify persons before God.[57] He viewed sin as the reason for mankind's tragic situation and not something from which persons could free themselves.[58] As Baird describes it, mankind's difficult and desperate situation moved Paul to mission to the point that he felt obligated to go and tell.[59]

There is no doubt that Paul had complete confidence in God's power and authority when he preached. However, it would be a mistake for church planters to believe that preaching with confidence alone will make them effective missionaries. Paul was well trained and had earned a reputation as a speaker before his conversion. No doubt, God used those skills along with his confidence as he preached Christ.

Allen outlines some of the recognizable patterns in Paul's preaching. Attempting to connect on a point of common truth or agreement, Paul opened with an appeal to his audience's past. Next, he typically made a statement of facts that could be easily grasped or understood, such as a concept concrete in nature or a story of life and death. Third, he answered questions his audience was inevitably asking in their minds.[60] Finally, he warned about the danger involved in rejecting God's message. Preaching was central to beginning new churches in the ministry of Paul.

[53]Ibid., p. 64.
[54]William Baird, *Paul's Message and Mission* (Nashville: Abingdon, 1960), p. 34.
[55]Ibid.
[56]Ibid.
[57]Ibid., p. 38.
[58]Ibid., pp. 40-41.
[59]Ibid., p. 41.
[60]Allen, *Missionary Methods*, p. 62-63.

GATHERING A CHURCH

What did Paul mean when he used the word "church" or *ekklēsia*? According to Robert Plummer in his book *Paul's Understanding of the Church's Mission*, Paul used it in two ways. First, he referred to "the entire community of persons redeemed by Christ" in all places and all times.[61] Second, he used the term to reference believers in a local setting such as the "church of the Laodiceans" or "the church of God that is in Corinth." This included those meeting in house churches or the believers in a city.[62] Plummer emphasizes that Paul saw his apostolic mission as tied closely to the local gatherings of these believers.[63] This is similar to Schreiner's claim that Paul viewed the local assembly of believers as a church.[64] Paul's frequent use of the term *ekklēsia*, according to Schreiner, indicates that Paul viewed the church as the "new Israel, the new people of God, the fulfillment of what God intended with Israel."[65] When Paul refers to churches (plural), he appears to be emphasizing the relationship between various churches, commending the solidarity among the churches, or pointing out when one church is misled on a particular issue.[66] In his book *Paul's Idea of Community*, Robert Banks observes that Paul's instructions to the church are not a list of tasks to complete but a lifestyle to live. Paul does not admonish believers to go to church to do the activity called "worship." Instead, he instructs them that worship is a whole life of sacrificing and giving of oneself in word and deed, not limited to special times or gatherings.[67] When Paul describes issues related to evangelism and social action, he does not prescribe programs or activities with starting and stopping points. Instead, he instructs believers to be "wise toward outsiders, making the most of the time."[68]

Within relatively short periods of time (five to eighteen months), Paul planted churches that were firmly established as congregations—not just as

---

[61] Robert L. Plummer, *Paul's Understanding of the Church's Mission: Did the Apostle Paul Expect the Early Christian Communities to Evangelize?*, PBM (Milton Keynes, U.K.: Paternoster, 2006), p. 44.
[62] Ibid.
[63] Ibid., p. 45.
[64] Schreiner, *Paul*, p. 332.
[65] Ibid.
[66] Ibid.
[67] Robert J. Banks, *Paul's Idea of Community: The Early House Churches in Their Cultural Setting*, rev. ed., (Peabody, Mass.: Hendrickson, 1994), p. 89.
[68] Ibid.

missions remaining dependent on other churches. Allen notes that Paul equipped these churches with the gospel and the ordinances of the Old Testament, being careful to not make the teaching so complicated it confused them.[69] In full agreement with Allen, Stott notes that Paul and Barnabas did not set up a mission organization; they set up a church, then left and "went home."[70]

Allen emphasizes that a large part of Paul's strategic success resulted from training his very first converts.[71] He describes Paul's work with these first converts as careful nurturing, making quality choices and careful investments in those that would carry on his (Paul's) work once he left. It is on this point that Allen is perhaps the most emphatic about Paul's key to success.[72] He points out that Paul's practice of preaching in a place for a few months required careful consideration of the church's leaders. Consequently, he was able to leave behind established churches that continued to grow and multiply.[73]

Charles Brock writes in *Indigenous Church Planting* that an indigenous church reflects its local culture and context. It is "native, domestic, national."[74] He goes on to offer a five-self description that should identify a local indigenous church plant: self-governing (makes its own decisions); self-supporting (takes care of needs through its members' offerings); self-teaching (members participate in the teaching and training, and public reading of the Bible); self-expressing (local culture is evident in its expressions of worship); and, last, an indigenous plant should be self-propagating (starts other churches).

These very helpful guidelines reflect the holistic establishment of Paul's churches. They protect against too much dependence on outside mission resources and redirect the church toward local and incarnational development.

---

[69]Allen, *Missionary Methods,* p. 89-90.
[70]Stott, *The Spirit, The Church, and the World,* p. 235.
[71]Allen, *Missionary Methods*, p. 82.
[72]Ibid., p. 82.
[73]Ibid., p. 83-84.
[74]Charles Brock, *Indigenous Church Planting: A Practical Journey* (Neosho, Mo.: Church Growth International, 1994), p. 89.

GATHERING AND TEACHING THE NEW CONVERTS

When people believed Paul's preaching, he gathered them for times of teaching and worship. Stott describes this teaching and exhortation to remain true to the faith as key to Paul's ability to establish enduring churches.[75] At all points, Paul acknowledges that the church was brought into being by God and belongs solely to God.[76] Schreiner asserts Paul's emphasis on "perseverance" in the faith for converts. It was not enough to lead someone to be a convert; it was essential that they persevere to the end. This was important to Paul's approach to planting churches. For Paul, it was not enough that churches be started, they must be established and persevere.[77]

THE FINANCES OF CHURCH PLANTING

Church planting almost always involves some type of financing, and Paul deals with the issue throughout his ministry. Addressing the complex issue of finances in the missionary endeavor, Allen acknowledges that the financial arrangements in any missionary activity have a serious impact on the relationships between the missionaries and those they are reaching with the gospel.[78] He notes the unique tone and direction when Paul wrote about finances compared to how missionaries in his day discuss them. Paul's tone toward money indicates it did not matter to him, but he did care about how much it mattered to those to whom he was ministering.[79] He did not critique those who took financial support, but he was extremely cautious of any appearance of taking money himself.[80] He did not allow himself to become indebted to any because of their donations. Allen emphasizes that Paul's example applied also to the churches depending on one another. Each church should support itself financially, and the believers should assist each other in times of need, rather than look to outside help.[81]

Allen views the churches' need to prove they are established a problem, writing that too much emphasis is placed on buildings and furniture.[82] He

---

[75]Stott, *The Spirit, The Church, and the World*, p. 235.
[76]Schnabel, *Paul the Missionary*, p. 233.
[77]Schreiner, *Paul*, p. 67.
[78]Allen, *Missionary Methods*, p. 49.
[79]Ibid.
[80]Ibid., p. 49-50.
[81]Ibid., p. 52; 2 Cor 8:13.
[82]Ibid., p. 52-53.

emphasizes that the value in the things used in missionary endeavors (equipment, buildings) or the power in them is not in and of themselves to "produce spiritual results." "The value of the outward things is derived from the spirit which animates them and gives them being."[83]

Allen's argument rings true in modern missionary practice. When even the most basic supplies are imported into a culture for use in worship—anything that a church could not resource on their own—this tends to create an immediate mindset of dependency among new converts.[84] Allen believes that small steps such as these eventually shape new converts into passive church participants (those who receive) rather than those empowered for gospel mission and work.[85] He also rightly points out another finances-related problem: when church planters have too many financial and physical resources, they "cease to be movable evangelists, and tend to become pastors."[86]

Allen highlights Paul's emphasis on churches sharing a "mutual responsibility" for every aspect—baptism, ordination, discipline, unity. "The Church was a brotherhood, and the brethren suffered if any improper person was admitted to their society."[87] Paul helped get them started but then released the church to carry on. "Just as he baptized three or four and then committed the responsibility for admitting others to those whom he had baptized, so he ordained three or four and committed the authority for ordaining others into their hands."[88]

PAUL LEAVING, VISITING AND FOLLOWING UP

Schnabel writes that because Paul's travels are so frequently referenced, often his pastoral investment in the churches he planted is underemphasized. "Paul's repeated visits to the churches which he had established demonstrates [sic] the significance of his 'anxiety for all the churches' (2 Cor 11:28) in his understanding of the missionary task."[89] His later writings and

---

[83]Ibid., p. 54.
[84]Ibid., p. 56.
[85]Ibid.
[86]Ibid., p. 57.
[87]Ibid., pp. 98-100.
[88]Ibid., p. 100.
[89]Schnabel, *Paul the Missionary*, p. 196.

visits with these churches indicate that Paul left churches well and was wel-
comed and respected when he returned. He exhibits no sign of regret that
he left these churches too quickly.[90] There is no sign that Luke, who recorded these journeys, felt that Paul had made mistakes or used poor
judgment in his missionary travels.[91] In fact, Luke describes Paul's travels as
"journeys guided by the Holy Ghost to a successful issue."[92]

What did Paul teach these first converts and disciples in his churches?
According to Allen, Paul kept it simple, focusing on the essentials that provided building blocks for continued learning. He began with a simple and
practical doctrine of God: the Father, Creator; the Son, Redeemer, Savior;
and the Holy Spirit, indwelling source of strength.[93] Paul appears to have
emphasized teaching about Holy Communion, Allen notes, with repeated
teaching on the significance of the death and resurrection of Christ. He
rarely taught on the parables or miracles of Christ.[94] Looking to Paul and
Allen's commentary for guidance in church planting requires discernment
regarding Paul's motives in adopting these emphases. As mentioned previously, Paul had a very clear intention to establish churches in relatively
short periods of time. His exclusion of Christ's miracles and parables should
not be seen as a dismissal of their value in the instruction of the church, yet
perhaps Paul did not see them of first importance in the early months of
planting a church. Clearly Paul emphasized equipping the believers to feed
themselves spiritually and to help them understand their place in the whole
story. Allen describes it as, "Paul was always calling out more and more the
capacities of the people in the church."[95]

In summary, Allen says that Paul left the churches he planted with the
basics of the gospel, the sacraments of the Lord's Supper and baptism,
emphasis on the death and resurrection of Christ, and further study in
the Old Testament.[96] Allen asserts that teaching the basics was very
strategic; the simplicity enabled the early converts to grasp the new faith,

---

[90] Allen, *Missionary Methods*, p. 16.
[91] Ibid.
[92] Ibid.
[93] Ibid., p. 87.
[94] Ibid., p. 88.
[95] Ibid., p. 89.
[96] Ibid., p. 90.

root themselves in it and move forward. [97]

Paul's teaching of these basics indicates he knew the material well and was able not only to prioritize it but also to communicate it simply. Moreover, he exhibited immense trust in the Holy Spirit and Christ, Allen writes: "It is characteristic of St Paul that he had such faith in Christ and in the Holy Spirit indwelling in the Church that he did not shrink from risks."[98]

Simply put, Paul did not stay long when he started churches. Allen notes, though it seems paradoxical, that the brevity of Paul's time with the churches he planted is likely what helped them succeed. He believes that had Paul stayed longer, he may have actually stunted the growth and progress of maturing believers. Paul's practice of planting a church, equipping new converts for a period of time, and then departing gave them room to grow into leadership roles in these new churches.[99] Bartholomew and Goheen describe Paul as having a "missionary pastor's heart" and being a leader who worked to see his churches become a "vibrant, witnessing community that would point to the coming kingdom of God in life, word, and deed."[100] Paul remained long enough to teach the new believers how to "embody the good news" so they could be faithful in their task.[101]

Allen emphasizes how much Paul depended on the Holy Spirit and trusted the discernment of the new converts to do the same. He did not encourage the development of a Christian subculture among these churches; in fact, the members of these churches were more immersed in their local culture than many churches today would feel comfortable being. Allen notes that Paul did not forbid these converts to continue in work that exposed them to intense idolatry nor did he urge them to retreat from the secular culture into a Christian subsociety. He did not insist that they remove their children from heathen schools or lead his early converts to escape from society.[102] Allen acknowledges that while it would have been easier for Paul to minister had these converts stepped away

---

[97]Ibid.
[98]Ibid., p. 91.
[99]Ibid., p. 93.
[100]Craig G. Bartholomew and Michael W. Goheen, *The Drama of Scripture: Finding Our Place in the Biblical Story* (Grand Rapids: Baker Academic, 2008), p. 187.
[101]Ibid., pp. 187-88.
[102]Allen, *Missionary Methods*, p. 119.

from so many idolatrous and heathen influences, evangelizing would have been more difficult.[103]

TEACHING THE EARLY CHURCH TO LIVE 'SENT'

Paul's example of going out and proclaiming the message of God's salvation was essentially a new, specifically Jewish-Christian endeavor.[104] Hengel and Schwemer describe a significant shift in the methods of Paul from his Jewish heritage. While Israel's history consistently shows God as a "sending God" (for example, sending help, kings, prophets and ultimately Jesus), the Jews as a religious people were not known as a people aggressively sent to non-Jews.[105] Rather, they were considered in Paul's day as an attractive religious option to many outside the Jewish tradition.[106] According to Plummer, Paul actively taught and expected these new churches to share the gospel message they had received. His writings indicate that he expected every believer to be intentional and proactive in sharing the message of Jesus and not to rely either on being observed for their good deeds or merely answering questions about their faith.[107]

In his letter to the Philippians, Paul celebrates that Christ is proclaimed. His language indicates he is referring to ordinary believers, not a missionary or clergy class of believers, writes Plummer.[108] In his letter to the Ephesians, Paul admonishes the church of Ephesus to be ready or prepared to move forward in sharing the gospel.[109] Finally, Plummer cites Paul's command to the Corinthians to imitate him by proclaiming the gospel to lead others to Christ and live as a missionary of the gospel—even to the point of enduring persecution.[110]

CONCLUSION

What does Paul's example mean in practical terms for those training and equipping future generations of church planters? Many lessons could be

---

[103]Ibid., p. 120.
[104]Hengel and Schwemer, *Paul Between Damascus and Antioch*, p. 75.
[105]Ibid.
[106]Ibid.
[107]Plummer, *Paul's Understanding*, p. 71.
[108]Ibid., pp. 73.
[109]Ibid., p. 77-79.
[110]Ibid., p. 84.

drawn—and whole books have been written on the subject—however, I will share four concluding thoughts. Based on Paul's model, we need to equip planters to be focused on the basics of the gospel, the nature of the church, flexibility of mission and passion for the nations.

The basics of the gospel. Every generation is called to share the good news of Jesus Christ with those who have never heard; there can be no successful church planting without gospel proclamation. For many modern planters, particularly in the West, there are many tools and resources available for helping to plant a church. Church starters can write out a strategy and marketing plan, but those who struggle to succinctly explain Jesus' gospel are not ready to plant Jesus' church. Here is a definition that I use to keep me focused on the priority of the work I am called to do:

> The gospel is the good news that God, who is more holy than we can imagine, looked upon with compassion, people, who are more sinful than we would possibly admit, and sent Jesus into history to establish His Kingdom and reconcile people and the world to himself. Jesus, whose love is more extravagant than we can measure, came to sacrificially die for us so that, by His death and resurrection, we might gain through His grace what the Bible defines as new and eternal life.[111]

Genuine church planting, as modeled by Paul, is gospel planting. Obviously, Paul's priority was clear. When describing his focus, he explained, "I delivered to you as of first importance . . . that Christ died for our sins" (1 Cor 15:3). He did not point to a strategy of urban planting; he pointed to the gospel. As we plant, we must do the same.

Planters must see the gospel, live it by the power of the Holy Spirit and lead others to this new life. If we aren't equipping planters for gospel-centered discipleship, why plant churches?

The nature of the church. Paul's legacy was simple: he preached the gospel and planted churches. Churches mattered deeply to Paul. He was not just winning converts; he was planting congregations so that "the manifold wisdom of God might now be made known to the rulers and authorities in the heavenly places" (Eph 3:10).

---

[111]Ed Stetzer, "EdStetzer.com: Gospel Definitions," www.edstetzer.com/2009/11/gospel-definitions .html (accessed August 30, 2012).

Paul planted churches—with leadership, functions and attributes. For many church planters, they need Paul's focus and commitment to the church and its being—a commitment to ecclesiology.

The flexibility of mission. Roland Allen reminded us that rapid reproduction requires empowered leaders and permission-giving structures. Today, that need remains. Rapid reproduction of churches in North America will never happen as long as we are focused on sustaining buildings, budgets and a bigger-is-better mentality. We must be advocates for all kinds of new church planters: bivocational, ethnic, lay, house churches and more.

As one example, bivocational-led church plants model what the Bible teaches: every believer is on mission, every member a minister. This is easier to grasp when the lead pastor is also a shop foreman or Web designer forty hours a week. Bivocational-led church plants will be the leaders in transitioning us from an attractional mindset to a missional one. A gospel-centered body of believers willing to carry the message of Christ to where the people are, rather than waiting to be found, is essential for reaching future generations with the gospel.

Passion for the nations. Paul's commitment to Spain has always fascinated me. He mentions it more than once. Yet, for me it is not simply a geographic destination. It is a spiritual yearning. Paul wanted to go to the Gentiles as far away as possible—and, in Europe at least, that was Spain. As Paul traveled with fellow workers, his desire was that he and they would go where the gospel had not been preached—to the unreached nations.

Paul certainly knew of the words of Jesus and chose his mission focus well. As a church planter (planting another church right now), I know the challenges of planting—organizing outreach, coordinating rental facilities, counseling new believers and working with leaders. It can be overwhelming for any planter. Yet, Paul's passion for the nations reminds me that the task cannot end with my church plant—my church cannot be a cul-de-sac on the Great Commission highway. Instead, my church (like the churches Paul planted) asks, how can we fulfill the words of Jesus?

> All authority in heaven and on earth has been given to me. Go therefore and make disciples of all nations, baptizing them in the name of the Father and of the Son and of the Holy Spirit, teaching them to observe all

that I have commanded you. And behold, I am with you always, to the end of the age. (Matt 28:18-20)

Paul said, "Be imitators of me, as I am of Christ" (1 Cor 11:1). With a focus on the basics of the gospel, the nature of the church, the flexibility of mission, and a passion for the nations, we do indeed hear the teachings of Jesus in the mission of Paul. As we join Jesus on mission, and follow Paul's example, Paul the planter teaches us yet again.

12

PAUL AND CONTEXTUALIZATION

♦♦♦

M. David Sills

Contextualization is a term that has caused a great deal of controversy in recent years. The controversy is surprising, both because contextualization is as old as the Bible itself and because it is impossible to reach, preach and teach the gospel among the nations faithfully without doing it. The controversy stems from a misunderstanding or misuse of the term. Unfortunately, some modern preachers utilize profanity or inappropriate humor in the pulpit and defend the practice by claiming that they are simply contextualizing their message to a modern audience. Other preachers react to such practice by denouncing contextualization. Unfortunately, neither side is correctly defining the term, and the necessary missiological tool of contextualization suffers, bearing witness to the truth of the African proverb, "When elephants fight, the grass gets hurt."

David Hesselgrave and Ed Rommen have defined contextualization as "the attempt to communicate the message of the person, works, Word, and will of God in a way that is faithful to God's revelation, especially as put forth in the teaching of Holy Scripture, and that is meaningful to respondents in their respective cultural and existential contexts."[1] Understood as

---

[1] David Hesselgrave and Edward Rommen, *Contextualization: Gleanings, Methods and Models* (Grand Rapids: Baker, 1989), p. 200.

faithfulness to God's Word in culturally appropriate ways, no one would disagree with contextualization. Such an understanding seeks to avoid the possibility of changing the gospel once for all delivered to the saints and the mistake of preaching in such a way that the hearers cannot understand it. Indeed, simply translating the Bible into the language of the target culture is the first step in contextualization, but it is just the first of many receptor-oriented processes.

CONTEXTUALIZATION AND CONTROVERSY

Ironically, some shy away from contextualization for fear of inadvertently changing the gospel. While contextualization does not change the gospel message, the failure to contextualize actually does. Indeed, though many avoid issues of contextualization in fear of unintentional alteration of the Truth, not contextualizing requires nationals to leave their culture and embrace another to hear the gospel, be discipled, study God's Word and worship God. When people refuse to contextualize in their environment, they become modern-day Judaizers, requiring others become like them before they can come to Christ.

New Testament-era missionaries did not utilize local cultural forms when planting churches but they did have to find effective ways to teach the truths of the Scriptures in other cultures of the Roman Empire, bring the Bible to bear on pagan practices and consider challenges they never faced in Jewish contexts. Introducing Christianity to other cultures is a risky business; teachers have to understand the meaning behind the forms they prohibit or include; otherwise they may communicate something they do not wish to teach. Schnabel points out, "Christians organized no processions or games in honor of their god in which the former Gentiles could have participated in festive celebration. The forms through which they could, together with other Christians, express their faith in God were baptism, the Lord's Supper . . . and prayer."[2] However, missionaries today must be careful when entering people groups that already have similar cultural religious forms. The simple truth is that cultures are not blank slates waiting for missionaries to write Christianity on their hearts.

---

[2]Eckhard J. Schnabel, *Early Christian Mission*, (Downers Grove, Ill.: IVP Academic, 2004), 2:1372.

The degree to which missionaries adapt to the local culture when introducing church forms, Christian culture and their ministry to host cultures is always controversial. The tendency is to think, "Anyone who does more than I do goes too far, and those who do less are not doing enough." In the Muslim contexts of the world today some "contextualization" strategies such as C5 and C6 strategies, Insider Movements and using the Koran in the Camel method of evangelism have resulted in more heat than light, but all perspectives in the controversy admit that some level of adjustment is necessary. Tim Keller points out,

> There is no "non-contextualized" Christianity. Jesus didn't come to earth as a generalized being—by becoming human he had to become a particular human. He was male, Jewish, working-class. If he was to be human he had to become a socially and culturally situated person. So the minute we begin to minister we must "incarnate," even as Jesus did. Actual Christian practices must have both a Biblical form or shape as well as a cultural form or shape. For example, the Bible clearly directs us to use music to praise God—but as soon as we choose music to use, we enter a culture. As soon as we choose a language, as soon as we choose a vocabulary, as soon as we choose a particular level of emotional expressiveness and intensity, as soon as we choose even an illustration as an example for a sermon—we are moving toward the social context of some people and away from the social context of others. At Pentecost, everyone heard the sermon in his or her own language and dialect. But since Pentecost, we can never be "all things to all people" at the very same time. So adaptation to culture is inevitable.[3]

Missionary contextualization seeks to utilize components of local culture that are not religiously charged, thus enabling nationals to understand Christianity and the gospel and avoid the impression that it is a foreign religion for outsiders. Of course using the local language is the first step to communicating this truth, but other aspects are music, leadership styles, financial matters and even preaching styles. Schnabel notes, "Paul disassociates himself from certain methods of public speech. It is obvious and unsurprising that he, a Hellenistic Jew, is knowledgeable of rhetorical

---

[3]Tim Keller, "Advancing the Gospel into the 21st Century, Part III: Context Sensitive," speech given to the Mission America Coalition, New York City, October 2003.

methods. A passage such as 2 Cor 11:4 demonstrates that Paul certainly was aware of the problematic nature and the appropriateness of rhetorical methods for the proclamation of the gospel."[4] Even Western styles of teaching must be adjusted to oral cultures where mentoring and master-apprentice styles are more effective.

Of all the diverse areas of Christianity that must be contextualized in the target culture, such as music, dress, worship times, leadership styles, church buildings, and language, the contextualization of theology seems the most risky when biblical fidelity is the goal. However, contextualized theology simply deals with issues that did not require detailed treatment in the missionary's home culture but do in the target culture. When the missionary is preaching and teaching the Bible in another culture, he may be required to address complex systems and worldviews related to polygamy or teach biblical models of Christianity in matriarchal cultures. Paul Hiebert's essay "The Flaw of the Excluded Middle" can aid missionaries seeking to reach and teach in animistic cultures with highly developed belief systems in spirits and sorcery.[5]

Contextualization also considers physical forms of Christianity and seeks to develop what would be most culturally appropriate in the local context. Outside of contextualization, the kind of building where the church meets is often not even considered by the missionary. He unconsciously thinks his background is normative and seeks to replicate the red brick church he knew at home, complete with pews, a piano and a sign behind the pulpit reporting how many were in Sunday School and brought their

---

[4]Schnabel, *Early Christian Mission* 2:1359.

[5]The "Flaw of the Excluded Middle" was developed by missiologist Paul Hiebert in an article in *Missiology* 10:1 (January, 1982): 35-47, which was later reprinted in chapter 12 of his book, *Anthropological Reflections on Missiological Issues* (Grand Rapids: Baker, 1994). There he identifies representational issues from the countless worldviews of the world's cultures. He notes the entities with which cultures note relationships, such as at the high end a creator deity, angels and saints; a middle level embraced by animistic cultures of the recently departed dead and created spirits that could be benevolent, malevolent or ambivalent; and a lower level of humans and animals. He also identifies a high level of cosmic forces accepted by different cultures such as kismet, fate, predestination and the will of Allah; a middle level accepted by animists and consisting of magic, rituals, sorcery, witchcraft, curses, fetishes, charms, amulets and the like; and a lower level comprised of the mechanical effects that physical objects have such as when we take an aspirin for a headache or an antibiotic for an infection. Hiebert stresses that the Western world emphasizes the high and low spectrums of these options to the exclusion of even acknowledging or recognizing the middle level. This flaw has resulted in a confused gospel that requires proper contextualization to correct.

Bible that day. Interestingly, some have gone to the other end of the continuum and have insisted on house churches on a global scale, even in regions where meeting in a house gives the appearance of being a cult. New missionaries reject the former missionaries' church forms and insist on the new without contextualizing; both extremes are ineffective if they don't consider the cultural context.

Missionaries certainly must adjust the ways they evangelize to the local context. Street meetings may serve well in some countries but be a fatal error in others. Even the practical aspects of living out the Christian life must take into account the matters of context. Speaking of Paul's teaching on Christian living, Schnabel wrote,

> Paul would have had to promote change in practical-theological matters as well: when Jewish believers continued to circumcise their children (which is a plausible assumption), they needed to understand that circumcision was no longer a sign of membership in God's covenant people. Jewish believers had to be instructed to recognize the central significance of Jesus' death on the cross as the normative criterion for the authority of God's revelation in the Torah of the "old" covenant. They had to understand, for example, that the purity laws and the food laws of the Torah are no longer valid, as holiness has been established and granted by Jesus Christ once and for all. This made true integration of Jewish believers and Gentile believers possible.[6]

No consideration of contextualization may overlook the constant vigilance required to remain faithful to the Bible and the unchanging message of the gospel. Tim Keller noted, "Paul does not change the gospel—but he adapts it very heavily. Sure this opens the door to abuses, but to fear and refuse to adapt to culture opens to abuses of the gospel just as much! The balance is to not, on one hand, 'succumb to relativism' nor on the other hand, think contextualization is really avoidable. Both are gospel-eroding errors."[7]

In our world of globalization, cultures are crashing together at increasing rates and in more complex ways. The many versions of Coca-Cola and McDonalds around the world are similar to their USA-based counterparts,

---

[6]Eckhard J. Schnabel, *Paul the Missionary: Realities, Strategies and Methods* (Downers Grove, Ill.: IVP Academic, 2008), p. 237.
[7]Keller, "Advancing the Gospel."

no matter where we find them, but they each have unique local nuances to make them fit wherever they are. Some refer to this dynamic as *glocalization* to indicate the local and global aspects present in the components of our Internet and air travel connected world.

THE BIBLICAL BASIS

Paul states in Romans 10:13, "For 'everyone who calls on the name of the Lord will be saved,'" and while this is comforting, he then asks a series of questions in Romans 10:14-15 that leave us uncomfortable. "How then will they call on him in whom they have not believed? And how are they to believe in him of whom they have never heard? And how are they to hear without someone preaching? And how are they to preach unless they are sent?" The truth is that receiving the gospel message is necessary to be saved. When a missionary from Germany preaches the gospel to Mandarin speakers in China, he has not fulfilled the Great Commission to reach and teach them unless he speaks to them in a language that they can understand. A missionary who does not speak in the language of his hearers may as well be speaking at a frequency that their ears cannot receive. He must make an adjustment, and this adjustment is not limited to the language he speaks, but rather it includes all the ways that humans communicate. This does not mean changing the requirements or content of the gospel, but rather changing the ways in which we communicate it.

While Paul emphasized the importance of retaining the unchangeable content of the gospel, he recognized the necessity of adapting its presentation so that those who heard it could understand it (1 Cor 9:22). "The manner in which the Evangelists and Paul communicated the gospel in the various cultural contexts gives evidence of the fact that a form of contextualization was practiced in the early church."[8]

Jesus was, is and will ever be God the Son, the second person of the Godhead, yet he took on human flesh and lived among us. This is the contextualization of God himself into the world of men. The Bible is God's contextualization of his message in a form we could understand—human language. John Calvin refers to the Bible as a form of baby talk that the

---

[8]Bruce Corley, Grant Lovejoy and Steve Lemke, *Biblical Hermeneutics* (Nashville: B&H Academic, 2002), pp. 374-75.

nurse uses with an infant in a crib.[9] God did not "dumb down" his message, but he did put it in terms and language that we could understand. Indeed, each book of the Bible communicates many of the same truths, but they are placed in one of several languages, in diverse historical situations and directed to particular audiences, and they even emphasize specific aspects of the truth as the Holy Spirit inspired them. Likewise, each of the four Gospels is unique and contains much of the same truth, but they are all contextualized to certain audiences for particular reasons. Paul's letters also carry similar truths, couched in unique forms, preaching necessary divine revelation tailored to the recipients of each.

THE PAULINE MODEL

Paul is the model missionary who crosses cultural boundaries and contextualizes his unchanging message to the particular contexts of his hearers. Paul knew that he could not assume the same level of monotheistic worldview, knowledge of Hebrew, familiarity with Jewish history and Pharisaic traditions, or even the acceptance of the truth about creation itself in the cities he entered during his missionary travels. He always began his ministry in the synagogues, knowing that people there would share the worldview of divine revelation—and because of an intense love for his fellow Jews. However, as he left the Jewish island of the synagogue and preached to polytheistic pagans, he had to adjust his message. The pastor who preaches to a congregation he has served for ten years may assume a certain level of knowledge but will preach the same truths with a different delivery style during the children's sermon or to his nursing home patients. If he were to preach the same basic sermon to an inner city rescue mission or on a mission trip to a lesser-reached people group, he would adjust it further still. The illustrations would be different; the level of knowledge assumed would not be as high; and, indeed, the language itself would have to be adjusted as he preached through an interpreter. With God's leadership

---

[9]"For who even of slight intelligence does not understand that, as nurses commonly do with infants, God is wont in a measure to 'lisp' in speaking to us? Thus such forms of speaking do not so much express clearly what God is like as accommodate the knowledge of him to our slight capacity. To do this he must descend far beneath his loftiness." (John Calvin, *Institutes of the Christian Religion*, ed. John T. McNeill, trans. Ford Lewis Battles, LCC 21 [Philadelphia: Westminster John Knox, 1960], p. 121 [Book I, Chapter 13, Article 1]).

and anointing, Paul was the master contextualizer, and this is why he communicated so clearly to his hearers and readers. When people accepted or rejected Paul's message, they did so because they understood it.

Paul not only preached the gospel message, he contextualized Christianity in the cultures where he planted churches. Paul did not seek to replicate the church of Syrian Antioch or Jerusalem when he went to new areas. Indeed, even those two churches had differing understandings of what a New Testament church should be, say and do, resulting in a major council of the church leaders in Acts 15. Paul's wise insights were essential aspects for the harmonious resolution reached for non-Jewish background believers. Flemming wrote, "The apostle Paul—missionary, theologian, interpreter of Scripture—is undoubtedly the key figure for an understanding of the process of doing contextual theology in the New Testament."[10]

Paul understood that new approaches would be needed to reach new areas of the world. While churches would still have to qualify as New Testament churches and the teaching should be the biblical gospel once for all entrusted to the saints, different contexts required culturally appropriate ministry forms. Barnett believes that Paul was uniquely used by God to spread Christianity in the first century, "Through the Holy Spirit this man 'in Christ,' who was steeped in the OT, and who had likely been catechized at his baptism, became the first theologian in the early church, and arguably the greatest in the history of Christianity. Paul's genius is not found so much in his innovation as in his adaptation and application of traditions that had come to him from the Lord . . . that he in turn reshaped for use in the churches, both by oral catechesis and by his letters."[11] Paul's thinking both inside and outside the Jewish box enabled him to establish Christian ministry and churches in forms that the Jerusalem mindset may not have recognized at first glance. Recognizing this reality, Barnett continues,

> From the beginnings of his new missionary thrust Paul adopted new approaches. He established churches in rapid succession as a means of spreading the gospel locally; he drew others into partnership with him as traveling coworkers and as envoys; he pioneered letter writing as a

---

[10]Dean Flemming, *Contextualization in the New Testament* (Downers Grove, Ill.: IVP Academic, 2005), p. 16.
[11]Paul Barnett, *Paul, Missionary of Jesus: After Jesus* (Grand Rapids: Eerdmans, 2008) 2:7.

means of instructing his churches in absentia. By far the most significant difference, however, was his deliberate outreach to rank pagans,
idol worshipping, temple-attending Gentiles. Soon his churches were
mainly composed of such Gentiles as well, no doubt, as synagogue-
connected Godfearers.[12]

Two passages that illustrate the nimble dexterity of Paul in maintaining
gospel purity but presenting it in different forms are Paul's sermon in
Psidian Antioch in Acts 13 and his address on the Areopagus in Acts 17. Paul
was not watering down the gospel or its requirements but couching it in
terms that his hearers would readily understand. "We misunderstand contextualization if we see it as an attempt to make the gospel more palatable. It
would be hard to imagine anyone accusing Paul of somehow sanitizing or
sugarcoating the message. The gospel is offensive, and the point of contextualization is not to change that."[13]

In Paul's writings and ministry, we see clear instances of contextualization in his presentation of the gospel. Osborne wrote of the Pauline
record, "we note evangelistic contextualization, the cultural attempt to be
'all things to all people' so as to 'save some' (1 Cor 9:22). This is also demonstrated in the preaching of Acts, with the very different approach to Jews
(Acts 2:14-36, 3:12-26) and to Gentiles (Acts 14:15-17; 17:22-31). In the Areopagus speech (Acts 17) Paul's utilization of Greek philosophers is an especially important example of contextualization, demonstrating what missiologists call 'redemptive analogies.'"[14] Van Rheenen considered Paul's own
guidelines for missionary ministry in 1 Corinthians 9 and then looked to
Paul's application of them in Acts: "We find in these words a profound willingness to adapt to cultural differences for the sake of winning men and
women to Christ. Paul would emphasize his Jewish background when
speaking to Jews (as we see him do in Acts 13:16-43). And he would set his
Jewishness aside when speaking to Gentiles (as he did in Acts 17:22-31)."[15]

[12]Ibid., 2:157.

[13]Tim Morey and Eddie Gibbs, *Embodying Our Faith: Becoming a Living, Sharing, Practicing Church* (Downers Grove, Ill.: IVP Books, 2009), p. 75.

[14]Grant Osborne, *The Hermeneutical Spiral: A Comprehensive Introduction to Biblical Interpretation* (Downers Grove, Ill.: IVP Academic, 2006), p. 413.

[15]Gailyn Van Rheenen, *Contextualization and Syncretism* (Pasadena: William Carey Library, 2006), p. 244.

Paul demonstrates his gifts and anointing to couch biblical truth in diverse forms for other cultures. Tim Keller presented an insightful comparative contrast of Paul's approach by analyzing his message to a synagogue crowd in Acts 13 and to pagans in Acts 14:

> In Acts 13 we see Paul sharing the gospel in a synagogue to those who believed in the God of the Bible, and in Acts 14 we see him sharing the gospel to a pagan, blue-collar crowd. The differences and similarities are striking. (a) His citation of authority is very different. In the first case, he quotes Scripture and John the Baptist. In the second, he argues from general revelation—[the] greatness of creation. (b) They differ in emphasis of content. [It is] hard to miss that with Jews and God-fearers he ignores doctrine of God and gets right to Christ; with pagans here and Acts 17, he labors the very concept of God. (c) Finally, they differ in even the form of the final appeal—how to "close" with Christ—is different. In Acts 13:39 Paul speaks of the law of God and says, essentially: "you think you are good, but you aren't good enough! You need Christ to justify you." But in 14 he tells them to turn from "worthless things"—idols—"to the living God" who he says is the real source of "joy"—he, not material things—is the real source. So he is saying, in effect: "you think you are free—but you are not! You are enslaved to dead idols." (d) Despite all these very profound differences (1) Both audiences are told about a God who is both powerful yet good (13:16-22; 14:17), (2) in both he tells the hearers they are trying to save themselves in a wrong way (moral people by trying to obey the law 13:39 and pagans by giving themselves to idols and gods that cannot satisfy 14:15) and (3) both tell hearers not to turn to some scheme of performance, but that God has broken in to history now to accomplish our salvation. Even the speech of chapter 14, which was a spontaneous outburst, though it doesn't mention Christ directly, still points to the fact that salvation is something accomplished by God for us in history, not something we do.[16]

Paul's Jewish background, though immensely helpful, did not guarantee success among the synagogue crowd. Flemming pointed out, "Luke's narrative in chapter 13 makes it clear that even though Paul shares the same basic culture and much of the same worldview as his audience, and al-

---

[16]Keller, "Advancing the Gospel."

though he communicates the gospel in language that is targeted to the Jews, the barriers to faith in Jesus are still substantial. Indeed, the very worldview and cultural assumptions of the synagogue community become a stumbling block to their receiving the good news. Now, as well as then, a shared cultural experience is no guarantee that our efforts at contextualizing the gospel will meet with a positive response."[17] This potential for failure, even in the midst of responsible cultural sensitivity, should give us comfort as it reminds us of our ultimate call to present the gospel in such a way that the cross might be the only stumbling block. The presence of failure despite culturally appropriate forms can serve for us, as it did for Paul, as a marker that the gospel has been presented to God's glory and without compromise.

The speech in Acts 17 attracts our attention because we find his audience to be similar to the hearers we find in our own modern context. Postmoderns who are skeptical truth tasters require a different approach than those who believe that there is one God and tremble, but who have not repented of their sins and placed faith in Christ. The scoffers we encounter must hear the truth in ways that resonate with their reason. Flemming found similar adjustments in the message Paul delivered: "The form and style of the Areopagus speech are exquisitely adapted to a sophisticated Gentile audience. In contrast with the frequent use of language and quotations from the Greek Bible that we find in sermons preached to Jews in Acts, this discourse reflects a more Hellenized style, which is suited to the occasion and hearers."[18]

Missionaries soon learn that praying the sinners' prayer does not reprogram the entire life history and worldview of new converts; until they are discipled and taught, they will continue to process and understand new information against the backdrop of all they have ever believed to be real, true and foundational in life. Paul's efforts to make Christian concepts understandable and harmonious with cultural differences did not stop once his hearers accepted Christ. Schnabel wrote, "Paul's theological instruction of Gentile Christians could refer to some elements of pagan conceptions of the divine, but only in very general terms. Basically, everything that Paul

---

[17]Flemming, *Contextualization*, p. 65.
[18]Ibid., p. 74.

needed to say about God and his revelation in the history of Israel, about Jesus the Son of God and the Messiah, about sin and the forgiveness of sins and about the identity of followers of Jesus as the people of God of the last days, was novel and unprecedented."[19]

Roland Allen described Paul's synagogue preaching with five elements: An appeal to the past, a statement of facts, an answer to the inevitable objection, an appeal to the spiritual needs of men and, finally, a grave warning.[20] He further characterized Paul's preaching as conciliatory, sympathetic, courageous, respectful and with unhesitating confidence in the truth of his message.[21] There was reasoning in his ministry adjustments for cultural reasons, but not cowardice, pandering or a low view of Scripture. While Paul taught the general admonition against the uncircumcised seeking circumcision to please the Judaizers or to seek favor from God, he still circumcised Timothy (even after Acts 15!), but not others such as Trophimus, which led to near martyrdom in Acts 21. Paul participated in purification rites (Acts 21:17-24), but rebuked Peter to his face for hypocritically drawing back from fellowship with Gentiles (Gal 2).

In 1 Corinthians 9:19-23, Paul establishes the purpose and the limits of contextualization. The purpose of the adjustments is "I have become all things to all people, that by all means I might save some" (1 Cor 9:22). He reveals the limits when he says, "I do it all for the sake of the gospel" (1 Cor 9:23). Clearly, Paul will not become a drunk to win drunks; that would bring reproach to the gospel. Likewise, we should practice contextualization to win as many as possible, but never do anything that would not be honoring to Christ. If we do, we have misunderstood our primary call to holiness. Flemming wrote of Paul's ministry, "On the one hand, he regularly associates with Gentiles, shares meals with them, even stays in Gentile homes, all without deference to boundary-marking Jewish food laws (cf. Acts 11:26; 16:15, 34, 40; 17:4-7). On the other hand, for the sake of his missionary work among Jews, Paul has his coworker Timothy circumcised (Acts 16:3), and later he consents to undergo the Jewish rite of purification

[19]Schnabel, *Paul the Missionary,* p. 237.
[20]Roland Allen, *Missionary Methods: St. Paul's or Ours?* (Grand Rapids: Eeerdmans, 1962), p. 63.
[21]Ibid., p. 64.

in the temple at Jerusalem (Acts 21:23-24, 26; cf. 18:18)."[22] Contextualization on behalf of pagans does not change the gospel to make it easier to embrace. Nothing could be further from the truth; contextualization allows a pagan to understand clearly the need to repent of the old and truly embrace the new. This concept, still often misunderstood today, was grasped generations ago by Roland Allen. He wrote, "St Paul distrusted elaborate systems of religious ceremonial, and grasped fundamental principles with an unhesitating faith in the power of the Holy Ghost to apply them to his hearers and to work out their appropriate external expressions in them. It was inevitable that methods which were the natural outcome of the mind of St Paul should appear as dangerous to us as they appeared to the Jewish Christians of his own day."[23]

CONTEXTUALIZATION AND THE ROLE OF MISSIONARIES

Proper and thorough contextualization requires missionaries to include discipled nationals in the practice of Christianity in the new context. When Chinese people convert to Christianity, who would be the best guide to disciple them away from ancestor veneration yet teach them still to follow the biblical counsel to honor their parents? A born again, discipled Chinese believer would better understand the mindset, dangers and limits of this aspect of Chinese culture as it is brought into submission to God's Word. Western missionaries have sometimes arrogantly considered themselves sufficient for tasks they did not understand, forbidding or allowing practices without understanding them, resulting in a syncretism of Christianity with paganism. Missionary ethnocentrism has not changed radically in this regard since Allen's day. He wrote,

> We have allowed racial and religious pride to direct our attitude towards those whom we have been wont to call 'poor heathen'. We have approached them as superior beings, moved by charity to impart of our wealth to destitute and perishing souls. We have used that argument at home to wring grudging and pitiful doles for the propagation of our faith, and abroad we have adopted that attitude as missionaries of a superior religion. We have not learnt the lesson that it is not for our

---

[22]Flemming, *Contextualization*, p. 56.
[23]Allen, *Missionary Methods*, pp. 6-7.

righteousness that we have been entrusted with the Gospel, but that we may be instruments in God's hands for revealing the universal salvation of His Son in all the world.[24]

This principle not only applies to teaching new believers; Allen also saw its use for administration of the churches. He wrote, "In our modern missionary practice we have constantly, almost invariably, violated this principle. We have constantly thrown the whole responsibility for the administration of baptism upon a foreign teacher who, as a stranger, is in the worst possible position to judge the real motives and character of those who offer themselves for baptism, and by so doing we have done much to weaken the sense of mutual responsibility among our converts."[25]

Critical Contextualization

Paul Hiebert recognized the dangers of not contextualizing at all—as well as the extremes of overcontextualization—and called missionaries to "critical contextualization."[26] He traced the era of noncontextualization from the colonial period when missionaries went out essentially as agents of their state church imposed by the colonial powers. These church forms were not concerned with local cultural understanding to properly contextualize the gospel but rather with "Christianizing" the populations with the colonial government's church. The resulting churches appeared foreign and closely tied to the abusive tendencies of the colonial powers.

The next era was one of contextualization as missionaries came to embrace many aspects of burgeoning interest in cultural anthropology and applied evolutionary theories to religions and cultures. Anthropologists became enamored with cultures and studied them as isolated silos with their own systems of right and wrong. Missionaries influenced by such thinking often allowed the local cultures too much freedom to establish the forms, practices and even content of Christianity in their local contexts.

Hiebert encouraged a four-part critical contextualization that consisted of investigating and thoroughly understanding the culture, studying the Bible to identify areas to address, involving discipled nationals in the

---

[24]Ibid., p. 142.
[25]Ibid., p. 98.
[26]Hiebert, *Anthropological Reflections*, pp. 75-92.

process of recognizing sinful practices and errant beliefs, and developing biblical and culturally appropriate responses for them. These functional substitutes would fulfill the needs once met by sinful practices, be biblically responsible and find ready acceptance since the nationals were part of the process of contextualizing Christianity in their culture. [27]

Although Roland Allen lacked Paul Hiebert's extra century of historical perspective, in a similar way he challenged the missions world of his day to look at the ministry of the apostle Paul with new eyes to reevaluate evangelism, church planting and Christian ministry among the cultures of the world. Recognizing the role of cultures, Allen called missionaries to be more sensitive to the Holy Spirit's guidance in international ministry. He knew that Christianity exported from the missionary's home church with no adjustments would lead to a foreign gospel and dependence upon the Western missionary forever. Kraft wrote of Allen, "He was convinced that the New Testament furnished the only sound model of mission in its emphasis on the power of the Holy Spirit to transform people into the living body of Christ in each local context."[28]

ROLAND ALLEN AND CONTEMPORARY CONTEXTUALIZATION

The most controversial elements of contextualization today are both beyond the scope of this chapter and after the time of Roland Allen. However, we see his genius in cautions he issued in his own day that apply as warnings and limitations even today. For example, the C1-C6 scale is a shorthand manner of referring to the degree to which a missionary contextualizes the gospel and Christianity in a Muslim context, with the degree of contextualization increasing more and more each time the number increases. By the time the C5 level is reached, the associated contextualization allows converts to continue in Islam in virtually every recognizable way, arguing that it will be easier for Muslims to accept Christianity in Islamic forms and that they will eventually find their way to true New Testament Christianity.[29]

---

[27]For a full discussion of Hiebert's model of critical contextualization see chapter 4 in Hiebert, *Anthropological Reflections*, pp. 75-92.

[28]Charles Kraft, *Appropriate Christianity* (Pasadena: William Carey Library, 1995), p. 44.

[29]Neither C1 nor C6 relate to the discussion of contextualization because they do not seek to contextualize. Rather, C1 simply brings a church to the target culture exactly as it was in a former culture and C6 does not seek to establish a church. C5 is the level that relates to the Insider Movement.

While C5 is the strategy of choice for some missionaries in Muslim contexts, it causes great consternation for more conservative missiologists. C5's use of the Koran to evangelize, using "Allah" to refer to the Triune God of the Bible, and the extremes of its contextualization causes quite an outcry among many. What would Allen think of such extremes? He wrote that Paul would not be in harmony with such methodologies. He acknowledged that although some have attributed to Paul a liberal understanding of the gospel or a low view of Scripture, especially in Paul's speeches in Lystra and Athens, this is unfair. Allen continued, "It also seems unfair to base upon them a theory that St Paul approached his Gentile hearers with great caution and economy, leading them gradually from heathenism by a semi-pagan philosophy to Christianity."[30]

Very closely related to C5 strategy are "Insider Movements."[31] Insider Movement proponents defend this method by pointing to early Christians who were both Jews worshiping in the Temple and Christians attending the church. They argue that even as it took the first believers a few decades to make a total break with Judaism, so we should allow Muslims and Hindus a generation or so to drift upstream to pure Christianity. Allen spoke to this strategy as well. He cited Bernard Lucas, *The Empire of Christ,* who believed that "we ought to receive the Hindu 'without demanding that exclusion from his social environment which baptism and the renunciation of caste involve.'"[32] Allen summarized their argument: "The work of the Christian missionary is not to call men from the heathen temple into the Church of God but to trim the dimly glowing lamp of God in the heathen temple, and to pour into it a few drops of the oil of Christian doctrine till it shines with a new radiance."[33] Allen responded to such thinking,

> Where this tendency manifests itself, it is due to the fact that we have lost the true conception of the nature and work of faith as preached by St Paul. As he taught, the one essential condition of life was faith in our Lord Jesus Christ. But faith in Jesus Christ involved, in itself, a breach with the past.

---

[30] Allen, *Missionary Methods,* p. 67.

[31] For a full background of the formation, history, development and resulting churches in the Insider Movement, see J. Henry Wolfe, "Insider Movements: An Assessment of the Viability of Retaining Socio-Religious Insider Identity in High-Religious Contexts" (PhD diss., SBTS, 2011).

[32] Allen, *Missionary Methods,* p. 70.

[33] Ibid., p. 71.

Faith was not a mere intellectual assent to a new theory of religion which could be held whilst the life remained in what it was before. . . . It meant the abandonment of the old conception of life, nay, of the very life itself as he before knew it. It meant the casting away of all the former things.[34]

Moreover, Allen believed that Paul would be adamantly against any strategy that allowed "converts" to add Jesus to what they knew before. He wrote of Paul, "He did not minimize the breach between Christianity and heathenism: he declared that the one was the kingdom of evil, the other the Kingdom of God, and that his work was to turn men from 'darkness to light and from the power of Satan unto God.'"[35] Allen did not see in the life of Paul any tendency toward a liberal contextualization that would intentionally allow the former religion to influence or have authority in a new Christian. C5 methodology and Insider Movement strategies would find no place in Allen's missiology or what he believed about the ministry of the apostle Paul.

Although Allen served as a missionary in China from 1895 to 1903, much of what he taught and emphasized does indeed resonate with missionary thought and practice today. He emphasized throughout chapter 6 of *Missionary Methods* the oft-cited contemporary stress on reproducibility and avoiding dependency. Although the chapter focuses on finances on the mission field, he weaves these two ideas throughout all that he has to say regarding the pitfalls of money in missions. Many missionaries stress today that if we utilize technology the nationals do not have, they will excuse themselves from ministry citing their lack of a laptop, projector or automobile. Others maintain the need to use only local funds so that they will not view their lack of money as a hindrance to starting new work. While Allen would principally agree with such thinking, his reasons were not merely pragmatic. He also argued that "missions financed from abroad naturally suggests that the religion which they represent is foreign."[36]

Allen listed crucial principles for practice in his chapter on the application of Paul's missionary methods. Of the five he listed, the first four are particularly applicable to the process of and need for contextualization. He wrote, "We have seen that the secret of the Apostle's success in founding

---

[34]Ibid.
[35]Ibid., p. 73.
[36]Ibid., p. 56.

churches lay in the observance of principles we can reduce to rules of practice in some such form as this."[37] The following are excerpts from each.

1. All teaching to be permanent must be intelligible and so capable of being grasped and understood that those who have once received it can retain it, use it and hand it on.

2. All organization in like manner must be of such a character that it can be understood and maintained.

3. All financial arrangements made for the ordinary life and existence of the church should be such that the people themselves can and will control and manage their own business independently of any foreign subsidies.

4. A sense of mutual responsibility of all the Christians for one another should be carefully inculcated and practised. The whole community is responsible for the proper administration of baptism, ordination and discipline.[38]

Parting Thoughts

Proper contextualization is essential for communicating the gospel. If there are any doubting holdouts still reading, keep in mind that simply translating the message from Hebrew or Greek to English and then to the language of your hearers are first steps in contextualization, and ones that are absolutely necessary. Donald K. Smith argued that there are twelve signal systems that cultures use to communicate; we all use all of them and each culture uses them in unique ways.[39] Language is just one of those systems. Just as we must put the gospel in the context's language, it is also helpful to contextualize the music, art, architecture, clothing, greetings and other expressions of the cultures where we are evangelizing, discipling and planting churches. There is no one Christian culture that is to be replicated all over the world. Kraft wrote, "The Gospel of Jesus Christ can be incarnated, given shape, lived out, in any cultural context—it is infinitely universalizable."[40] Just as there is no culture whose members do not need to hear the saving gospel message, there is none that cannot receive its truth in an understandable way.

---

[37]Ibid., p. 151.
[38]Ibid.
[39]See Donald K. Smith, *Creating Understanding* (Grand Rapids: Zondervan, 1992), pp. 144-65.
[40]Kraft, *Appropriate Christianity,* p. 187.

As we learn cultures and contextualize the gospel among them, we learn more of it ourselves. There are supracultural aspects of the gospel and Christianity that must not be changed or influenced by the myriad cultures of the world, and unity in these essentials will provide the basis for fellowship among all Christians in Christ's Body. No one culture has a corner on the Truth. Each culture will understand some nuance of Christian truth in their corner of the kingdom in a way that will add to the Body's understanding. As a symphony of worshipers, together we are richer and fuller than we are when separate. New Testament churches understand the gospel and worship in Quichua culture in all of the essential aspects, but with nuances not seen in New England culture and vice versa. Kraft wrote, "This 'translatability' of the Christian Gospel and Christian Church entails something broader, deeper and more pervasive than mere communication of a message."[41]

Missionaries who study missiology and modern methods in a world that has the advantage of reflection on preceding generations' research and experience often arrive in mission field settings where the early missionaries did not know to contextualize. The ministries they inherit are not what the missionaries wish they were. Perhaps the first missionaries ministered during the days of "missionary compound mentality," or of replicating the sending church from another country, or using financial resources to maintain control and loyalty among the national church. None of the earlier missionaries intended negative results or patronizing mentalities, but they occurred and remained just the same. Some newer missionaries often feel it would be easier to go and start afresh elsewhere. What should the new missionary in such a setting do? Allen wrote of this challenge for the young missionary with a different perspective,

> He cannot possibly ignore that situation. He cannot act as if the Christian community over which he is called to preside had had another history. He cannot desert them and run away to some untouched field. He cannot begin all over again. Nevertheless, if he has the Spirit of St Paul he can in a very real sense practise the method of St Paul in its nature, if not in its form. He cannot undo the past, but he can amend the present. He can

---

[41]Ibid., p. 188.

keep ever before his mind the truth that he is there to prepare the way for the retirement of the foreign missionary. He can live his life amongst his people and deal with them *as though he would have no successor.* He should remember that he is the least permanent element in the church. He may fall sick and go home, or he may die, or he may be called else-where. He disappears, the church remains.[42]

It is possible for a missionary to enter a ministry setting where contextualization was not done, where dysfunctional relationships or beliefs are rampant, to first decontextualize and then properly recontextualize. This will not be easy, but it can be done. Only when the gospel, Christianity and Christian ministry are understood and practiced in culturally appropriate and sensible ways will the missionaries be able to say that they have finished the task. The Great Commission is to reach and teach others everything Christ commanded, discipling them. Only with this goal of critical contextualization are missionaries truly able to take the things God has taught them and "entrust to faithful men who will be able to teach others also" (2 Tim 2:2).

---

[42]Allen, *Missionary Methods,* p. 153, emphasis in original.

13

Paul and Leadership
Development

♦ ♦ ♦

Chuck Lawless

I have served as a church consultant for more than fifteen years. The work has been steady, as few churches on the North American continent (or around the world, for that matter) are fully healthy. The weaknesses in most churches are several, including a lack of evangelism, a failure to disciple, a focus turned inward and a myriad of other issues. At the core of most concerns, however, is a singular pressing issue: a failure in leadership.

Sometimes the leader is no leader at all; he finds himself in a position that demands more than he can give. At other times, he has the gifts to lead, but he has lost a vision to do so in his current setting. Congregation difficulties, personnel issues and stagnant church growth have taken a toll on the leader who once dreamed of making a significant Great Commission impact.

More often than not, those in leadership positions have not considered the issue of multiplication and mentoring; that is, they have not intentionally prepared leaders to follow in their footsteps. Their focus is present tense, with little attention to the future. Seldom is there in place a leadership development strategy for the future. To my regret, I have often seen the same unhealthy pattern in churches around the world.

Against that backdrop, the goal of this chapter is to examine the leadership development strategy of the apostle Paul. His plan, as we will see, was multidimensional: individual and corporate, immediate and long-term, internally and externally focused.

PAUL'S CALLING: A MANDATE TO MULTIPLY

The book of Acts includes three accounts of the apostle Paul's conversion experience on the road to Damascus (Acts 9:1-30; 22:5-21; 26:12-18). The latter is the least detailed account, with no mention of Paul's blindness or his visit to Ananias in Damascus. Instead, the focus is on Paul's calling as Jesus first verbalized it to him: "But get up and stand on your feet. For I have appeared to you for this purpose, to appoint you as a servant and a witness of what you have seen and of what I will reveal to you. I will rescue you from the people and from the Gentiles. I now send you to them to open their eyes so they may turn from darkness to light and from the power of Satan to God, that by faith in Me they may receive forgiveness of sins and a share among those who are sanctified" (Acts 26:16-18).[1]

This truncated version of Paul's calling emphasized his Great Commission mandate "to bring the light of Christ to all people."[2] His commission—to be a witness to Jew and Gentile alike (Acts 20:21), with emphasis on the Gentiles (Acts 9:15)—was a mandate similar to God's callings to Jeremiah (Jer 1:7) and Ezekiel (Ezek 2:3).[3] Moreover, the calling to "open their eyes so they may turn from darkness to light" (Acts 26:18) echoed the servant song of Isaiah 42:6-7, where the Servant of God brings light to the nations. Thus, Paul was to do his work as a representative of the Messiah, the Servant of God.

The One who called Paul was the Son of God, who himself had uttered the Great Commission at least four times while on the earth (Mt 28:16-20; Mk 16:15; Lk 24:45-49; Jn 20:19-23; Acts 1:6-8).[4] Jesus Christ, in whom "the

---

[1] Unless otherwise indicated, all scripture quotations are from the Holman Christian Standard Bible (Nashville: LifeWay, 2010).

[2] John B. Polhill, *Acts*, NAC (Nashville: Broadman & Holman, 2001), p. 501-2.

[3] Simon J. Kistemaker and William Hendriksen, *Exposition of the Acts of the Apostles*, NTC (Grand Rapids: Baker, 1991), p. 898.

[4] Included in these texts is Mark 16:15. This discussion inevitably raises the question of the original ending of Mark's gospel. See *Perspectives on the Ending of the Gospel of Mark: Four Views*, ed. David Allen Black (Nashville: Broadman & Holman, 2008). The space limitations of this chapter prohibit

entire fullness of God's nature dwells bodily" (Col 2:9), had been given "all authority" (Mt 28:18) to command obedience to the Great Commission. In the words of Christopher Wright, "The identity and the authority of Jesus of Nazareth, crucified and risen, is the cosmic indicative on which the mission imperative stands authorized."[5] That is, Paul was to do the Great Commission because the living Son of God demanded that he do so.

Paul's task, like that for all of Christ's followers, was to proclaim the gospel to all nations. Without question, proclamation—that is, verbally speaking the message—is essential to doing the Great Commission. That should not be surprising, if one rightly believes Romans 10:14: "But how will they call on Him they have not believed in? And how can they believe without hearing about Him? And how can they hear without a preacher?" Apart from hearing the gospel, no person in any people group of the world can be saved; thus, proclaiming the Word is imperative. As John Piper has rightly noted, "The frontline of missions is the preaching of the Word of God, the gospel."[6]

Moreover, Paul was not to omit the necessary teaching that followed conversion (Mt 28:20). He—again, like all believers—was to teach new believers to obey what Jesus taught, thus helping to assure that future generations heard the gospel and saw it demonstrated in holy lives. New Testament scholar Robert Plummer describes this responsibility of the church as follows: "The apostles are to teach the converts everything that Jesus has commanded (Mt 28:20). If the young converts are to become mature disciples, they must continue to be schooled in the apostles' teaching—enabled by Christ's indwelling Spirit to love God and love neighbor (Mt 22:37-40)."[7] So clearly is this task described in the Scriptures that D. A. Carson has concluded, "The NT can scarcely conceive of a disciple who is not baptized or is not instructed."[8]

---

tackling this complicated issue sufficiently. I have chosen to include Mark 16:15 because it generally reflects the remaining unquestioned texts. For a more extensive look at the Great Commission texts in the New Testament, see Chuck Lawless, "To All the Nations," *SBJT* 15, no. 2 (2011): 16-27.
[5]Christopher J. H. Wright, *The Mission of God* (Downers Grove, Ill.: IVP Academic, 2006), p. 60.
[6]John Piper, *Let the Nations Be Glad!* 3rd ed. (Grand Rapids: Baker, 2010), p. 84.
[7]Robert L. Plummer, "The Great Commission in the New Testament," *SBJT* 9, no. 4 (2005): 4. Plummer points out that the command was to teach *all that Jesus commanded*—including the Great Commission itself. If the disciples' students were themselves to do the Commission, the argument that Mt 28:18-20 was intended for only the disciples has little credibility.
[8]D. A. Carson, *Matthew*, EBC (Grand Rapids: Zondervan, 1984), p. 597.

The enormity of this task was surely incomprehensible to Paul. No man, regardless of upbringing, training or ability, could do this work alone. The urgency of lostness demanded immediate and full obedience to the Great Commission, but the nonbelieving population in the Roman Empire sorely outnumbered the church. In addition, Paul knew himself as a former blasphemer (1 Tim 1:13) and the worst of all sinners (1 Tim 1:15). His only hope of fulfilling God's call on his life rested on two matters: God's presence in his life and God's plan for carrying out his calling.

Paul understood that God indwells his followers through the Spirit (Rom 8:9-11), pouring out his love to them through his intimate presence in them (Rom 5:5). It is that Spirit who sets believers free (Rom 8:2), produces evidence of His presence in them (Gal 5:22), empowers their words (1 Cor 2:4) and seals them as God's children (Eph 1:13-14). Tom Schreiner thus summarizes Paul's teaching on the Spirit's power as follows: "The power of the Holy Spirit is the only means by which believers can do what God commands. In Pauline letters, commands are often given after Paul has detailed what God has accomplished in Christ for his people. In other words, the indicative precedes the imperative."[9]

Given that Paul understood the Spirit as, in Schnabel's words, "the power of God's gracious presence who helps believers to live lives pleasing to God (Rom 8:1-17)," we can rightly assume that Paul sought the Spirit's guidance about the topic of this chapter: leadership development.[10] The task was immense, and Paul was but one man. Only through training a next generation of leaders could he move toward accomplishing his calling. The remainder of this chapter focuses on how he did that.

PAUL'S METHODOLOGY: A MULTI-DIMENSIONAL APPROACH

Church planting expert J. D. Payne reminds church planters that they should always be asking the question, "If I were walking down the street and were struck by lightning and died, what would happen to the newly planted churches?"[11] While the question is a graphic and startling one (in-

---

[9]Thomas R. Schreiner, *Paul: Apostle of God's Glory in Christ* (Downers Grove, Ill.: InterVarsity Press, 2001), p. 316.

[10]Eckhard J. Schnabel, *Paul the Missionary* (Downers Grove, Ill.: InterVarsity Press, 2008), p. 204.

[11]J. D. Payne, *Discovering Church Planting* (Carlisle, U.K.: Paternoster, 2009), p. 117.

tentionally so), it is a proper question for all church leaders. Leaders with no plans to develop current and future leaders leave a church with a significant void to fill. Such leaders are, in fact, not leading well—and have likely not learned much from the apostle Paul's approach to developing leaders.

New convert training. Roland Allen's classic work, *Missionary Methods: St. Paul's or Ours?* was as much a criticism of the mission station approach to missions as it was a call for a return to what Allen understood to be Paul's methods.[12] Included in that critique was a strong caution against unhealthy dependence on missionaries and an equally strong call to establish a congregation's own leadership at its inception: "The secret of success in this work lies in beginning at the very beginning. It is the training of the first converts which sets the type for the future. If the first converts are taught to depend upon the missionary . . . , the infant community learns to rest passively upon the man from whom they receive their first insight into the Gospel."[13]

The implications of this conclusion extend beyond the issue of dependency. What is true regarding dependence is likewise true regarding leadership development. Producing leaders in the church is based on a strong foundation for new converts. In his review of Paul's teachings for new converts—and correspondingly, on Paul's teachings on basic ecclesiology, Allen concludes that Paul taught a "tradition or elementary creed," the sacraments, the Orders (church ministers), and the Holy Scriptures.[14] His training was neither elaborate nor complex, but it was intentionally focused. It was leadership development beginning where it should begin—at the start of one's walk with Christ and one's entrance into the church.

The creed was essentially the simple gospel, including doctrines "of God, the Father, the Creator; . . . Jesus, the Son, the Redeemer, the Savior; . . . [and] the Holy Spirit, the indwelling source of strength."[15] Essential to

---

[12]For another strong evaluation of the mission station approach, see Donald A. McGavran, *Bridges of God* (London: World Dominion, 1955).

[13]Roland Allen, *Missionary Methods: St. Paul's or Ours?* 2nd ed. (Grand Rapids: Eerdmans, 1962), p. 81.

[14]Ibid., p. 107.

[15]Ibid., p. 87. Schnabel, *Paul the Missionary*, pp. 198-99, includes these teachings: God's revelation in Christ; the condition of human beings without faith in God; God's gift of righteousness in Christ; the necessity of repentance and forgiveness; the identity of believers in Christ and their communal fellowship; the consequences of the gospel for everyday living; the transformation of the mind and behavior of believers; the return of Christ and the final consummation.

this gospel were the facts of the death and resurrection of Jesus: "For I passed on to you as most important what I also received: that Christ died for our sins according to the Scriptures, that He was buried, that He was raised on the third day according to the Scriptures, and that He appeared to Cephas, then to the Twelve. Then He appeared to over 500 brothers at one time; most of them are still alive, but some have fallen asleep. Then He appeared to James, then to all the apostles. Last of all, as to one abnormally born, He also appeared to me" (1 Cor 15:3-8).

Paul's gospel "always focuses on the significance of Jesus' death on the cross and of his resurrection from the dead. . . . [Paul] insists that the news of Jesus the crucified Messiah and Savior is the foundation of the faith of followers of Jesus."[16] Some scholars, in fact, assert that these concepts formed a primitive statement of faith that the early church used.[17] That message was grounded in the authority of the Scriptures—particularly the Old Testament, whose promised blessings to the nations through Abraham (Gen 12:1-3) were now being fulfilled in the good news of the Messiah.[18]

That good news was portrayed and recalled through the sacraments of baptism and communion, and all believers were expected to participate in both. Schreiner uses numerous phrases to explain how important the act of baptism was for new believers according to Paul's writing: "the rite of entrance into the new community," "part of the commencement of the Christian life," "the badge of entrance into the Christian community," "a boundary between their old and new life."[19] The Lord's Supper—addressed only in 1 Corinthians in Paul's writings—then commemorates the core of the gospel while also looking forward to the return of Christ. Neither sacrament was to be observed independent of the church: "both involve sharing the common life in the body of Christ with all other believers, and carry with them serious ethical corollaries which Christians ignore at their peril."[20]

---

[16]Schnabel, *Paul the Missionary*, pp. 398-99.

[17]Simon Kistemaker & William Hendriksen, *Exposition of the First Epistle to the Corinthians*, NTC (Grand Rapids: Baker, 1993), p. 528.

[18]Schreiner, *Paul*, p. 190, also points out that the death and resurrection constituted the fulfillment of Old Testament promises.

[19]Ibid., pp. 371-76. While asserting the significance of baptism and the Lord's Supper, Schreiner does not affirm baptismal regeneration, arguing instead that those who do so exalt baptism over the gospel. Allen's attention to the sacraments tends to betray his Anglican background.

[20]F. F. Bruce, *Paul: Apostle of the Heart Set Free* (Grand Rapids: Eerdmans, 1977), p. 285.

Regarding what Allen called the "Orders," the apostle Paul and his companions not only planted churches, but they also assisted in establishing leadership for the new churches. Acts 14:21-23, for example, indicates that Paul returned to cities where he had planted, strengthened the believers with further teaching (including a word about suffering and hardship) and appointed elders for the church. Scholars debate whether Paul or the congregation appointed the elders. It is conceivable that "in new areas leaders were appointed, but in established areas leadership traits had a chance to be manifested and be affirmed by the local church."[21] Regardless of the chosen method, though, the early church elders were selected from the congregations to which they belonged. They were known members of the body set apart to lead the body, and Paul taught new converts about this significant role.

Schnabel likewise reviews Paul's instructions to new converts, summarizing those teachings in terms of theological instruction, ethical instruction, instruction concerning life in the church and evangelistic outreach.[22] The lattermost component demands further attention here. Praising churches with a missionary heart (e.g., Phil 1:5; 1 Thess 1:8,), Paul expected believers to stand ready to speak the gospel (Eph 6:15). The conduct of spouses (1 Cor 7:16), elders (1 Tim 3:7), older women (Tit 2:3-5), slaves (Tit 2:9-10) and all believers was to undergird rather than discredit the gospel. Young or old, newly born again or maturing, all believers were to share the gospel.

Continuing leadership training. The nature of Paul's leadership development strategies has fostered considerable debate. At the center of this debate is the question of the missionary's responsibility and methodology to raise up leaders in the church. Allen describes the position that most concerns him as follows:

> On the one hand, there are those who hold that it is our prime duty to establish in each country a church, not necessarily very widespread, nor very numerous, but highly educated, . . . that we ought to concentrate upon a few within the church . . . establish them in our doctrines and ethics, and so prepare them to direct the church in its great missionary work when time is ripe and the church so founded has advanced to such

---

[21]R. J. D. Utley, *Luke the Historian: The Book of Acts*, SGC (Marshall, Tex.: Bible Lessons International, 2008), p. 178.
[22]Schnabel, *Paul the Missionary*, pp. 236-48.

strength that it is not only able to take over all the work which we have begun but to carry it forward into all the corners of the land.[23]

Such an approach, says Allen, fosters dependence, promotes paternalism and professionalism, and inhibits spontaneous growth. It is, in fact, a lack of faith, evidenced by an unspoken belief that the Spirit of God cannot grow and equip his church without the assistance of the trained church leader. "We believe that it is the Holy Spirit of Christ which inspires and guides us; we cannot believe that the same Spirit will guide and inspire them," writes Allen.[24]

Hence, Allen negatively critiques the practice of devolution, or "the notion of gradually delegating rights, authority, power, and privileges to native churches over an arbitrary period of time."[25] Such a process not only slows spontaneous expansion of the church, but it also leads to inevitable discontent in the church. The missionary wrongly believes that the time to turn over the church to indigenous leaders—that is, after they have been sufficiently trained—will be obvious to all, but "those who are seeking to gain authority never agree to wait until those who hold it think that they are sufficiently prepared."[26] Filled with the Holy Spirit, the new believers are thus "not so incapable as we [missionaries] suppose."[27]

Toward this end, Allen argues that the apostle Paul generally "preached in a place for five or six months and then left behind him a church, not indeed free from the need of guidance, but capable of growth and expansion."[28] Paul accomplished this task by "teaching the simplest elements in the simplest form to the many," thereby fostering a reproducible process that facilitated rather than hindered planting new churches.[29] The apostle planted and taught the young church, moved on quickly to his next ministry destination and made himself available to minister as needed to the planted church via his writings or his emissaries. The leaders he left behind were not necessarily highly educated; they were simply Holy Spirit-filled men.

---

[23]Roland Allen, *The Spontaneous Expansion of the Church and the Causes which Hinder It* (Grand Rapids: Eerdmans, 1962), p. 20.

[24]Allen, *Missionary Methods*, pp. 143-44.

[25]J. D. Payne, "The Legacy of Roland Allen," *Churchman*, 117 no. 4 (2003): 321.

[26]Allen, *Spontaneous Expansion*, p. 25.

[27]Allen, *Missionary Methods*, p. 146.

[28]Ibid., p. 84.

[29]Ibid., p. 90.

An analysis of Paul's process for developing leaders is now in order here. First, it is fair to conclude that Paul did not fully describe either the role or the training process of church leaders. Again, Schreiner is helpful as he considers the purpose of Paul's Pastoral Letters:

> Another feature, mentioned previously, distinguishes the Pastorals from church manuals: practically nothing is said about the specific functions of the leaders. Virtually all of the attention is devoted to the character of the appointed (1 Tim 3:1-13; Tit 1:5-9). One hardly writes a church manual and leaves so much about the leaders' specific functions up in the air. Details were probably not filled in because Paul left it to individual churches to work out the concrete circumstances of church life. He did not intend to prescribe everything but left much up to the spiritual wisdom and good sense of the congregation.[30]

That is to say, Paul left many issues undiscussed, "probably because Paul left the details to Timothy and Titus and to churches themselves."[31] What details the Scriptures do provide are thus somewhat general, yet nevertheless significant.

Second, Paul did not abandon the churches he planted, even though he continued his missionary journeys. Allen describes the churches in this fashion: "they were no longer dependent upon the Apostle, but they were not independent of him."[32] For example, Paul and Barnabas ministered in Lystra where Paul was stoned and left for dead (Acts 14:8-22); nevertheless, the apostle later returned to the area to strengthen the believers in that region. By doing so, he illustrated the necessity and significance of follow-up and continued training for new believers.[33] They were to remain faithful

---

[30]Schreiner, *Paul*, p. 389. See also Allen, *Missionary Methods*, p. 149: "He [Paul] never did things for them, he always left them to do things for themselves. He set them an example according to the mind of Christ, and he was persuaded that the Spirit of Christ in them would teach them to approve that example and inspire them to follow it."

[31]Schreiner, *Paul*, p. 389.

[32]Allen, *Missionary Methods*, p. 111. At the same time, Allen was careful to contend that Paul's sending representatives to his churches cannot be equated with sending someone to catechize believers and administrate the sacraments: "St. Paul was careful not to lose touch with his new converts. They sorely needed visits and instruction, and they received them. I have no doubt that he was in constant communication with them by one means or another. But there is an immense difference between dealing with an organized church through letters and messengers and occasional visits, and exercising direct personal government" (Ibid., p. 86-87). This general statement has validity, but it seems to miss the deep concern Paul had for proper doctrine, right living, etc., in the churches he planted.

[33]Polhill, *Acts*, p. 318.

to God even in the midst of opposition and persecution. A further visit to Lystra would result in Timothy's beginning his training with Paul (Acts 16:1-5), and "strengthening all the disciples" would be the purpose of even another follow-up visit (Acts 18:23).[34]

Paul's relationship with the church at Corinth is another illustration of his longer-term commitment to discipleship, training and follow-up. The apostle planted this church during his second missionary journey (Acts 18:1-11), staying with the church at least eighteen months (Acts 18:11, 18). After continuing to Ephesus, Paul sent the Corinthians a letter—now likely lost—after having heard of a series of troubles in the congregation. Further correspondence with the church led to Paul's writing 1 Corinthians and sending Timothy to the city.

The troubles did not cease, however, and Paul made a difficult visit himself to Corinth (2 Cor 2:1). Further letter writing and a visit from Titus continued Paul's relationship with the Corinthian church, resulting in his joy when the church did repent (2 Cor 7:8-16). A later generous offering from believers in the region of Corinth to aid the believers in Jerusalem suggests that a third visit from Paul was a positive one (2 Cor 13:1-2).

The point is clear: despite his commitment to taking the gospel where it had not been preached (Rom 15:20), Paul neither ignored nor abandoned the churches he planted. Via personal visits, correspondence and representatives, he stepped back into the lives of his churches when necessary. Even in cities such as Philippi and Thessalonica where Paul spent only a brief period, he left behind leaders who would minister in his place.[35]

Schnabel's conclusions describing Paul's ministry to believers helpfully summarize Paul's approach:[36]

1. Paul constantly quotes or alludes to the Scriptures, that is, the Old Testament. . . . suggest[ing] that the reading and exposition of Scripture was a regular feature of the churches which Paul established.

2. Paul taught the new converts "the whole counsel of God" (Acts 20:27) both "publicly and from house to house" (Acts 20:20).

---

[34]Richard Longenecker, *John and Acts*, EBC (Grand Rapids: Zondervan, 1981), p. 489.
[35]Neil Cole, *Journeys to Significance* (San Francisco: Jossey-Bass, 2011), p. 106.
[36]Schnabel, *Paul the Missionary*, pp. 198-200.

3. Paul seeks to promote the spiritual growth of the believers, in terms of not only promoting their theological understanding of the gospel but also helping them to pray, to worship and to be serious and consistent about living out the truth of the gospel in their everyday lives.

4. Paul works to strengthen the fellowship of local believers as the people, the temple and the household of God, as the body of Christ and as the community of the Spirit.

Indeed, Schnabel concludes that theological instruction of believers was a "first major focus" for Paul.[37]

The following summary from Schnabel is a lengthy but significant analysis of Paul's approach to continuing leadership training:

> Paul was not content to preach the gospel to unbelievers and to establish new communities of followers of Jesus. He continued to be concerned about the churches that had come into existence and about the believers who were meeting in these local churches every week— concerned for their doctrinal authenticity and for their moral consistency, for their faith and for their life, for their leadership and for the new converts. Paul is concerned that the teachers of the churches teach correctly and that the believers in the churches believe correctly— this is why he writes his letters and why he discusses one-sided or misleading beliefs that some Christians propagate.[38]

The inclusion of Schnabel's summary here is not intended to deny many of Allen's concerns about contemporary missiological practices. Allen is correct in asserting that too often converts are taught that only "duly appointed ministers may preach."[39] It is right that congregations should determine who is admitted as a member or set apart as an elder.[40] Moreover, some attempts at leadership development and training certainly do remove leaders from the people they must lead and the nonbelievers they must seek

---

[37]Ibid., p. 237.

[38]Ibid., p. 207. See also Cole, *Journeys*, pp. 108-9: "I am not arguing for lifelong service in one place as a missionary. I do not believe that anyone who actually has an apostolic gifting could do that anyway. But I am finding that if a church is started and the missionary leaves before leaders can be mentored and established, the church feels abandoned and inadequate, which fuels a desire for dependency, not less."

[39]Allen, *Missionary Methods*, p. 76.

[40]Ibid., pp. 97-100.

to reach.[41] At the same time, however, even Allen recognizes that it is through believers teaching other believers that the church is equipped.[42] Legitimate teaching should lead to right doctrine and right praxis, to obedience to the gospel.

The Schnabel summary above does, however, raise issues with those who argue that Paul's work was always rapid, with little attention to the care and development of the congregation left behind as he journeyed on.[43] There can be little question that Paul "was often torn between his urgent call to establish new work and his concern for the well-being of the congregations he had already founded," but the apostle worked to address both concerns.[44] Great Commission leadership development demands nothing less.

Mentoring leadership development. Paul the church planter is perhaps best known for developing leaders via mentoring young men in the ministry. Indeed, he invested his life in several men, including Timothy and Titus. For the purpose of this chapter, the focus will be on Paul's mentoring relationship with Timothy.

The Scriptures give few details about the events that led to Paul's mentoring Timothy.[45] The apostle was traveling through the city of Lystra on his second missionary journey when he announced that he wanted Timothy traveling with him (Acts 16:1-5). It is possible that Timothy had converted to Christianity during Paul's first trip through Lystra in his first missionary journey, but it is not clear when Timothy became a believer. His mother and grandmother were believers who trained young Timothy in the Word of God (Acts 16:1, 2 Tim 1:3-5, 3:14-17). His father, a Greek, was likely a nonbeliever.[46]

This introduction to Timothy provides insight into Paul's approach to leadership development through mentoring. First, Paul took the lead in establishing the mentoring relationship; thus, the leader led the way in

---

[41]Ibid., pp. 106, 119-20.

[42]Ibid. See, e.g., pp. 89, 96, 157.

[43]See, e.g., Gunther Bornkamm, *Paul* (Minneapolis: Fortress, 1995), p. 54, who asserts that Paul "founded churches and traveled farther, instead of taking time to care for them and train them." To be fair, Bornkamm does recognize Paul's use of letters and representatives to minister to the churches, but he sees those approaches as less significant than Paul's personal presence.

[44]John Polhill, *Paul and His Letters* (Nashville: B & H Academic, 1999), p. 99.

[45]Some portions of this section are found in Chuck Lawless, *Mentor: How Along the Way Discipleship Can Change Your Life* (Nashville: LifeWay, 2011).

[46]Kistemaker and Hendriksen, *Acts of the Apostles*, p. 578.

calling out the next generation of leaders. Paul apparently remained alert for believers who showed promise, and Timothy caught his attention. Perhaps he had heard from church leaders who recognized Timothy's giftedness (1 Tim 1:18, 4:14). In Allen's words, Paul took men like Timothy with him "to act as his assistants and ministers that they might receive from him deeper lessons of Christian doctrine and practice than they could learn at home."[47]

Second, leadership development through mentoring produced a profound connection between Paul and Timothy. The general silence in the scriptures about Timothy's father suggests that he did not have a strong influence in Timothy's life or that he had died by the time Paul invested in Timothy.[48] A review of the terms Paul used for Timothy, however, reveals that their mentoring relationship developed a deeply held bond:

> "He [Timothy] is my dearly loved and faithful son in the Lord" (1 Cor 4:17).
>
> "Timothy, my true son in the faith" (1 Tim 1:2)
>
> "Timothy, my dearly loved son" (2 Tim 1:2)
>
> "I [Paul] constantly remember you in my prayers night and day. Remembering your tears, I long to see you so that I may be filled with joy" (2 Tim 1:3-4).
>
> "He [Timothy] has served with me in the gospel ministry like a son with a father" (Phil 2:22).

Paul went so far to say that he had no one who was as like-minded with him as Timothy (Phil 2:20). Leadership development was thus much more than a program; it was a relationship. The connection between Paul and Timothy was a divine intersection that must have been difficult to deny. So close were Paul and Timothy, in fact, that six letters of the New Testament bear their names as coauthors. It was also this closeness—particularly evidenced in Paul's appreciation for, commitment to and encouragement of Timothy—that gave Paul the right to challenge his protégé to use his gifts (2 Tim 1:6).[49]

---

[47]Allen, *Missionary Methods*, p. 101.

[48]Kenneth O. Gangel, *Acts*, HolNTC (Nashville: Broadman & Holman, 1998), p. 266.

[49]Michael T. Cooper, "The Transformational Leadership of the Apostle Paul: A Contextual and Biblical Leadership for Contemporary Business and Ministry," *CEJ* 2, no. 1 (Spring 2005): 58.

Third, Paul recognized Timothy's areas of needed growth. Within Paul's writings are hints about Timothy's struggles. Timothy was a young man (perhaps in his 30s) whose youth apparently became an obstacle for some in his ministry, and Paul encouraged him to overcome that obstacle through faithful speech, conduct, love, faith and purity (1 Tim 4:12).

Moreover, Timothy apparently battled "youthful passions" (2 Tim 2:22), including, but not limited to, sexual desires. These desires might have included useless arguing and impatience.[50] Again, Paul reminded Timothy that he could counter his youthful desires by intentionally being gentle and patient while pursuing righteousness, faith, love and peace. As one writer concluded, "Timothy's character, and not his age, would determine his authority to lead."[51]

Other writings of Paul suggest that Timothy was a timid and perhaps unhealthy person. Paul reminded him that God had not "given us a spirit of fearfulness" (2 Tim 1:7), and he warned the Corinthians not to create fear in Timothy when he visited their congregation (1 Cor 16:10). Frequent illnesses and stomach problems also haunted Paul's protégé (1 Tim 5:23). Whatever the illnesses were, they were recurrent enough that Paul was aware of them—but they did not stop Paul from calling Timothy to be a leader.

Fourth, Paul invited Timothy into his life. The book of 2 Timothy is considered to be Paul's last will and testament—his final words to Timothy as the apostle awaited his death in a Roman prison. This letter is emotional, gripping and personal. Timothy, who had seen Paul's "teaching, conduct, purpose, faith, patience, love and endurance, along with the persecutions and sufferings" (2 Tim 3:10-11), may have even been present when Paul was persecuted and left for dead in Lystra.[52] He also knew of times when Paul was whipped, beaten with rods, confronted with danger on all sides, and still found God's strength ever present in his weakness (2 Cor 11:23-30). Hence, Timothy learned from Paul on the mountaintop and in the valley.

---

[50]Tommy Lea and H. P. Griffin, *1, 2 Timothy, Titus*, NAC (Nashville: Broadman & Holman, 2001), p. 219.

[51]Bruce Barton, David R. Veerman and Neil Wilson, *1 Timothy, 2 Timothy, Titus,* LABC (Wheaton, Ill.: Tyndale House, 1993), p. 87.

[52]Allen, *Missionary Methods*, p. 145, argues that a primary role of the teacher is to "awaken a spirit, to teach the pupil to realize his own powers, by setting before him difficulties, and showing him how to approach and overcome them." Paul did so by allowing Timothy to be with him in his struggles.

It was in the context of that life-on-life leadership development that Paul called Timothy and others to imitate him as he followed Christ (1 Cor 4:16, 11:1; Phil 3:17-21; 2 Thess 3:7-9). Paul knew that he personally had room for growth, but he was also confident enough in his walk with God to call others to walk beside him. Paul was thus an example to his followers, who themselves would become an example to others (1 Thess 1:6-7).[53] The result was, as Kenneth Boa points out, followers who themselves became leaders:

> The apostle Paul understood the crucial role of mentoring in leadership development. He reminded the Thessalonians that he had done more for them than impart spiritual truth. Paul had internalized his beliefs to such an extent that those who followed in his steps could be confident that they were following Christ. It is important to note that the chain didn't end with the Thessalonians. After following Paul, they became a 'model to all the believers in Macedonia and Achaia' (v. 7). The followers became leaders. Those who had been mentored became mentors to others.[54]

Fifth, Paul challenged Timothy to fulfill his own calling. Paul called Timothy to travel with him and learn from him, but he did not allow Timothy to remain with him. Knowing that Timothy was gifted—so gifted that the church had affirmed him and set him apart for ministry—Paul trained him, sent him out to do ministry and often reconnected with him between tasks.

A quick review of Timothy's work shows how much Paul trusted him. Timothy accompanied Paul on portions of two of his missionary journeys, and he accepted Paul's assignments on the apostle's behalf. Timothy and Silas stayed in Berea to minister after the crowds ran off Paul (Acts 17:14). Later, after the men rejoined Paul in Athens, Paul sent Timothy out again to check on the churches planted in Macedonia (Acts 19:22). When Paul could not go to Corinth, it was Timothy his "dearly beloved and faithful son in the Lord" (1 Cor 4:17) that he sent.

From prison, Paul sent his mentee to Philippi to get a report on that good

---

[53]Payne, *Discovering Church Planting*, pp. 106-7, views this process as a reproducible model in church plants.
[54]Kenneth Boa, "Leadership Development," http://bible.org/seriespage/leadership-development.

church (Phil 2:19-20). He also trusted Timothy to deal with false teachers in the church at Ephesus (1 Tim 1:3-4). This ministry travelogue shows that Timothy played a vital role with Paul, a role that Allen describes in some detail: "It is absolutely essential that the founder of churches should keep in close touch with the communities which he has established, so that he may be able at any moment to intervene in any crisis or serious difficulty which may arise. St Paul needed Timothy and Titus, and we sorely need zealous and capable lieutenants whom we can dispatch with haste to any point of our missions where the less educated and less trained leaders may be in danger of falling into error."[55]

It is even more telling that Paul very much wanted Timothy with him as he faced his impending death (2 Tim 4:9), evidenced in the apostle's giving Timothy his final leadership charge (2 Tim 4:1-8) even as he faced his own departure. That charge was both a testimony of Paul's life and challenge to Timothy. The connections between the charge and the testimony are obvious, as the chart below shows:

Figure 13.1

TESTIMONY OF PAUL	CHARGE TO TIMOTHY
There is reserved for me in the future the crown of righteousness, which the Lord, the righteous Judge, will give me on that day (2 Tim 4:8).	I solemnly charge you before God and Christ Jesus, who is going to judge the living and the dead, and because of His appearing and His kingdom (2 Tim 4:1).
For I am already being poured out as a drink offering, and the time for my departure is close. I have fought the good fight, I have finished the race, I have kept the faith (2 Tim 4:6-7).	Proclaim the message; persist in it whether convenient or not; rebuke, correct, and encourage with great patience and teaching. . . . Be serious about everything, endure hardship, do the work of an evangelist, fulfill your ministry (2 Tim 4:2, 5).

---

[55]Allen, *Missionary Methods*, pp. 84-85.

Paul knew that he would be facing the judge of eternity, but he was prepared to do so because he had fought his fight and finished his race. Now, he wanted Timothy to be found faithful, too, until the end. He understood that Timothy's calling would grow increasingly difficult, as people would not want to hear the Word of God; even so, he challenged his protégé to proclaim the message regardless of the cost. As a prisoner now being sacrificed like an offering poured out to God, Paul could with integrity call Timothy to that level of obedience.

The apostle was ready to die, and he would not miss his opportunity to teach his mentee about living and dying. Leadership development thus continued until the mentor died.[56]

Paul's writing to Titus further illustrates this concept as it applies within the local congregation (Tit 2:1-8). The church in Crete was apparently poorly organized and facing the threat of false teachers within their midst. In that context, Paul called the church to adopt a leadership development strategy: leaders teaching those who would become leaders. Older believers were particularly to teach younger believers, thus establishing discipleship and "building up the inner life of believers as the best antidote against error."[57]

First, older men were to model Christian living by being clearheaded, respectable and sensible. It is likely that these older men were old enough to have raised families of their own, and their life was to be characterized by good judgment and Christian dignity. Their faith was to be grounded in true doctrine, their love for God and others genuine and their patience under trial obvious. The context of this passage suggests that the older men were particularly to model their faith for the younger men in the church.

Second, older women were to live a life of reverence, not gossiping or overindulging in wine. They were to teach "what is good"—not so much by formal schooling, but by informal life-on-life modeling. More specifically,

---

[56]See Stacy E. Hoehl, "The Mentor Relationship: An Exploration of Paul as Loving Mentor to Timothy and the Application of This Relationship to Contemporary Leadership Challenges," *Journal of Biblical Perspectives in Leadership* 3, no. 2 (2011): 35. Hoehl concludes, "Throughout the duration of this relationship, Paul ensures that Timothy is the right person for the job, equips him for ministerial tasks, empowers him for success, employs him in a challenging environment to develop effectiveness, and communicates to Timothy the value of their relationship."

[57]D. E. Hiebert, *Ephesians through Philemon*, EBC (Grand Rapids: Zondervan, 1981), p. 435.

it was their responsibility to train younger women how to live out their Christian faith, teaching them to love their husband and children, to be self-controlled and pure, to take care of their homes in kindness and to graciously follow their husband's direction. By living holy lives and teaching others to do the same, the older women would be honoring the Word of God.

Titus was himself a younger man, yet he was also to model Christian faithfulness for other young men. That is, the older men in the church in Crete and the younger men who were growing in their faith—like Titus— were to invest in the other younger men. Again, Titus was to model basic holy living by doing good deeds, believing right doctrine and exhibiting dignity and seriousness. His speech, whether in formal teaching or in informal conversation, was to be so biblical and consistent that even his opponents would have no case against him. In the end, Titus was to train others as he had been trained. Mentoring would continue to be a primary method of leadership development.

Conclusion

It has rightly been said that the true test of a leader is the legacy he leaves behind. A team of researchers from the University of Dallas, Texas Wesleyan University and the University of North Texas evaluated Paul's leadership according to 1 Thessalonians on this basis, and their conclusion follows:

> The measure of the Apostle Paul's leadership is the changed lives of those to whom he ministered: "You also *became* imitators of us and of the Lord, having received the word in much tribulation with the joy of the Holy Spirit, so that you *became* an example to all the believers in Macedonia and Achaia" (1 Thess 1:6-7). The key point here is that the Thessalonians became imitators. Just as Paul was transformed by his personal encounter with the risen Christ and became an imitator of Him, the Thessalonians were transformed by their encounter with Paul. As discussed earlier, they were "marked" and in turn became examples for others who were thus transformed. By being worthy of imitation, Paul created a legacy that continues to provide an example of leadership that creates other leaders who themselves are worthy of imitation.[58]

---

[58]J. Lee Whittington, Tricia M. Pitts, Woody V. Kageler, and Vicki L. Goodwin, "Legacy Leadership:

That is indeed the goal of leadership development—to produce leaders who themselves model leadership as they train others. Paul accomplished this task as he trained congregations and individuals, as he taught in the immediate context and trained for the future, and as he ministered to churches internally even as he propelled them outward. Given the failure of the contemporary church to produce such leaders, continued reviews of Paul's leadership strategy are needed. Only through the healthy development of new generations of leaders will the church fulfill the Great Commission that so motivated the apostle.

The Leadership Wisdom of the Apostle Paul," *The Leadership Quarterly* 16, no. 5 (October 2005): 759; italics added.

Postscript

Roland Allen's *Missionary Methods* at One Hundred

♦ ♦ ♦

J. D. Payne

"C̶an I read your writings, Grandfer?" The adolescent Hubert J. B. Allen asked his grandfather.

"Yes, you may read them. But you won't understand them," the older provocateur replied. "No one will understand them until after I've been dead for ten years."[1]

So wrote the younger Allen in the only biography written about the legendary Anglican behind the creation known as *Missionary Methods*.

Allen died in 1947, and while it was not completely a decade after his death, it was a few years later before his work began to catch on among churches and missionaries across the globe. He was a misunderstood prophet. While the years of his missionary efforts in China and labors in both England and Nairobi were not many in number, Allen had a keen mind and a pen with an unlimited supply of ink. He was a man who knew both his times and the Scriptures and who wrote quite extensively about the missiological problems of his day. Even fifteen years after the publication of *Missionary Methods*, Allen was still convinced of both the challenges of his

---

[1] Hubert J. B. Allen, *Roland Allen: Pioneer, Priest, and Prophet* (Grand Rapids: Eerdmans, 1995), p. vii.

day and the necessity of the apostolic paradigm. Commenting on the apostle Paul, he wrote, "We must allow to his methods a certain character of universality, and now I venture to urge that, since the Apostle, no other has discovered or practiced methods for the propagation of the Gospel better than his or more suitable to the circumstances of our day. It would be difficult to find any better model than the Apostle in the work of establishing new churches. At any rate this much is certain, that the Apostle's methods succeeded exactly where ours have failed."[2]

MISSIOLOGY OF THE MAN

Since other writers in this book have addressed Allen's missiology, I will not do so at length, but only reference what is necessary to provide a summary and illuminate his influence over the last century. Priscilla M. Allen provided the best summary of her father's work: "There are three themes in the life of Roland Allen which overlap like the tunes in a fugue: he was a missionary and a critic of missionary methods; he was a parish priest and found that he could not square this with his conscience; and he became more and more conscious of the inadequacy of the professional, whether missionary or cleric."[3] These themes greatly influenced his missiology and should be kept in mind when reading his works.

Though Allen's book *The Spontaneous Expansion of the Church* would not be written until 1927, the missiology behind *Missionary Methods* was consistent with his later work. Allen desired to see the natural multiplicative expansion of the church occurring across the world as people naturally shared the gospel and planted churches.

The way of Jesus. While Allen has the reputation of being focused on the apostolic labors of Paul, he recognized that the necessary elements conducive to the spontaneous expansion of the church did not begin with Paul. Allen understood that most of the Jerusalem apostles had been trained by Jesus and imitated what had been modeled before them. This paradigm had also been passed on to Paul.

Apostolic paradigm. Allen was convinced that the way of Paul was de-

---

[2]Roland Allen, *Missionary Methods: St. Paul's or Ours?* 2nd ed. (Grand Rapids: Eerdmans, 1962), p. 147.
[3]Priscilla M. Allen, "Roland Allen: A Prophet for this Age," *The Living Church* 192, no. 16 (1986): 9.

rived from the model of Jesus and was the proper way to plant indigenous churches. Michael Don Thompson noted that "Allen found in Paul the perfect prototype of the missionary who believed wholeheartedly in the power of Christ, and then lived and ministered in a way which clearly reflected that belief."[4]

The missionary was to practice retirement. Like the apostle Paul, he was not to remain a permanent fixture providing leadership to new churches. Rather, he was to practice the ministration of the Spirit, by teaching the new churches and their leaders how to rely on the Spirit's guidance. His writings on the importance of the Spirit led David Bosch to conclude that he was "one of the first theologians to have stressed the missionary dimension of pneumatology."[5]

Allen never advocated that the missionaries abandon new churches shortly after their birth. It would be appropriate for the missionary to continue in relationship and training with the churches, but he was not to remain with them but rather to continue his labors elsewhere. Just as the Apostle left behind the Creed, Sacraments, Orders and Scriptures, the contemporary missionary was to provide a similar foundation before moving on to other areas.

The missionary was to give priority to evangelism. While Allen recognized that there was much benefit to other forms of missionary expressions such as educational work and medical practices, he understood that preaching the gospel was paramount: "Of the reasons for supporting evangelistic missions I need not speak at length. I believe that they are in themselves supreme, and that without them no educational or medical missions would ever have come into existence. . . . Christ, the beginning, the end; the need for Christ; the hope in Christ; the desire for His glory; the conviction of His sovereignty; the impulse of His Spirit—these are some of the reasons for evangelistic missions, and however we may express them, they are, as I said, in their nature supreme."[6]

---

[4]Michael Don Thompson, "The Holy Spirit and Human Instrumentalilty in the Training of New Converts: An Evaluation of the Missiological Thought of Roland Allen" (PhD diss., Golden Gate Baptist Theological Seminary, 1989), pp. 69-70.

[5]David J. Bosch, *Transforming Mission: Paradigm Shifts in Theology of Mission*, 20th Anniv. ed. (New York: Orbis, 2011), p. 41.

[6]Roland Allen, "The Relation Between Medical, Educational and Evangelistic Work in Foreign Mis-

Missionary faith. Encompassing all of the Apostolic paradigm was a faith in the power of the Holy Spirit that would enable the missionaries to avoid any paternalistic methods and thus empower and release the new churches to labor in their fields apart from any outside control from the West. Unless missionaries were able to trust the Spirit to accomplish His work in the new churches, then they would maintain control over the churches and only gradually turn over such control, a common practice known as devolution.

Indigenous churches. Building on the momentum created by Nevius, Anderson and Venn, Allen emphasized that an indigenous church was a church at the moment of birth. Such churches were free to have their own leaders and practice the Eucharist. Allen was quick to note that indigenous churches were not a complicated matter, as the Western tradition had created them to be.

> In the New Testament the idea of a Church is simple. It is an organized body of Christians in a place with its [leaders]. The Christians with their officers are the Church in the place, and they are addressed as such. This is simple and intelligible. That Church is the visible Body of Christ in the place, and it has all the rights and privileges and duties of the Body of Christ. Above it is the Universal Church, composed of all the Churches in the world and of all the redeemed in heaven and on earth. The Apostolic idea of the Church is wonderfully intelligible to men everywhere. . . . The Apostolic system is so simple, that it can be apprehended by men in every stage of education, and civilization.[7]

And for him, the indigenous church so "makes itself at home, that it grows and expands on the soil without any external aid, spontaneously."[8]

Spontaneous expansion. Allen's missiology pointed in the direction of the natural growth of the church apart from outside control. In his book *The Spontaneous Expansion of the Church,* published in 1927, he defined this as "the expansion which follows the unexhorted and unorganized activity of individual members of the Church explaining to others the Gospel which they have found for themselves; I mean the expansion which follows the

---

sions," *Church Missionary Society* (March 1920): 57.
[7]Roland Allen, "The Priesthood of the Church," *The Church Quarterly Review* 115 (1933): 240.
[8]Roland Allen, "The Use of the Term 'Indigenous,'" *International Review of Missions* 16 (1927): 264.

irresistible attraction of the Christian Church for men who see its ordered life, and are drawn to it by desire to discover the secret of a life which they instinctively desire to share; I mean also the expansion of the Church by the addition of new churches."[9] He described such growth as a "very simple thing," asking for no "elaborate organization, no large finances, no great number of paid missionaries."[10]

Allen believed that such growth was possible only if the missionaries were practicing an apostolic approach, built upon the way of Jesus. The churches they planted had to be indigenous churches, led by their own people, empowered by the Spirit and taught to rely on that Spirit. As long as such churches were in place and the missionaries were manifesting the missionary faith, then spontaneous expansion was possible.

THE PAST CENTURY

In the 1950s, Episcopal priest Joseph Moore attempted to apply Allen's concepts to rural areas of southern Indiana, and later, in Nevada and Alaska. However, traditional expectations from established churches and clergy offered much resistance to the unconventional approach. Allen influenced the pioneering work of Roman Catholic Vincent Donovan among the Masai in East Africa. Bishop R. O. Hall of Hong Kong staffed his entire diocese with voluntary clergy, drawing from Allen's influence. Bishop K. H. Ting credited Allen's work for influencing the Three-Self Movement in China. The Student Volunteer Movement in the United States drew much from *Missionary Methods* and *The Spontaneous Expansion of the Church*. In the 1960s, several bishops in Alaska were able to establish an Allen-inspired approach to ministry to the Native peoples. The results achieved by some of these bishops influenced Episcopal leaders to apply Allen's ideals in Episcopal labors in Central and South America. Bishop Adrian Caceres credited *The Spontaneous Expansion of the Church* as providing the missiological guidance that resulted in the growth of the Episcopal Church from 394 members, with no local clergy, to two dioceses, 240 congregations of 20,000

---

[9] Roland Allen, *The Spontaneous Expansion of the Church and the Causes which Hinder It,* American ed. (Grand Rapids: Eerdmans, 1962), p. 7.

[10] Ibid., p. 156.

baptized members with 48 indigenous clergy in the years of 1971 to 1988.[11]

In the early 1960s, David M. Paton wrote in the foreword to *The Ministry of the Spirit: Selected Writings of Roland Allen,* "Roland Allen is perhaps now at last coming into his own, and is indeed acquiring an interested public of astonishing ecumenical width."[12] In 1963, Charles Chaney wrote, "Since the end of World War II, Allen's thought has undergone a fresh and enthusiastic revival. His major books have been reprinted, and his theories have exerted more influence, received greater acceptation and experienced wider practical application than ever before. Today it is an oft repeated truism that Roland Allen's influence is more extensive than it ever was during his life."[13]

While acknowledging that the Allen revival was taking place in part due to the fact that the ecumenical movement and the rise of biblical theology "strengthened concerns for those things which Allen contended" and the reality of the lack of missionaries and money available, Chaney commented that there were two other yet "primary reasons." He believed that Allen's influence increased because post-WWII missions were on the defensive. Societies and missionaries were being forced to address many of the paternalistic matters Allen wrote against. Second, the rapid multiplication of conservative faith mission societies was also a primary factor due to their emphasis on the Bible as a guide for missionary practice, importance of the Holy Spirit, and a priority on evangelism and church planting.[14]

Over the past century, many church leaders have read Allen's works. He ranks as one of the most influential missions theorists in the history of the Church. His advocacy for the place of the Holy Spirit in the lives of new churches has appealed to many who, agreeing with Allen, maintain that indigenous churches have everything they need to be and exist as the church from the moment of their birth. His writings helped facilitate the need for indigenous churches to exist in non-Western lands free from Western control.

---

[11]The examples provided in this paragraph were taken from Charles Henry Long and Anne Rowthorn, "The Legacy of Roland Allen," *International Bulletin of Missionary Research* 13 (April 1989): 68.

[12]David M. Paton, ed., *The Ministry of the Spirit: Selected Writings of Roland Allen* (Grand Rapids, Eerdmans, 1970), p. vii.

[13]Charles Chaney, "Roland Allen: The Basis of His Missionary Principles and His Influence Today," *Occasional Bulletin from the Missionary Research Library* XIV, no. 5 (1963): 1.

[14]Ibid., pp. 9-10.

His lesser-known writings such as *Voluntary Clergy, The Case for Voluntary Clergy and Voluntary Clergy Overseas* all contributed to a surge of interest related to releasing the laity for the work of the ministry in building up the Church. In 1958, Hendrick Kraemer referenced Allen's *Spontaneous Expansion* in his important work *A Theology of the Laity*.[15] David M. Paton noted in 1968 that the interest in Allen's writings had been increasing. Even many Roman Catholic missionary leaders in the 1960s turned their attention toward what Allen had published.[16]

While both a shortage of full-time ministers and financial compensation struck the Anglican Church, David M. Paton and Charles Long noted that such matters paved the way for the Church to become more open to Allen's views on the nonprofessional clergy. By the early 1980s, Paton and Long noted that among many Anglican dioceses there were many nonstipendiary priests and the beginning developments of locally ordained ministry "which is put up by the congregation and recognized by the Bishop and fostered by the Diocese."[17]

Possibly the greatest missiologist of the twentieth century and father of the Church Growth Movement, Donald A. McGavran, credited Allen as being one of the individuals who highly influenced his views. He believed so strongly in Allen's writings that he exhorted all missionaries serving among people movements to read his books.[18] Another individual who found Allen's writings to be of much value was Lesslie Newbigin. Newbigin, among other noteworthy contributions, was influential in providing the theological and missiological foundation that resulted in the Missional Church Movement. Newbigin even penned the foreword to the 1962 American edition of *Missionary Methods*. Realizing the power of Allen's words, he offered a warning to the reader: "I have thought it right to enter these two words of caution, because the reader should be warned that he is embarking on a serious undertaking. Once he has started reading Allen, he will be compelled to go on. He will find that this quiet voice has

---

[15]Hendrik Kraemer, *A Theology of the Laity* (n.p.: Regent College Publishing, 2005, reprint), p. 20.
[16]David M. Paton, ed., *Reform of the Ministry: A Study in the Work of Roland Allen* (London: Lutterworth, 1968), p. 7.
[17]David M. Paton and Charles Long, eds., *The Compulsion of the Spirit: A Roland Allen Reader* (Grand Rapids: Eerdmans, 1983), p. viii.
[18]Donald McGavran, *The Bridges of God* (New York: Friendship Press, 1955), p. 136.

a strange relevance and immediacy to the problems of the Church in our day. And I shall be surprised if he does not find before long that any of his accustomed ideas are being questioned by a voice more searching than the word of man."[19]

It is now commonplace for many popular authors, particularly those writing in the area of church planting, to make reference to Roland Allen. For example, Rick Warren credits Allen in his book *The Purpose Driven Church* when he writes, "The task of church leadership is to discover and remove growth-restricting diseases and barriers so that natural, normal growth can occur. Seventy years ago Roland Allen, in his classic text on missions, called this kind of growth 'the *spontaneous* expansion of the church.' It is the kind of growth reported in the book of Acts. Is your church spontaneously growing? If that kind of growth is not happening in a church we should ask, 'Why not?'"[20]

In his book *Organic Church*, Neil Cole draws attention to *Missionary Methods*.[21] David Garrison, in *Church Planting Movements*, cites both *The Spontaneous Expansion of the Church* and *Missionary Methods*.[22] Alan Hirsch quotes Allen in his book *The Forgotten Ways*.[23] And there are several other popular American authors who are referencing Allen as well.

Anecdotally, I am finding more and more people in the United States interested in learning about Roland Allen. I often hear of how Allen has influenced people's thinking and actions regarding missions in the twenty-first century.

In 2010, I shared with the executive leadership of the Evangelical Missiological Society the need for our annual theme in 2012 to be that of "missionary methods," in recognition of the centennial of the book's publication. It was a unanimous decision to focus on this topic for 2012. When Missio Nexus, the largest evangelical missions network in the United States

---

[19] Allen, *Missionary Methods*, p. iii.

[20] Rick Warren, *The Purpose Driven Church: Growth without Compromising Your Message and Mission* (Grand Rapids: Zondervan, 1995), pp. 16-17.

[21] Neil Cole, *Organic Church: Growing Faith Where Life Happens* (San Francisco: Jossey-Bass, 2005), p. 110.

[22] David Garrison, *Church Planting Movements: How God is Redeeming a Lost World* (Midlothian, Va.: WIGTake Resources, 2004), pp. 249, 268.

[23] Alan Hirsch, *The Forgotten Ways: Reactivating the Missional Church* (Grand Rapids: Brazos Press, 2006), p. 83.

heard of our EMS theme, they also decided to craft their annual meeting on this topic.

The January 2012 volume of *Evangelical Missions Quarterly* was dedicated to the theme "missionary methods." I was honored to have been invited to write the editorial related to the one-hundredth anniversary of Allen's book.[24] In April of 2012, I published *Roland Allen: Pioneer of Spontaneous Expansion,* a brief book on the life and missiology of the man.[25] The journal *Transformation*, published by the Oxford Center for Mission Studies, dedicated the theme of their July 2012 edition to articles about Roland Allen. I have also heard that editors from another missions journal are planning a volume in 2012 dedicated to Allen.

Recently, the Episcopal Church in the United States declared June 8 as the day to recognize Roland Allen on their Calendar of Saints. While it is unlikely that Allen would have approved of such attention, clearly the times have changed. The man who was seen as a radical and was understood by few during his day now has annual recognition alongside of names such as Hilary of Poitiers, Phillips Brooks, Thomas Aquinas, Cyril and Methodius, Martin Luther, Gregory the Great, Patrick, John Calvin, Dietrich Bonheoffer, Augustine and John Bunyan, just to name a few.

Much can happen in one hundred years. Even though Allen sleeps, he still speaks—but this time people are listening.

---

[24] J. D. Payne, "'Messing Up' Missionary Endeavors: Celebrating Roland Allen's *Missionary Methods,*" *Evangelical Missions Quarterly* 48, no. 1 (2012): 6-7.

[25] J. D. Payne, *Roland Allen: Pioneer of Spontaneous Expansion* (n.p.: CreateSpace, 2012).

CONTRIBUTORS

Lizette Beard is research project manager at LifeWay Research and a PhD student in missions at Southeastern Baptist Theological Seminary.

Michael F. Bird is lecturer in theology at Ridley College in Melbourne, Australia.

David J. Hesselgrave is emeritus professor of missions at Trinity Evangelical Divinity School and cofounder of the Evangelical Missiological Society.

Don N. Howell Jr. is professor of New Testament at Columbia International University.

Craig Keener is professor of New Testament at Asbury Theological Seminary.

Chuck Lawless is vice president for global theological advance at the International Mission Board of the Southern Baptist Convention.

Benjamin L. Merkle is associate professor of New Testament and Greek at Southeastern Baptist Theological Seminary.

J. D. Payne is pastor of church multiplication for The Church at Brook Hills in Birmingham, Alabama.

Robert L. Plummer is associate professor of New Testament interpretation at Southern Baptist Theological Seminary.

Michael Pocock is senior professor emeritus of world missions and intercultural studies at Dallas Theological Seminary.

Eckhard J. Schnabel is Mary F. Rockefeller Distinguished Professor of New Testament Studies at Gordon-Conwell Theological Seminary.

M. David Sills is associate dean for Christian mission and professor of Christian missions and cultural anthropology at Southern Baptist Theological Seminary.

Christoph W. Stenschke is lecturer in New Testament at Forum Wiedenest, Germany and *professor extraordinarius* at the University of South Africa.

Ed Stetzer is director of research and missiologist in residence at LifeWay Research.

John Mark Terry is professor of missions at a seminary in the Pacific Rim and visiting professor of missions at Southern Baptist Theological Seminary.

Scripture Index

Paul the Missionary

*Realities, strategies
and methods*

Eckhard J. Schnabel

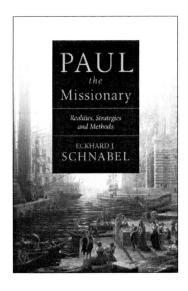

ISBN: 978-1-84474-349-0
518 pages, large paperback

Eckhard Schnabel's two-volume *Early Christian Mission* is widely recognized as the most complete and authoritative contemporary study of the first-century Christian missionary movement. Now in *Paul the Missionary* Schnabel draws on his research and provides a manageable study for students of Paul as well as students and practitioners of Christian mission today.

Schnabel first focuses the spotlight on Paul's missionary work – the realities he faced, and the strategies and methods he employed. Applying his grasp of the wide range of ancient sources and of contemporary scholarship, he clarifies our understanding, expands our knowledge and corrects our misconceptions of Paul the missionary.

In a final chapter Schnabel shines the recovered light of Paul's missionary methods and practices on Christian mission today. Much like Roland Allen's classic *Missionary Methods: St. Paul's or Ours?* of a century ago, Schnabel offers both praise and criticism. For those who take the time to immerse themselves in the world of Paul's missionary endeavour, this final chapter will be both rewarding and searching.

For more information about IVP
and our publications visit
www.ivpbooks.com

Get regular updates at **ivpbooks.com/signup**
Find us on **facebook.com/ivpbooks**
Follow us on **twitter.com/ivpbookcentre**

Inter-Varsity Press, a company limited by guarantee registered in England and Wales, number 05202650. Registered office IVP Bookcentre, Norton Street, Nottingham NG7 3HR, United Kingdom. Registered charity number 1105757.